KIM PHUC PHAN THI

FIRE ROAD

The Napalm Girl's Journey through the Horrors
of War to Faith, Forgiveness & Peace

TYNDALE
MOMENTUM™

The nonfiction imprint of
Tyndale House Publishers, Inc.

Visit Tyndale online at www.tyndale.com.

Visit Tyndale Momentum online at www.tyndalemomentum.com.

TYNDALE, Tyndale Momentum, and Tyndale's quill logo are registered trademarks of Tyndale House Publishers, Inc. The Tyndale Momentum logo is a trademark of Tyndale House Publishers, Inc. Tyndale Momentum is the nonfiction imprint of Tyndale House Publishers, Inc., Carol Stream, Illinois.

Fire Road: The Napalm Girl's Journey through the Horrors of War to Faith, Forgiveness, and Peace

Designed by Dean H. Renninger

Edited by Bonne Steffen

The author is represented by the literary agency of Alive Literary Agency, 7680 Goddard St., Suite 200, Colorado Springs, CO 80920, www.aliveliterary.com.

Scripture quotations are taken from the *Holy Bible*, King James Version.

For information about special discounts for bulk purchases, please contact Tyndale House Publishers at csresponse@tyndale.com, or call 1-800-323-9400.

ISBN 978-1-4964-2429-7 (hc)
ISBN 978-1-4964-2430-3 (sc)

Printed in the United States of America

23 22 21 20 19 18 17
7   6   5   4   3   2   1

For my three families:

My parents and siblings,
whose compassion made a little girl's suffering bearable

My husband and sons, my daughter-in-law and my grandson,
whose unconditional love heals me a little more every day

My Faithway Baptist Church family,
whose prayers help me stay the course.

—◁◈▷—

Contents

PART I: A BODY ABLAZE

PART II: A LIFE EXPLOITED

War, and Peace

I have been dreaming about this book for nearly a decade, perhaps even longer than that, if I include the literary longings I felt but reflexively pushed aside when my sons were still young children who demanded constant care. "When they are older, I shall pursue that dream," I reasoned, an appropriate response to that season of life. My sons are older now.

Ms. Denise Chong wrote a book about my story titled *The Girl in the Picture*, a marvelous and detailed account of Vietnam's civil war that affected me, most notably the famous picture that was taken of me as I fled a certain napalm attack. What a thorough job Ms. Chong did as it relates to history and to geography, to dropping of bombs and to victims of war. But there was a story beneath the story told there, a divine underpinning that for many decades even I could not detect, a set of spiritual stepping-stones that, unbeknownst to me, were paving a path to get me to God.

That is the story I wish to tell in these pages. I wish to tell of God's faithfulness, when I was enveloped by mind-numbing fear. I wish to tell of his kind provision for me, when I was shelterless and hungry and cold. I wish to tell of his pursuit of me, when I was sure I would live the sum of my days marginalized and unloved. But mostly, I wish to tell of his peace, the "peace of God, which passeth all understanding,"[1] the peace that shall keep our hearts and minds through Christ Jesus. For what I desired more than healing for my wounds and hope for my heart was peace for my troubled soul. *Peace!* Yes, I must write about that peace.

I should say here that because I longed so deeply for peace and then—miracle of miracles—actually *encountered* peace, my approach to all of life centers on being *at peace*. I want to receive God's gift of peace each day; I want to allow that peace to infiltrate my thoughts, my reactions, my work; I want to carry that peace with me wherever I go; and I want to share that peace with whomever I should meet.

What this means for you, my dear reader, is that if you came to this book in hopes of picking up weighty opinions on war, I fear I will disappoint you. I suppose there was a time when I did possess such opinions—and when we come to those bygone eras, I shall return briefly to that frame of mind—but across the nearly four decades that have elapsed since then, I have found peace a more captivating topic. My belief is that a careful study of peace will have a far greater unifying effect than even the most exhaustive excavation of the horrors of war. Living a life at peace, and being a people of peace, is how problems get solved.

My highest aim in writing down the words of this story? It is that you will fully know and fully live with the peace that I have found. If we shall meet at some point in the future, face-to-face, do you know how elated I would be to hear that my story pointed you to *peace?* There could be no greater compliment, I assure you!

A final duo of admissions before you begin. First, while I wish my memory were sharper for occasions now four decades old, perhaps it is God's grace in my life that at times, while working to recreate scenes and events for you, I pondered and strained and came up short. When possible, I consulted relevant parties, in an effort to present the most accurate picture of how things went, but I acknowledge openly that because my story has been told thousands of times by as many storytellers, some of the information I present in these chapters will surely fail to square with the other accounts that exist. I stand behind what I have written here.

Second, I have been told by my friends who are fluent in English that I speak in a very distinct manner, one that is not commonplace in the world today. "Oh, yes!" I say with a giggle, "I have heard this many times before!" As you might guess, I grew up speaking Vietnamese, which is still the tongue that comes easiest for me. Later on, my story took me to Cuba, which explains how I am also fairly well versed in Spanish, and then to Canada, though I still am woefully ignorant of French. While living in Toronto, one of the most diverse cities in all the world, I began to study English, and while I truly applied myself—"Come, now, Kim," I would exhort myself, "you must get this right!"—it is not a simple language to grasp. So many rules! So many exceptions! So many confusing conjugations to recall!

My writing partner, my editor, my publisher, and my agent all have assured me that my book indeed makes sense, but just in case a few stumbles and bumbles slip through our collective cracks, I ask you to forgive the mistakes as mine.

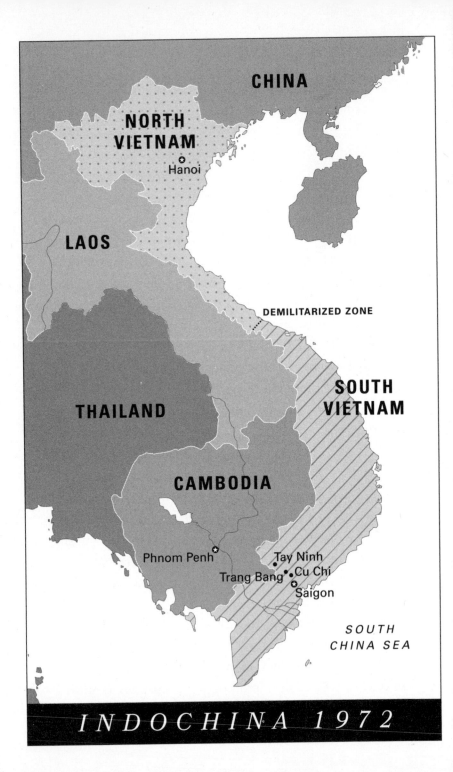

CHINA

NORTH
VIETNAM
⊛ Hanoi

LAOS

DEMILITARIZED ZONE

THAILAND

SOUTH
VIETNAM

CAMBODIA

Phnom Penh ⊛

Tay Ninh
Trang Bang ● Cu Chi
⊛ Saigon

SOUTH
CHINA SEA

INDOCHINA 1972

Beloved, think it not strange concerning the fiery trial which is to try you, as though some strange thing happened unto you: But rejoice, inasmuch as ye are partakers of Christ's sufferings; that, when his glory shall be revealed, ye may be glad also with exceeding joy.[2]

**THE APOSTLE PETER,
TO VARIOUS CHURCHES IN ASIA MINOR**

The aim of the wise is not to secure pleasure, but to avoid pain.

ARISTOTLE

In Pursuit of Smooth Skin

I do not think I will ever get used to this.

I should be welcoming this dramatic shift in weather. Florida is known for its warm winds, its temperate climate, its sunny and easygoing days. And yet as my husband, Toan, and I go through this process of leaving our residence in Canada again, zooming through the sky to Miami International Airport, where we are hit with an oven-like blast, the scars that have defined me these forty-four years scream out, enraged by humidity, by heat. Yes, my skin was tighter hours ago in Toronto's winterlike scene, but at least things were holding steady. I knew precisely what to expect. And so it is not merely Miami's warmth that harms me; it is that it is different from what I have left behind.

I spot the various reporters from news outlets waiting to cover my trip and muster courage to approach those microphones to greet them—all smiles, all peace. Following a brief press conference in the terminal, I am ushered toward a waiting vehicle that will transport me to the hotel where we always stay.

"How are you feeling today, Kim?" the reporters had asked. And, "Are these laser treatments really healing your scars?" During the twenty-minute commute to my destination, I reflect on the depth of those probes. How *am* I feeling? I wonder. Is this process helping at all? Truthfully, I am not sure. *I shall not assess until all seven treatments are complete*, I tell myself, aware that if I render an evaluation too early, I will need to concede that I am not where I had hoped I would be. "We keep going!" I had said with a confident fist pump to the pool of reporters back at the airport. "We keep trusting that my skin will be smooth!"

The following morning, Toan and I are transported to the clinic of Doctor Jill Waibel, the dermatologist conducting my treatments. I am welcomed by still more reporters, each of whom is eager to update their beat: How, exactly, would I characterize the progress that has been made so far? What will today's treatments hope to improve? How long will I be "out" for the procedure? How much pain do I experience while Doctor Jill does her work?

To that last question, I force a grin and answer earnestly: "Even the best pain medicines can only cloak 30 percent of the pain. I feel the other 70 percent. It is as if I am placed on a barbecue grate and grilled to within inches of my life."

The hard truth of these laser treatments is that in order to help heal my burn scars, Doctor Jill has to burn my skin all over again. During each lengthy procedure, thousands of microscopic holes are drilled into my scars, in hopes of promoting in those wounded areas blood flow that I have not known since I was a child.

"It is necessary, Kim," Doctor Jill explained to me during

our first meeting nearly a year ago. "Pain with a purpose, you might say."

Here in Miami for the fifth time in eight months, I try to ignore the lighthearted banter emerging from the clinic's lobby as the reporters swap tales over crudités and sandwiches while they wait for me. I focus my attention on the task at hand: *Today will move you closer to wholeness and health, Kim. Pain with a purpose. There is great purpose in this pain.* I change into a hospital gown, I lie down on the cold, grey examination bed, I exhale the trepidation that seems always to come to me in these seconds before treatment begins, and I choose to take Doctor Jill at her word.

Part I

A BODY ABLAZE

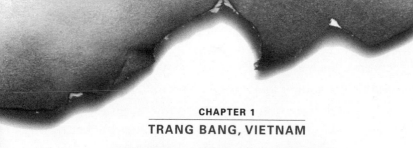

WAR? WHAT WAR?

SPRINGTIME 1972

I am a girl of eight, skipping home at the end of a typical school day, having completed the kilometer-long trek with a few other village kids and, on occasion, my brother—Number 5. In large families such as ours, numbers are easier to remember than names. I am Number 6. We make our way along the dirt path that has been carved through the overgrown fields, our progress only interrupted by a heavy-burdened cow being driven by a farmer eager to get his bundles of fresh vegetables or grain to town, or by a rich man seated high atop a motorbike, eager to remind the rest of us of his wealth.

As I emerge from the dense canopy of trees and set foot onto the giant cement patio that my father poured with his own two hands, I marvel at how much of the ground is covered. Such a thing is a rarity in my village and a not-so-subtle declaration that we, too, have found wealth. I am thinking nothing of weapons systems and strategic advances, of tactical zones and attempts to seize, of the Easter Offensive and waning United States support, anything even remotely related to war, save for my persisting curiosity over those distinctive tire-tread sandal prints my grandma points out some mornings. Viet Cong fighters have made yet another middle-of-the-night raid through my family's property, most likely in search of rations—bandages and medicines, I am told, or else rice or soap.

It was always at night that they came, creeping about the jungle in their black pajamas, silently avoiding South Vietnam's gaze. They would emerge from the elaborate tangle of underground tunnels they had dug in order to obtain supplies or to deliver verdicts to local villagers who had refused to comply with their demands. "We have a message for you to deliver," they would say to my eldest sibling, Loan (Number 2), on many an occasion. (There never is a "Number 1" in South Vietnamese families. We are a quirky bunch, I agree.) Loan—Hai, we called her—had been trained as a schoolteacher and was one of the few literates among most of the adults in our area, thus making her a prime puppet for the conveyance of dissident decrees. Her allegiance, of course, was to the South, but she knew better than to stand her ground. She valued life, as we all did. With resolve summoned, she would clear her throat and read the decree.

"You are hereby informed that, as penalty for failure to assist Viet Cong's efforts in this, our civil war, you shall suffer imminent death," she would be forced to say to one neighbor or another. I cannot imagine having to choke those words out, but my sister did.

Because of the pavement surrounding our home, my brothers and sisters and I would head over to Grandma's house, a five-minute walk away, to take in the fresh prints. She and Grandpa still had a dirt perimeter around their house, and oh, the imprints we could see. "Look! Look there!" my *ba ngoai* would implore us, pointing at the muddy, rutted ground.

My siblings and I—there were eight of us total, nine if you count dear Tai who died as a little baby—would *ooh* and *ahh* in wonder, the mythology ever expanding in our minds surrounding these warriors from our beloved South Vietnam homeland who had had the audacity to join forces with armies from the North. I imagined massive armies of soldiers having traipsed through in the dead of night, even though, in reality, it may have been a small band of eight or ten.

Of course, we kids were merely playing off of the adults' explanations and reactions to all goings-on related to war, for only my very oldest siblings Loan and Ngoc had any context for such things. Our enthusiasm for the discussion waned as quickly as it was stirred. After all, who had time for talk of battlefields and air strikes when there were games to play, books to read, and a tangle of guava trees to climb? How I miss those beloved trees.

—◊◊◊—

During my growing-up years, to step onto my family's property was to enter a charming countryside paradise, a refuge brimming with sufficiency and splendor. Whenever my closest friend, Hanh, walked home from school with me, I would drop my book bag at the gated entrance, scale like an energetic monkey one of the forty-two guava trees that outlined our home's perimeter, select two of the plumpest, ripest guavas from the citrine clusters dotting the limbs, and sink my teeth into the first while tossing the second down to Hanh. We both would giggle in satisfied delight as guava juice trickled down our chins. Literally, my name, Kim Phuc (pronounced "fook"), means "golden happiness," and that is exactly how life was—bright, cheerful, holding unparalleled value. I loved my days and my years. (The "Phan Thi" portion reflects my family's surname, and in my homeland, that "last" name actually comes "first." For years, I did indeed go by "Phan Thi Kim Phuc," eventually shifting to the current construction to simplify things for Western audiences.)

My parents—Nu and Tung are their names—raised more than one hundred pigs at a time, selling piglets off as they matured, and on any given afternoon, chickens, ducks, swans, dogs, and cats roamed the two-plus-acre grounds with those pigs, as though the lot of them owned the place. In addition to the guava trees, we grew bananas, and I distinctly remember multiple occasions when my siblings and I would gorge on an entire bunch as soon as they were ripe, for the simple reason that they were there and we were hungry. There were coconut trees and durian fruit trees, and the grapefruits we grew were as big as my head and sweeter than any I have tasted since. Nearly every night my mother brought us surplus vegetables, chicken, and rice from her noodle shop in town, served with a side of fresh fruit. We ate well every day, like the royalty I believed we were.

In actuality, "royalty" would not be a fitting description of the life my family and I lived, but relative to our surroundings, we were well off, indeed. I attribute our former status to the back-breaking labor of my ma. Even before my parents were married, my father could not help but notice Ma's delicious noodle soup. In 1951, soon after their wedding, an idea was hatched.

"Your soup is so good that I believe people will pay you to eat it," my father told my ma, who was all too eager to put his theory to the test. She quickly gathered her small mud oven and the necessary ingredients—pork and anchovies, spices and herbs, vegetables, noodles she made by hand—and squatted rent-free in front of a kind local storeowner's shop, her vat of soup ready to dish out.

By the time my parents had saved up enough money to move out of my grandparents' home and purchase a place for themselves, Ma was able to stop squatting in the market and rent a soup stall, complete with tables and stools. She had an official sign that hung above the modest structure: *Chao Long Thanh Tung*, it read, which referenced both her specialty—*chao long*, the pork-and-rice porridge Ma used as her soup's base—and her husband, Tung. Business began to boom.

Within seven years, Ma was able to purchase not only her stall, but the two stalls that flanked hers. She increased seating capacity to eighty people, she replaced bamboo furniture with carved wood, and she capitalized on the era's influx of American soldiers, all hungry, as it seemed, for good soup. To keep up with demand, my ma would rise long before dawn, often after only two or three hours' sleep. She would silently slip out the back door, careful not to wake her snoring children, and she would make her way by fire lamp to the market to purchase ingredients for the day's soup.

She would return home late in the afternoon or in the early-evening hours, tend to the chores of our farm, manage the business side of her shop, see to it that the family's laundry was done, and then put us children to bed. Indeed, Ma was busy every moment of every day, but even in the spare seconds of deep night, when she would allow me to cuddle into her side as she at last lay down for sleep, my emotional well would be filled to overflowing. She was safety and security for her adoring little girl.

My father was also a wonderful cook who prepared food on handmade barbecue grills he formed out of mud. He'd fuel them with charcoal and kindling, and then lay white fish that he had caught on top, searing them to absolute perfection. While the fish was sizzling, he would toss whatever vegetables were available into a stir-fry pan, making even our most meager meals possess a special flair. While my dad was a tender man and a gentle disciplinarian, my relationship with him lacked intimacy, owing to his prioritizing Ma's increasingly profitable noodle shop and the juggling of both Viet Cong and South Vietnamese soldiers' demands over frivolities such as playing with one's children. As a wealthy member of our village, warriors looked to him to supply even more of their needs, which was a daily burden for my dad. His goal for his family was survival, one which, miraculously, he achieved.

My great-uncle lived with our family and took care of us kids when Ma and Dad were gone. On sunny days, I would head for the book nook I had created in the trees, where I would devour pages from *Te Thien Dai Thanh*—in English,

The Monkey King. At mealtimes Great-Uncle would holler my nickname—*My,* meaning "beautiful," which had been bestowed on me by my grandmother—in order to pull me away from my book and to the lunch table, where rice and grilled fish awaited. But rather than making my whereabouts known to him, I would just grin there in my secret reading spot, sinking deeper into the pages I held. When Ma came home from work, she would scold me for having refused food all afternoon long, even as, unbeknownst to her, I had made meals of fresh, delicious fruit most days in my treetop perch.

When I did leave my book nook, it was generally for mischief. Between the two houses that sat on the property—a large entertaining house, as well as my family's smaller-structured residence—was a cement courtyard connecting them. It was a lovely, relaxing place, and often my great-uncle would doze off there in the hammock for an hour or two following lunch.

A favorite pastime of mine was waiting until he was deep in sleep, evidenced by his rhythmic snoring, and then sneaking up next to him with a pouch of salt and a spoon in hand. I would load up that spoon to overflowing, pour the entire sum into his open mouth, and then run off as fast as my legs could carry me, screaming delightedly with every step. "My! My!" he would holler behind me, his restful nap having been disrupted once again. "*Myyyyyy!*"

On especially sweltering days, Great-Uncle slept in the hammock without a shirt on. Number 5 and I would hunt down a tube, pour very cold water into it, and then slowly drip it into the sleeping man's belly button. More shrieking. More chasing. More fun.

Eventually the heat would be tempered by violent rainstorms that were prone to erupting without notice, and each time those welcome drops fell, my siblings and friends and I would rush to the cement courtyard in our bare feet, wait for the slab to be completely wet, and then hydroplane around and around and around, laughing hysterically with each lap. My childhood was everything a childhood should be: carefree, cherished, whimsical, provisioned, enjoyable, abundant, *alive*. I could not possibly have known that all of that would change, and in the blink of an eye.

—⁓—

As spring gave way to summer in 1972, the war in Vietnam regained some of the momentum it had lost following the Tet Offensive, a major military turning point four years prior. Back then, in the spring of 1968, communist forces had attacked the American embassy in our capital city of Saigon, which enraged both US and South Vietnamese leaders alike. I was only five years old at the time and did not know that these events had unfolded or what they meant for my family and me. The significance of Tet would reveal itself years later, when retribution was leveled in my hometown. For now, in my protective bubble, the war was "over there," far, far away from here, and thus far away from me.

If I had been paying closer attention, I would have recognized that my family was beginning to receive more and more guests across those late-winter and early-spring months. I called our visitors "forest people," for they always arrived from the heavily treed area to the northeast of our village, the mountain region that was proving to be a perfect hideout for Viet Cong rebels. I had never seen the forest people's villages myself, but as I got older I would come to understand that as the war stretched farther toward the Cambodian border, additional families were being forced on the run as refugees, their homes having been destroyed by bombs.

As a young child, I did not know the reason these people were surfacing; I knew only that my ma and dad would take them in, give them small plots of land on our property to call their own, serve them home-cooked meals of pork and cassava, of sweet potatoes and organic fruit. Our guests were provided a sturdy stepping-stone for a time—weeks, or sometimes months—on their journey toward wherever they were headed next.

The cause of the forest people's heartache was a military initiative called the Easter Offensive, which occurred in March 1972 and saw communism advance to within one hundred kilometers of Saigon. They were *serious* about unifying Vietnam under their political system, and regardless of how many troops it cost them to reach their goal, they were prepared to pay that price. "You will kill ten of our men, and we will kill one of yours, and in the end it will be you who tire of it," revolutionary communist leader Ho Chi Minh had said to his opponents nearly three decades prior—a battle cry that rebel fighters still embraced.

I did not understand these things at the time, but my parents certainly did. Did they know that there would be fire and terror, agony and death to suffer? They did not. But they knew that trouble was brewing. And they feared that it was coming for us.

—⁓—

The morning of June 6, 1972, I woke while it was still dark outside to my ma's voice urgently whispering my name. "My! My!" she said. "Come, we must leave."

That's strange. Ma is always gone by now to tend her noodle shop. "Why have you not gone already?" I asked her through the fog of unfinished sleep, to which she said, "Shh, My! Quiet. You must ask nothing, child."

I would later learn that the Viet Cong had been at my house all night. Their troops, malnourished and disheveled though they were, had arrived just after midnight, intent on occupying my family's home for the purpose of digging further tunnels that would position them closer to the main road. At the sight of them en masse, no longer a stray band of rebels here or there, my ma knew that our village was now unsafe. But where to take her family? Immediately, she thought of our temple, just on the outskirts of the village. It was close enough to allow her access to our home, in the event that she could return to care for our animals or gather up additional possessions, but far enough away to hopefully ensure safety until the war passed.

Standing with feet firmly planted and gaze fixed on the rebel commander who was barking out his demands, my ma said quietly, "I will allow you to enter, but may I first take my family from here?"

"No!" the commander spat at her. "If you leave now, the South will know where we are."

There were always eyes on everyone, belonging both to Viet Cong and South Vietnamese. These troops needed us to be still so that they could complete their work undetected by the enemy they intended to rout.

"Three, four hours," he shouted at my ma. "We build our tunnel, and *then* you go."

The truth was that my great-uncle was suffering a terrible stomach ailment, and my ma feared he would not survive the night. This added stress and upheaval would do nothing to help him out. Had she known she had access to a listening God that night, I know she would have called out in prayer. As it was, she did the only thing she could do: She settled in for a four-hour wait.

It was after she had been given the signal to go that my ma woke me, and together we collected my brothers and sisters and as many of our belongings as our arms could carry. We then took our caravan outside, which is when I noticed that our home no longer had any doors—the Viet Cong had removed them hours before. Peeking around a corner, I saw a man in those unmistakable Viet Cong black pajamas, and behind him, more pajama-clad men standing beside a haphazard mound of guns.

"Oh, Ma!" I cried, frightened of all that would surely unfold, but she only shushed me more passionately and tightened her grip on my hand as we rushed into the night.

Within moments, my family had relocated to the comfort and familiarity of our local temple, where we had attended ceremonies my entire life. It was a logical choice for a hideout, given the significance it held for our village. Not only did its imposing architecture make it the largest structure for miles, but it was also sacred. Set apart. Surely the safest place on earth.

As my siblings and I barreled through the temple doors on that Tuesday morning, the terror of the day's early hours was tempered some by the surroundings I had come to love. There above me was the brightly painted arched ceiling. Before me were the ornate pillars, festooned in giant molded dragons of fuchsia, orange, turquoise, and gold. Below my feet were the hand-laid marble tiles, arranged in a dizzying pattern of white and wheat that stretched from one end of the room clear to the other. Sometimes during worship ceremonies, I would attempt to count those tiles, always failing to get them all in. How grateful I was in this moment for their sturdiness in holding us up when the entire world seemed to be falling away.

Trang Bang's temple of CaoDai—we pronounce it "cowdie," with emphasis on the second syllable, though its meaning relates neither to cattle nor to their death—represented more than mere religious symbolism for my family. My grandparents—my ma's mother and father—had originally donated the large plot of land to CaoDai elders from other villages who wanted to expand to Trang Bang, and it was on that land that the temple was built. Both my grandma and my grandpa were very important leaders within the religion and as such drew enormous respect from our entire community. Following in their footsteps, my parents, who had grown up knowing no religion except CaoDai, also devoted themselves to temple service. Yes, they were extraordinarily busy people, but on high holy days, which occurred twice monthly and then on three or four additional days each year, they pushed aside every other obligation in order to spend hours upon hours in worship.

CaoDai's official position regarding its beliefs states that as a universal faith, it recognizes all religions as having "one same divine origin, which is God, or Allah, or the Tao, or the Nothingness," (or Macrocosm, or Yahweh, or Ahura Mazda, or Monad, or the mountain gods, or the gods of nature, or our own long-since-deceased ancestors . . . or all of the above), and sees all religions as different manifestations of "one same Truth."[3]

You might say that we were equal-opportunity worshipers, giving any and every God/god a shot. In terms of practical application for us Caodaists, this wide tolerance equated to three goals: first, to prize love and justice above all other things; second, to honor all religious leaders as equals; and third, to apply ourselves to the practice of what they called "self-purification," which from what I could tell meant we needed to do good; not do evil; and avoid eating meat during specified periods of time, lest you render yourself defiant and risk returning someday in a reincarnated state to whatever animal you had harmed and consumed. "You are god, and god is you"—this is a mantra that was ingrained in us, which was quite empowering to a young person, I must admit. But as I cultivated eyes to see the truth of that matter, which centered on evildoers being summarily dismissed from our fellowship, never to return again, I grew leery of declaring myself my own god. What if I failed in my pursuit of self-purifying, do-good perfection? What would life look like for me then? I would find out, soon enough.

On those "special" days when my parents forsook all other plans in order to spend the day at temple, we honored the legacies of the founders of the world's five major religions, as well as the first female cardinal of CaoDai and the French novelist His Eminence Victor Hugo, the author of such works as *Les Misérables* and *The Hunchback of Notre-Dame*. To us, he was much more than a famous writer; he was a highly influential spiritist who held to our same religious beliefs—that morality was the ticket to a successful spiritual life and that there is no need to offend *any* of the gods. After all, what if you should need their intervention someday?

Looking back, I see my family's religion as something of a charm bracelet slung 'round my wrist, each dangling bauble yet another god. When troubles came along—and every day, it seemed, they did—I was encouraged to rub those charms in sequence: the Jade Emperor, Dipankara Buddha, Taishang Laojun, Confucius, Jesus Christ . . . and do not forget Victor Hugo, little My, while crossing my fingers that help would arrive. It would take me years and years to realize the futility of such an approach. At the time, I was an eager adherent, grooming myself to be the best Caodaist there possibly could be. I would out-devote the most devoted in our midst; eventually, that would be me.

But I was not there quite yet. As a young child, I wrestled to keep my attention focused on such lofty goals—understandable, given the aesthetics of a typical worship service. The lush décor; the intricate patterns; the welcome chill of the marble floor; the stark-white pants and tunics of the worshipers set against the vibrancy of the inner sanctum—oh, how marvelous it all appeared. Some followers of CaoDai—those who had been elevated to the level of priest—achieved special status and were allowed to don temple robes of bright yellow, green, or red, colors that really draw a person's eye and beckon the onlooker's attention to stay put. Throughout the ninety-minute services, when I was supposed to be focused on the sections of the Holy Word we were being asked to recite, I would study the priests instead, marveling at their reverence; their righteousness; their deep and sincere bows, which I took to reflect a deep and sincere faith. Their apparent holiness was magnetic to my young, impressionable soul, even as I had no idea quite yet what the concept of "soul" even meant.

I would have guessed that the splendor and veneration characterizing CaoDai gatherings would elicit from all onlookers the sense of awe and allegiance I experienced time and time again, but my siblings were living, breathing proof that one can call himself or herself religious while having no use whatsoever for the religion being espoused. Yes, my brothers and sisters would make an appearance on the holy days; yes, they would recite the Five Pledges—May CaoDai be proclaimed widely, may salvation be granted to all, may God bless with forgiveness all his disciples, may peace be granted for all mankind, may security be delivered for our temple—yes, they would feign interest as the leader presented his or her sermon and congregational announcements were made; yes, they would move their lips in unison as songs of praise were raised.

But I? I knew the truth. I was far more devoted than they. Or I was *preparing* for grand devotion, anyway.

I was in the temple chorus, for example, which meant I would stay after service to practice religious songs. Eventually, I would be attending service not a handful of times each year, but rather a handful of times each *day*, including a worship gathering that began at the stroke of midnight, an occasion that for a time I rarely, if ever, missed.

Certainly, during my growing-up years that laid the foundation for that ensuing devotion, I did not fully grasp all that it meant to be Caodaist. I knew only that my grandparents loved CaoDai. My parents loved CaoDai. My siblings at least *pretended* to love CaoDai. All of my neighbors and friends and fellow villagers loved CaoDai. And so I, young Kim Phuc, would choose to love CaoDai too. I would love it with all my heart.

As Ma led us through the worship area to the outbuildings situated on the back of the temple grounds, we encountered two smaller structures that housed the temple's caretakers. This pair of servants was very important to our assembly, as they were responsible for preparing post-ceremony meals and serving them in the dining area that adjoined their two homes. The sight of that stocked kitchen was a real encouragement to me, for my family and I loved to eat. *We will be well-fed here. We will be safe. Things will work out okay.*

The rear perimeter of the temple grounds was lined with a thick stand of tall bamboo stalks flanked by lush guava and jackfruit trees. The well for fresh water sat in the center of the vegetation, and the sight of so much life was a welcomed hint of hope. Inside of our new home away from home, as Tuesday morning slipped into Tuesday afternoon, bellies began to grumble. Cobbling together rice, vegetables, crackers, and any bits of protein they could find, the women assembled lunch, made sure that everyone had a bowlful, and then urged us kids to run and play.

Given the lack of real toys in our village, the games that my friends and I played were heavily reliant on an active imagination. We played "prince and princess," using dwarf cobs of corn as the husband and wife, still smaller cobs as their passel of children, and bamboo stalks, banana leaves, and stray tree branches to build dollhouses they could call their own. We chased blackbirds all over the place, pretending they had magical powers or that we, too, could fly.

To be sure, there was a certain intensity in the air due to the adults' well-founded fears over what was underway outside those temple walls. But for us kids, as soon as we could no longer see with our own two eyes the Viet Cong rebels, we forgot to feel afraid. All that we knew for sure was that there were a whole lot of children in one space, there was a whole lot of time to be spent together, and our parents kept exhorting us to play. *What an adventure!* I thought. It would be the closest thing to summer camp I would ever know.

Of special interest to me was my three-year-old cousin Danh, my ma's sister Anh's little boy and a treasured friend to me. He was the cutest, chubbiest child I had ever seen, and at some point along the way, I took him in as one of my own siblings, teaching him to form his letters, his numbers, his first smiley face.

"Ma!" he had identified that first face, gripping the pencil tighter and adding to the scene. He then drew dozens more smileys, representing his father, his siblings, his grandparents, his cousins, his aunties, his uncles, his life. I loved nothing more than creating art with Danh. Or eating with Danh— "Danh! Eat this," I would cheer, as I offered him something, only to see the finicky eater scrunch up his face.

"Ewww!" he would squeal. "I do not like it, My!" Or playing chase with Danh and making him giggle so intensely that everyone within earshot would fall into waves of laughter too. Danh was innocent, loving, and perfect—a delightful boy to call *friend* and a joyous distraction for me there at the temple.

The older boys in the group played "war," which took little imagination, given the dozen or so actual soldiers armed with serious-looking weaponry that flanked us all throughout the space. Those military men had been deployed from a nearby South Vietnamese unit for the purpose of protecting our village's citizens and took their role very seriously, informing the moms and dads at every turn of the goings-on near and far. I would later learn that each time a bomb was dropped in the region, the soldiers would alert my ma and the other adults, explaining what had been hit and where.

The bombs were dropped always in pairs—two over this particular section of forest, two over that small village. While the damage they caused was significant, we as a group were never once ushered into any of the bomb shelters that undergirded the temple grounds. When I focus on what I remember of that stay in the temple—for three days, we would stay tucked inside—I distinctly recall the sounds and smells of burning: burning fields, burning houses, burning trees. Perhaps I should have been alarmed, but I was not. We were in a holy, protected place.

By Thursday, the eighth of June, I was missing home. It was summertime, my favorite season of the year, and I longed for the security of my favorite tree—not just any tree, but *my* tree. I missed evening dinners, just my family and me, and my father's cooking, which I deeply loved. I also missed my dad. He had not been with us for three full days now, and whenever I noticed his absence, I was reminded that all was not well.

For many weeks, my father had been residing with a family friend who lived in Trang Bang proper, several kilometers from the area encompassing both the temple and our family home. Dad had tried to stay with us in order to keep the family together, but Viet Cong soldiers looked to him to supply an exorbitant amount of their goods. With their needs on the rise, my dad feared that if he stayed put, he would be abused and even killed, should he ever decide to refuse the rebels' request. And so each day, as sunlight waned and dusk emerged, he would take off, leaving my ma to care for the homestead—the trees, the pigs, the chickens, the ducks, and a large collection of energetic kids.

That arrangement had been difficult enough for us all, but then came the intensified military action closer to home, which meant major parts of the main road leading into Trang Bang had been cut off to all forms of transportation, foot traffic included. Now, not only was my father missing at night, but also during the three days when we needed him most. Still, I distinctly recall receiving the explanation for his absence plainly, with mature understanding. In the same way that people who live in rural settings know better than to allow their pets to wander too far from home during night-time hours, for fear of those small dogs and cats becoming dinner for a hungry predator, we in South Vietnam knew that the night belonged to the Viet Cong. They were ravaging beasts on a mission, willing to devour anyone or anything that got in their way. We never saw them during daylight, but as night fell, we made our way inside. They would always surface, come dark. My dad was wise to stay put.

In the years that have passed since that unexpected temple stay, I have been asked why the Viet Cong did not treat my ma with the same forcefulness and greed, to which I always point to a cultural norm: In the Vietnam I grew up in, the highest position in a home belonged to the man, and all dealings had to pass through his hands. In the end, of course, rebel fighters did come to my ma, they did lay out wild demands, and they did occupy our home. But from my father's perspective, his absence significantly delayed that inevitable turn of events.

From *my* perspective, those Viet Cong must have known how brave and fierce my ma could be, choosing to come to her only as a last resort. They must have known how determined she was to protect her family; how committed she was to seeing her children thrive; how resilient she was, even in the face of the awful circumstances that always accompany war.

By way of example, mere months before my family was pushed from our home, my ma had been working in her noodle shop when a wedding party of nineteen people stopped in for soup. Their mood was joyous and celebratory as they found seats and settled in for their meal, but within moments of their arrival, the scene turned from glorious to gruesome. Inexplicably, Viet Cong in the area parked a bicycle packed with explosives outside, and when the dynamite went off, every last guest was killed. My poor ma had watched the entire situation unfold, right before her eyes. What a terrible thing to witness!

Still worse was what happened later, after the scene had

been cleaned up. South Vietnamese leaders came and arrested Ma, shouting, "You are Viet Cong! You are with the Viet Cong!" They put her in jail for a full month, an outright travesty, given the flimsy claims. Still, she waited patiently for things to sort themselves out. She nodded politely when both the mayor and the senior-most official from the police bureau of Trang Bang, tipped off to the false arrest by one of my dad's good friends who worked for the government, came to her holding area and said, "We have been alerted to a misunderstanding." She calmly returned to her noodle shop, which had been shut down for thirty-one days' time, and began turning a profit again.

Ma's fortitude was my fortress there at the temple. If Dad had to be away for now, I had the best possible alternative at hand: In the shadow of my ma, I knew I would be fine.

For much of the morning, heavy rains and an uptick in increasingly closer bombings kept the thirty or so of us who were living at the temple hunkered down inside. I could see on the adults' faces the growing concern for our safety. With each passing day, I noticed more and more occasions when the air was pierced by the heart-stopping sounds of explosions. Following those sounds were sights that are difficult to explain: a blood-red sky, a wall of flames licking the heavens, the landscape being overwhelmed by smoke. This did not feel fun or adventuresome anymore. I wanted to go home. I wanted the sights and sounds to stop. And yet that is not at all what happened. On the eighth of June, what I wanted, I would not get.

An hour or so after lunch, a military plane descended

overhead and swooped down abruptly to within feet, it seemed, of the outbuilding where we were. In its wake, a smoke grenade detonated, coating the scene in bright purple and gold. It was a signal to the South Vietnamese pilot who was trailing behind: Drop your bombs on this very spot.

A color-mark made within the temple grounds? This had to be an error. Why would our country's troops be attacking their own?

Sensing a shift in the room's energy, I glanced up from my play to study a nearby soldier's expression. As he took in the emerging situation through the glass of a small, painted-frame window, his eyes widened and his lips formed around not a name but a curse: "Jesus Christ."

SOLDIER'S ORDERS

08 JUNE 1972

"Chay ra mau len!
"Chung ta phai roi khỏi noi nay, khong co an toan o day nua,
"Chung no se huy diệt cai chua nay.
"Di nhanh len!
"Con nit chay trước di di ngay bay gio!"

Get out! Run!
We must leave this place! It is not safe here!
They are going to destroy this whole place!
Go! Children, run first!
Go! Go now!

"TOO HOT! TOO HOT!"

08 JUNE 1972

From what I could tell, this "Jesus Christ" whom the soldier summoned must have been occupied with other business that day, for neither he nor any of the other gods I had worshiped as a child were able to curtail the circumstances that came our way.

The soldier's commands left no room for ambiguity, and so we who had been living in the temple did as we were told: With us children leading the way, we fled the outbuildings; we ran toward the front of the temple grounds; we made our way from the property onto the adjacent road, Trang Bang's Route 1; and we pedaled our legs as fast as they could carry us as hell rose up to clutch earth.

Seconds later, I caught sight of an airplane closing in on me. It was jolting to take in something so immense, so fast, and so earth-shatteringly loud, and the magnitude of its presence left me paralyzed there on the road. My jaw fell open as the plane whizzed past, its massive grey underbelly temporarily eclipsing whatever traces of sunlight had broken through the morning's storms. Perhaps I would have stood there for an eternity, my feet unable to move, my entire being fixed to that gravel road, were it not for what I saw next.

The fly-by was not an inconsequential event, for falling from that underbelly were four large ice-black bombs. And as the bombs softly made their way to the ground, landing one by one, somersaulting end over end—*whump-whump, whump-whump, whump-whump, whump-whump*—I knew I had to flee. These were not bombs that fell heavily from the sky, as I had heard that bombs would do; no, these bombs all but floated down. There was something sinister in those cans.

"Nooo! Nooo!" I screamed to nobody but the air surrounding me, all of the other children and soldiers having disappeared into the dense clouds of smoke that now encroached. Route 1 was known as the longest stretch of the famous Asian Highway Network, running through Tokyo and Korea, through Hong Kong and Bangladesh, through Afghanistan and Iran, even to where Turkey meets Bulgaria, and yet out of all the possible stretches along that road I could have found myself, I had to be *here,* in Trang Bang, where Route 1 and all its inhabitants were dissolving into explosions of raging fire. *I will die here on this road. I will be taken to death in these flames.*

—⁓—

If you had asked me on June 7, 1972, the day before those bombs fell, about the worst pain I had ever known, coy, quiet, shy little Kim Phuc Phan Thi probably would have bashfully shrugged her shoulders, cut her eyes this way and that, and eventually said, "Em . . . falling from my bicycle and scraping my knee?" Then she would have nervously giggled over the attention being paid her.

This was the nature of my childhood, or at least the eight-year span that was marked by love, laughter, and precious few discomforts to report. But after June 8, 1972, my answer forever would change. What a difference a day makes, indeed.

At the center of my experience that summer day was a certain terrifying and tactical weapon known as napalm, so named for the two primary components that give it its gelling quality, the things that make it so thick: naphthenic and palmitic acids. Despite its prevalence during my country's civil war, I had never heard of napalm before it invaded my province and my body, but after that isolated introduction, I can tell you it is the fiercest adversary a human being ever could meet.

The trouble with napalm is twofold: First, its sticky nature causes it to adhere in unrelenting fashion to anything and everything it touches—including human skin; and second, once it adheres, it burns to dust whatever that target once was.

Neither my immediate caregivers that day nor I fully grasped the mechanics of how napalm burned; all we knew was that I was on fire, badly in need of help. Years later, I would learn that this was no ordinary fire. Water boils at two hundred and twelve degrees Fahrenheit, and an average building fire, at its hottest, burns somewhere between twelve hundred and fifteen hundred degrees. But napalm? It burns at *five thousand*. Napalm means business every time it shows up. Unfortunately, it came to my village that day.

The flames first chased me from behind. My legs were propelling my body up the road as fast as they could take me, but I was neither the swiftest of runners nor known for being a vigorous child. I was wearing typical clothing for the region, a loose-fitting, tunic-style cotton blouse over wide-legged cotton pants, and the fact that I did not have on a heavy flak jacket, as the soldiers all wore, may have well saved my life. The flames clung to the synthetic material of those jackets and refused to let go, creating something of a high-temperature oven for the soldiers wearing them. Their death was quick and sure. But the very flames that took their lives were partially extinguished in the fibers of my clothes. As the fire whisked away my garments, the licks of heat that remained on me had already lost much of their force.

Still, the effects of the napalm had done much damage, and as I continued to run up Route 1, now naked and shrieking in pain and fear, anyone and everyone who caught sight of my backside—my neck, my back, my arm—received quite a shock indeed. My skin had burned away as though it were simply a swimsuit peeling off, and in plain view was the pale, thin underlayer of skin that had never before seen the light of day. I continued rushing ahead, having no idea where I was going or what I would find once I arrived.

Where is Ma? Where are my siblings? Where are the armed men who had been charged with protecting my family from this very threat? Why is this happening to us . . . to me? How will I survive such heat?

I had no idea how I had arrived here naked, afraid, and alone.

Shell-shocked soldiers shoving us out of the temple.

The roar of engines blasting across the sky.

Metal monsters descending to earth: one, two, three, four.

Flames licking, tasting, devouring the rain-soaked road.

Nothing but fire.

Too hot! Too hot!

Before I could take in all that was happening, fire had crept up my arm, and in the same way you might brush off a pesky bug that happens onto your sleeve, reflexively I reached my right hand over to my left arm and whisked the flames away. Of course I did not know that I was brushing away sticky napalm, which is why today, in addition to the more penetrating scars that run up and down my left side, I still bear on my right hand the searing pain associated with burns of this sort.

Eventually, my stamina ran out. I felt so weary that I had no option but to stop there in the middle of the road, despite everything inside of me begging me to plow ahead. As the distance between the fire and me grew, the smoke cloud surrounding me began to dissipate, and I could see there at my side two of my brothers, two of my cousins once-removed, a group of stunned South Vietnamese soldiers, and various reporters, journalists, and photographers dressed in military fatigues who now were on the scene.

"Nóng quá! Nóng quá!" I shouted, hopeful that some-one—*anyone*—would come to my aid. "Too hot! Too hot!" I was screaming. I was desperately, painfully hot. From the inside out, I was hot. Although no flames were visible on my

body, napalm had worked its way deep into my skin, torching everything in its path. I was being cooked down to my bones, and in that moment, I wanted more than anything in the world to escape the torment.

One of the reporters present, a man I would later learn was a Mister Christopher Wain from the British Broadcasting Corporation, reached for his canteen and began pouring small sips of water down my throat, and with each swallow, I hoped that the liquid would snuff out the volcano erupting inside of me. How I longed for the agony to end. And yet it would only get much worse.

Moments after those cherished gulps, kind Mister Wain, hearing my continued pleas for help, for someone to help me not be so hot, then lifted his canteen over my head, tilted it so that the cool fluid could wash over me, could extinguish all my fires, the water raining down my head, my neck, my back, my legs. Neither of us could possibly have known then what we both fully understand today: Because napalm partially combusts oxygen wherever and whenever it encounters it, dousing me with water, whose molecular structure includes oxygen, was the worst possible thing to do. I caught on fire all over again.

There on the main road leading into my beloved village, standing in what was once the place of beauty and abundance I had called home my entire life, surrounded now by well-meaning onlookers desperate to see me survive the type of burn that nobody ever survives, I fainted dead away.

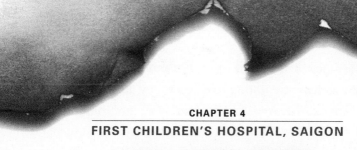

THE VIEW FROM INSIDE THE MORGUE

11 JUNE 1972

I do not remember being placed inside the morgue at the First Children's Hospital in Saigon, but the reality that I was left for dead while still quite alive would haunt me for three decades. I had been comatose upon my arrival, slipping momentarily in and out of consciousness although never entirely coherent. I had been unable to say to the hospital staffer, "No, no, do not take me to the morgue. I am not dead yet! I know it looks like I am dead—or at least on my way to dead—but I am still here! I am in here somewhere."

If only Ma or Dad could find me.

What I did not know was that Ma, my dad, and Number 5 *were* frantically searching for me, having no idea where I had been taken—and by whom.

Three days earlier, just after the napalm bombs dropped,

my great-uncle had caught up to me and the reporters and photojournalists attempting to come to my aid.

As one of the Associated Press (AP) photographers, Huynh Cong "Nick" Ut, was wrapping a borrowed raincoat around my bloody, skinned body, Great-Uncle approached and hollered, "The children! Please take the children to hospital!"

Despite my undeniable debilitation, I had not been the only child injured that day. Hearing the exhortation, the photographer led me to his AP van, carefully got me and the others inside, and told the driver to rush toward town.

Nick Ut (pronounced "oot") was only twenty-one years old and had been on the scene somewhat accidentally, having decided to come to Trang Bang on a whim the night before. The battle between South Vietnamese forces and the Viet Cong for control of my village had been raging for three days, and the young photographer figured that perhaps it was ready to come to a head. At 8:00 a.m. he drove to a spot only a kilometer or so from the temple where my family and I were hiding and set up his camera, capturing for several hours shots of smoke rising from bombings in the distance; of military jets overhead; of rivulets of frantic refugees fleeing Trang Bang, trying to avoid certain death.

Uncle Ut, as I would come to call him, had been mostly self-trained in photography, deciding at age seventeen to follow in the footsteps of his brother, an AP wartime photographer who had been killed on assignment in 1965 when communist forces overtook the Mekong Delta. Although Uncle Ut was not an especially skilled photographer, he was teachable. He had worked his way up from being a darkroom assistant to being a field photographer, determined to make his brother proud.

Uncle Ut would later tell me that he had planned on turning back and heading for Saigon just before lunchtime on June 8, that he had enough photos to call it a day. But as he was packing up his cameras and batteries and film, crimson and gold streaks flashed in his peripheral vision. "That is not a bomb," he said aloud. "That is a signal."

He dropped his bags to the ground and positioned himself to document what was happening, first capturing the four bombs dropping from the Skyraider; then the wave of fire and smoke; then soldiers and civilians running for their lives; and then, as it turns out, me. As I ran along Route 1, Uncle Ut snap, snap, snapped his camera shutter, wondering as I got closer why I wore no clothes. It was only when I passed him that he could see my body was burned.

"I am dying! I am dying!" he heard me cry, prompting him to set down his camera and come help me. Not only did he save my life that afternoon—he also logged proof of my days. The sum of what I know from that day and the days to follow, I owe to Uncle Ut. His memories became my memories when I fell unconscious.

—m—

As soon as the AP van sped away, Great-Uncle went to find my parents and convey to them three terrible truths: Their daughter had been burned; she had passed out from shock; and she had been taken by some stranger to some hospital, somewhere in South Vietnam.

My brother and my parents traveled on foot from our

village of Trang Bang to Saigon, joining those refugees who were also running away. Route 1 was a crush of people attempting to escape the inferno that our province had become in the swift moment it took for that single plane to appear overhead. But I have to believe my parents were the most desperate of them all. When Ma and Number 5 questioned the staff at the closest clinic they could find, Bac Ha Hospital in Cu Chi, a town twenty kilometers from where I was located, they were told, "The girl is not here." When Dad questioned the staff at Cho Ray, Saigon's largest general hospital, he was told, "The girl is not here."

Unbeknownst to Ma and Dad, they both were heading to First Children's Hospital—a journey of just over fifty kilometers that had taken three long days to cover. On June 11, my parents arrived within hours of each other, each one convinced they had finally located their daughter. When the staff there told my ma and brother, "She is not here," a sense of quiet resignation threatened to overtake them. My ma did not give in, though, instead whispering to my brother, "We look anyway." And so they did, searching all eight floors of the facility, room by room, determined to find their little Kim Phuc.

During that search, Ma happened upon a man who worked in custodial services for the hospital. "Have you seen a young burn victim, a girl of nine years?" she sputtered out, anxious for any indication of my whereabouts. "She would have been admitted in the past two or three days."

Wartime burn victims rarely survived, a fact this man must have surely understood. In response to my ma's plea for answers, he lazily pointed his mop toward a small structure just outside the hospital's main doors and mumbled, "That room there? That is where they put the ones who die."

My ma gathered her strength and walked toward the outbuilding, having no idea what awaited her behind the closed door.

—⟋⟍⟍—

In fact, Uncle Ut had tried to find help for me in Cu Chi, but the nurses there had refused to accept me. They did not have the staff to tend to me, they told him, nor did they possess the resources to treat severe burns. Uncle Ut showed them his media credentials and issued to them a not-so-subtle threat: "You will treat this girl today, or else you will find great trouble tomorrow."

As Uncle Ut pocketed his credentials and turned to rush to the AP office where he would file the day's stunning shots, the nurses at Cu Chi accepted me at once.

In that hospital staff's defense, they did their best to address my needs, bandaging my wounds and arranging my transfer to Saigon's First Children's Hospital, a larger, more sophisticated facility that in their minds would be better equipped to manage my care. But in the end their actions were a death wish issued on my behalf; the doctors and nurses there in Saigon looked me over, assessed the third- and fourth-degree burns that had seared all three layers of my skin as well as the muscles and ligaments that held together the bones of my small body, and determined I was a hopeless case. They had seen scores of similar situations already throughout the tragic war years, and napalm-burn victims never survived. And so, in my unconscious state and with nobody present to advocate on my behalf, I was left to die.

———⟋⟍⟍⟍⟋———

Inside the hut that had been designated as First Children's morgue, I lay curled into myself on a small cot. My hair had been singed and was now clumped by pus and blood. My face was swollen to three times its normal size. The bandages that had been wrapped around my neck, arm, and back at Cu Chi were soaked through, the fluids from my wounds gluing them to my charred skin. And my skin was beginning to rot, filling the air with a nauseating metallic stench.

There was a young boy lying on the cot beside mine, and despite my horrifying state, he was worse off still. He had sustained deep burns from firecracker-play gone awry, and his wounds had gone untended for so long that maggots now feasted on his flesh. My ma would tell me later that some of those maggots had made their way to my cot, my face, and my inner organs, now exposed. The sight of creatures devouring her daughter caused her to shiver in disbelief.

Pulling her shawl up to cover her nose, my ma came to my side and lifted my burned body onto her lap. She wept then, knowing nothing else to do. Her little girl was gone, and she had not even said goodbye.

My ma was not alone in the room, for seated next to her was the little boy's mother, there to grieve the loss of her child as well. After many minutes spent in silence, the woman glanced up at my ma and asked with a whisper, "If I may: Who is Danh?"

A certain darkness came over my ma's already somber

countenance. My precious three-year-old cousin, Danh, the little boy I loved as a brother, had not been fast enough to outrun the fire. In the rush from the temple, mothers and grandmothers had scooped up the babies from our village who could not yet walk. Danh was made to run on his short, chubby legs that were accustomed to toddling about, not moving quickly with balance and grace. Danh made it several feet out on the open road before a tenderhearted soldier caught sight of him and swept him up into his arms. The soldier ran and ran, but could not find his way out of the smoke. The fire overtook the soldier's entire body, burning him up and causing him to drop Danh to the ground.

By that time my grandmother had caught up to Danh and picked him up from the road. But it was too late; every inch of Danh's frame had been scorched. As Grandma ran with him toward safety, her bare feet slapping the puddles that dotted the ground, the skin of the little boy in her arms peeled off and flapped in the breeze, giving him the appearance of a molting animal. Danh was dead.

My aunt Anh lost two sons as a result of the napalm bombs—Danh that day, and nine-month-old Cuong, who died two months later. Like me, she had suffered burns, and the scars on her left leg and left hand would be a constant reminder of the horror.

"Danh is my nephew," my ma replied. "He died in the bombing of our village three days ago."

The woman looked with sympathy at my ma and said, "Your daughter has been silent except for once yesterday, when I heard her scream, "Danh. Wait, Danh. Danh! I go with you."

ALIVE, IF NOT COMPLETELY WELL

SUMMER AND MORE, 1972

It is said that even a tiny baby still housed in her ma's womb can recognize and will respond to the sound of her ma's voice. If true, this phenomenon may at least partially explain why, when nothing else could tug me out of unconsciousness and toward at least a semi-alert state, the sound of my ma's reply to that woman did the trick. I remember hearing her say of Danh, "He died." I remember her soft whispers, one grieving mother to another. I remember her professions of love for me as I lay there secretly wishing I could die like Danh.

I stirred then, to my ma's sweet voice, a flower bending itself toward the sun, and with that subtle movement my ma's hopes were revived. I was alive. Her My was alive!

In a matter of minutes, a series of events I now regard as "miraculous" then unfolded. My ma and my brother, realizing there was life left in me, scooped me up to carry me back into the hospital, which is when they literally ran into my dad. In rapid-fire sentences, Ma updated my dad on all that had unfolded and urged him, "Quickly! We must find help!"

My dad rushed back into the main hospital, intent on locating someone who might assist them with their almost-dead-but-not-dead-yet daughter, which is when he found a doctor who was ending his shift for the day and heading home. "Sir!" my father cried as he tugged on the doctor's laboratory coat. "My daughter was placed in the morgue, but she is still alive. You must help us! She needs your assistance . . . *please!*"

As the doctor's eyes met my father's eyes, both men were taken aback. Momentarily disoriented by seeing each other here, in a hospital corridor, in the midst of this crisis involving a child, they strained to sort out how they knew each other. For several seconds they simply stared at each other, blinking recognition but incapable of naming the connection. "University!" the doctor finally said with a finger-snap, his broad smile celebrating his powers of recall. And so it was that my father and his classmate from twenty years prior were reunited in Saigon.

Within half an hour, an ambulance arrived at the front doors of First Children's Hospital to transport me to Cho Ray's Center for Plastic and Reconstructive Surgery in Saigon, known by locals as the Barsky Unit, in honor of the center's founder, the late American doctor Arthur Barsky. There were fifty-four beds in the unit, and my parents and Dad's doctor friend hoped that one would be available for me.

Staffed primarily by local doctors, the Barsky Unit had already effectively treated more than thirty-five hundred children who had been wounded in the war. My father's friend had not called ahead, fearing that if he phoned the Barsky and asked permission to bring me over, the request would be denied. The unit did not "receive" new patients; it "invited in" new patients, and their backlog was nearly four hundred names long. Furthermore, nobody expected me to survive. Admitting me would mean assigning valuable resources to me, and the Barsky was already stretched thin.

When my ambulance arrived, staffers assumed they would turn it away, sending it on to some other hospital in Saigon that might have more resources, more room. But that is not at all what occurred. One of the on-call surgeons, Doctor Le My, looked at me and knew that if the Barsky could not help me, then nobody could. There simply was no other facility equipped to handle the needs I so clearly had. She saw me and saw my burns and saw the plea in my parents' eyes. She swallowed hard the hospital's regulations and official protocol. And she said quietly, "I will try to help."

First, I needed blood. My parents did not know my blood type (or theirs), and finding viable blood in my burned body to test was nearly impossible. The doctor finally extracted a sample from my heart and determined I was type A. Further quick tests proved Ma was a match, and she was prepped to donate. Because nearly all of the veins in my upper body had collapsed, Doctor Le My made an incision in a vein near my right ankle. When the first drop of Ma's blood entered that vein, my body responded and my vital signs improved. Everyone knew. *I was going to survive.* Still I had a long road ahead. Over the next few days, the initial treatments for my burns began, preparing me for the first of the sixteen surgeries I would undergo while a patient there. A seventeenth operation would take place in Germany many years later, when I was twenty-one years old. But here, now, at the Barsky, nobody knew I would ever see age twenty-one.

There is much I do not remember about my stay at the center—the people I met, the patients I shared space with, the surgeries I was made to endure—but a memory that will never leave me is that of my daily burn baths. The goal, according to what my parents were told, was threefold. Burn baths had been proven to improve the elasticity of burned skin. They were known to increase the patient's range of motion and ability to engage with the demands of physical therapy. And they created a greater sense of comfort and well-being for the sufferer. (Hospital staff did not mention to my parents that before the "comfort" part of the equation showed up, the patient would have to endure outright torment first.)

Every morning just after sunrise, two or three nurses would appear at the foot of my painted-metal recovery bed with grim news on their lips. "Kiiiim," one of them would all but whisper. "Good morning, little Kim. It is bath time, sweet Kim. Kiiiim, are you awake?"

In fact, I had been awake for many minutes by then, having heard their encroaching footsteps. I was not intending to deceive them by lying there motionless, eyes closed. Rather, some force deep inside me resisted all that was to unfold. I did not like the burn bath. I did not like the tormenting pain when the water contacted my wounds. I did not like any aspect of this treatment, and so I lay there aching for another way.

"Kiiiim? Hello, Kim?" the nurse was saying. "Kim, we will put you on gurney now."

And so my day would begin, in the same way every day began, for weeks and weeks on end. My naked body would be hoisted from the hospital bed onto the transport bed, which never so much as creaked underneath my light weight. One of the nurses would slowly wheel me into a sterile bathroom, where a stainless steel tub waited. As we entered the room, I could hear the mechanical hum of heaters and the rumble of jets that sloshed healing solution through the bath; the sounds struck me as something of a death march. "You are about to suffer," they said.

Once in the bath, a nurse would increase the agitation of the jets to full blast, and I would be submerged for a full thirty minutes' time as the water softened my skin.

The sting of those baths was so unbearable to me that nearly every morning, I passed out moments after being placed into the tub. One of the nurses would have to hold my head aloft so that I did not slip underwater and drown. The body tends to develop a tolerance to pain medications over time, and so with the exception of the first bath—and the most horrific, given how much charred flesh needed to be softened and removed—there was nothing the nurses could offer me in order to numb my body's pain receptors, save for reassuring smiles and tender hands. There was no morphine. No oxycodone. No *nothing* to subdue the full brunt of swirling water pounding unprotected nerve endings.

When my half-hour was up, nurses on either side of me would reach for my underarms, pulling me as gently as possible out of the tub and back onto the transport bed. Back in my room, different nurses holding sterile medical scissors cut away all the dead skin. In a rhythm I came to despise, as soon as enough rotted skin had been cleared, another skin-grafting operation would take place.

On several occasions, my father donned the hospital-issued sterile coverings and entered the bathroom with me, even as he was helpless in the face of my pain. Ma never once stood guard over the procedure, for the simple reason that our family needed income, and my burn bath always coincided with her busiest time in the noodle shop.

My oldest sister, Hai, did come to visit me at the hospital one morning, intending to support my burn-bath routine, but as soon as she saw me enter the waters, she herself fainted there on the spot. "We do not have adequate staff to care for your daughter *and* her visitors," the head nurse admonished my father, a clear signal that guests of mine had better come equipped with nerves of steel. The squeamish-stomached were not allowed; had I been better able to communicate my own state of mind, I, too, would have been evicted from the place.

Still today, whenever my pain comes to me I flash back to those burn baths and think, *Regardless of how terrible I feel in this moment, at least I do not feel as badly as I did then.* Oh, if there is a more fitting demonstration of the phrase "hell on earth" than the burn bath, I do not want to know what it is. Those baths were worse than death itself. Dying is far worse than death.

During that first week, my ma would shuttle back and forth between Saigon and Trang Bang—about a ninety-minute trip by bus—doing her best to manage her noodle shop while at the same time supporting her struggling child. Daddy would sit at my bedside from morning to night, leaving only just before my bedtime, when hospital staff informed him that visiting hours were over. He would then shuffle out the hospital's front doors to the stone bench he used for a bed, make himself as comfortable as possible for the few hours he was forced to be away from me, rest as best he could, and then, as soon as the hospital doors opened in the morning, make his way right back to my bedside.

For nearly forty days, I remained in critical condition at the Barsky, leaving doctors and nurses and my parents wondering if I would ever truly recover, if I would "come back to myself." I received 100 percent of my food intravenously, I could not wear clothes, and while rehabilitation efforts eventually commenced, progress was painfully slow. I could not stand. I could not walk. My head could not swivel. My hands could not grip. I was an invalid, disabled in every conceivable way.

Whenever Ma and Dad were together, they carefully surveyed my situation. More than 30 percent of my body had been deeply singed; my organs were extremely vulnerable to infection; I had sluggish circulation throughout my torso and limbs, which meant my mobility was terribly compromised; and because my body was using all its resources to try to heal my skin, my strength day by day was sapped.

"If she will be so disabled all of her life," my ma would whisper to my dad when they were beyond my ear's range of hearing, "then I think it better that she die."

Equally resolved that he did not want his child to suffer for the rest of her days, my adoring father would soberly nod his head in agreement. *Yes, I agree. Who would wish such pain on his little girl?*

And so it was, that across that span of tumultuous critical-care days, Ma begged the gods of CaoDai, "Please, take my daughter from this life."

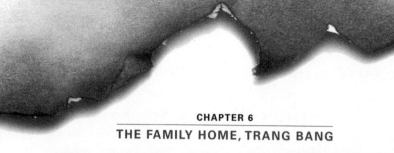

CHAPTER 6

THE FAMILY HOME, TRANG BANG

THE CURSE CALLED DIFFERENT

AUGUST 1973

When the war came to my village of Trang Bang, it was as if someone flipped a grand light switch into the off position; what had been bright and beautiful was now decimated and dim. Gone were the laughter and whimsy; gone were those thriving fruit trees; gone were lazy days and innocence; gone was abundance in all its forms. Those napalm bombs were dropped, and everything exploded—our resources, our freedoms, our lives.

Contrary to Ma's desperate prayers that I would be taken from this life, and defying all the smart doctors' hypotheses regarding my survival, I did get discharged from the hospital—even if a full fourteen months after my admittance. And upon arriving back home, I saw with my own two eyes what my parents had reported to me all along. We really *had* lost everything. We were now officially poor.

Technically, my family's house was still standing, but the roof was so compromised that I could now see the night-time stars while standing within the remains of my bedroom. Walls were so sporadic throughout the home that people could come and go as they pleased, which was fine if those people were friends and not thieves.

On one occasion, thieves did come, tying up my great-uncle, two of my brothers, and me, and threatening to murder us if we did not comply with their demands for the money they believed we had, as though we had anything at all to give.

"We must tie you here until you tell us where the money is!" one of the men shouted at Great-Uncle, who later speculated aloud that the men had heard from chatty people in the area that my family was receiving financial assistance from kindhearted people who wanted to help fund my rehabilitation.

The truth was that those funds never made it to us. Mysteriously, between the philanthropists' hands and my parents' hands (and the government's facilitation of the exchange in between), those monies disappeared.

As I sat there with bound wrists and surges of pain running up and down my arm, watching the robbers overturn what remained of our furniture while hissing at us to remain silent, I could only blink in disbelief.

"Quit lying to us!" the thieves barked at my family. "We will kill you if you do not speak the truth!"

Thankfully, Great-Uncle suspended his fear long enough to realize that the ill-intentioned men had not properly tied up Number 5.

"Too loose! They tied you too loose!" he whispered repeatedly to my brother. "Work out that knot. It is loose! Get out!"

My brother took advantage of the distracted state of the robbers, who were frantically searching other rooms to find riches. Within five minutes of the thieves' arrival, Number 5 had sprung free and fled for Grandma's. Moments later, my grandmother, my grandfather, and my aunt descended on our property, yelling for anyone and everyone to hear, "Robber! Robbers inside! Robbers are trying to kill us! Robbers! Help us! Help us, please!"

Those robbers, sensing they would soon be outnumbered, tripped over themselves trying to get out. I can still see them in my mind's eye, racing empty-handed into the bright sunlight.

My grandfather rushed to my side and began working on the heavy knot, careful not to tug on my wounds, all of which were throbbing now. We were relieved that we had survived the ordeal, but the experience left a deep mark on me. As terrible as it was to live in the hospital for more than a year, I actually longed to return there, where I was cared for, well-fed, and safe.

As far as how people fared throughout Trang Bang, we were the lucky ones. For many friends and neighbors, all they could claim as the year 1973 unfolded was a giant hole in the ground, one bomb or another having completely erased any proof of their having lived there. Still, as days crept on, I felt anything but lucky. Gone were the indoor washrooms we once took for granted. Gone was the refrigerator to cool our food, and the freezer from which we had gathered ice—an especially meaningful loss, given the heat my scorched skin produced and the headaches that now plagued me daily. Gone were the days when my parents had discretionary monies, which we now could have put toward medicine for my pain and therapy for my skin. Oh, how I longed to fully stretch out my arm and make a fist with my hand. But I couldn't.

We had little food—only what Ma could afford to bring home at the end of her day from her shop. We had been thriving before, but since the war had come to us? We were not thriving anymore.

———

My discharge from the Barsky Unit came in the summer, and while I had initally been elated about all the things I would do—climb my favorite tree, eat my beloved guava, pick up the bound love stories in my book nook, and play with my dear friend Hanh—life back home was not nearly as charming as I hoped. For two years' time, my brothers and sisters and I endured abysmal living conditions, showering outside in a hose-fed puddle, subsisting on bits of leftover rice and cold vegetables, shivering in fear each night from thoughts of more thieves returning.

For my part, things were made far worse by the fact that I was in debilitating and constant pain. The pain was sharp those days, the sharpest I had known. In order to find any relief at all, I had to rapidly pound my flesh. I could use my right fist to a certain extent, but on more occasions than not, I had to beckon one of my brothers or sisters to pound me with their fists in an attempt to stimulate my body's blood flow.

My skin was clearly angry with me. It was thick. And tight. My range of motion was minimal. My skin was hot—too hot, because I could not sweat since my hair follicles had been burned off. And I was itchy, *so* itchy, with an itch that could not be scratched. My body was weeping its refusal to be soothed. I hated those burns, those scars, that pain. I craved relief that never would come. And yet despite every last external circumstance that threatened to overtake me—mind, body, and soul—the most agonizing pain I suffered during that season of life dwelled in my heart.

Before the war, my dear friend Hanh and I would play together each afternoon, two giggly girls soaking up life and talking of love. Together, we dreamed of the moment when we would meet our long-awaited princes—oh, the beautiful brides we someday would be! We adored each other as much as any two sisters, and in fact, we *were* related somehow, she being my ma's second cousin's daughter, or some connection such as that. I treasured Hanh, and Hanh treasured me.

When I returned to Trang Bang, to my family's home, even before I made a proper survey of my post-war room or my post-war guava tree, I looked up the road, eager to catch sight of Hanh's face. Surely she had witnessed my arrival; surely she soon would be coming to play. We would talk and laugh and climb and play. *Come, Hanh, come! Come to my house! I wait here for you!*

Glancing southward along Route 1, I saw sweet Hanh's face a good distance away. *My friend!* I thought. *I am home! We now can play!*

Hanh saw me bobbing toward her, my enthusiasm carrying me along the road, but in response to my cheers and wide smile and waving arm, she stood there, fixed to her spot. She was not also cheering. She was not also smiling. She was not also waving her arm at me, but rather was frozen there, standing in place. I slowed to a trot and then to a slow walk and then to a disillusioned stop. My dear friend did not want me to come closer. She did not want to be my dear friend anymore.

"Oh," I whispered to the thick air surrounding me. "It is true. Hanh has heard all the reports. I am burned. I am scarred. I am not normal now."

Months later, Hanh's father happened to be at our house and observed me trying to sip broth from one of the porcelain teacups Ma had brought home from her shop. I was making progress in my healing, but that left hand of mine still had a mind of its own. For instance, despite my brain asking it to grip the handle of that cup, it simply refused to curl around the cup's form. On that day, the cup slipped out of my grip altogether, crashing to the floor. The hot soup splashed up onto my leg, which made me cry. The tears were not due to the pain, however; they were due to my embarrassment. Here I was, a girl of ten, who could not even hold a cup.

Hanh's father looked at my ma and said, "You need a coconut husk for the girl to drink from. It is the only way to protect your fine dishes!"

I did not hear him say those words in the moment. No, it would be years and years later when my ma would tell me what he had said. Even then, the syllables would sting. They would sting as sharply as had that napalm, and napalm stings worst of all.

Sometime after returning home from the Barsky, I was able to reflect on the afternoon of the bombings, to sit with my memories of that June day and consider all that had transpired. My family would ask me questions, prompting me to piece together what I recalled, and time and again, the single thought I remember thinking, even as I was racing from the temple up Route 1 was this: *I am ugly now.* I was not thinking about fire, or about my family, or about matters of life and death. I was thinking only about the scars I would have and about how terrible those scars would look.

To some extent, my awareness of physical beauty— firmly instilled in me even by age nine—was a natural part of Vietnamese life. In my culture, women care for their bodies, hair, and skin with greater attention than in any other culture I have seen. As a young child, I would watch my ma prepare for her workday by allowing her long, dark tresses to fall from a bun in order to dry properly in the air. She would carefully smooth oil into the ends and then brush the strands until they lay perfectly flat. After gently rubbing cream into her cheeks, her forehead, and her chin, she would dress in her smart *ao ba ba*.

Ma did not choose the floral patterns preferred by other women, favoring instead the straightforwardness of black wide-legged pants and a stark-white tunic top. The bell sleeves that tapered out toward the wrist and the slits from hip bone to waist together formed a stunning silhouette around Ma's slender frame. I did not know what I wanted to be when I grew up, but I surely hoped it involved looking like Ma. And yet now, what hope was there for me, an alien in my own land?

If only I could have returned to the hospital, where *everyone* did not fit in. There, every person had a problem, an ailment, a disability, a scar, a pain. I fit in so well among those misfits! But here? Even my closest friend was too frightened by my appearance to come near.

I now understand why Ma had prayed for me to die.

———ᴍ———

I made an agreement in those moments when the napalm scorched my clothing and then my skin and then the fat and muscle and other tissue that had once thrived in layers below my skin, that because I would now and forever be seen as "different," I was unfit to be loved.

My pale beautiful skin was now appalling, mushy and bumpy and red.

I am unfit to be loved.

My long, glossy hair, which once cascaded halfway down my back, was now a crunchy, uneven bob.

I am unfit to be loved.

I no longer looked anything like the other girls.

I am unfit to be loved.

I would never be normal or acceptable.

I am unfit to be loved.

As days turned into weeks and months and my "healing" began to take place, I would come to understand that my suffering, which had begun on that fateful 1972 day, would not be confined to a thin slice of time.

"This suffering, unfortunately, will stay with you," doctors would tell me there at the burn clinic where I was being made well. "You will always have scars, you will always have challenges, and you will always have very high pain."

You might think such news would have alarmed me,

given that I was still only nine and then ten years old. But the underlying message I heard loud and clear shook the foundation of my life even more. *You are unfit to be loved now, Kim.*

That is the message I heard.

Years later, womanly curves would replace my board-straight frame as I entered the teenage stage, and that inner vow of being unfit for love only lodged itself deeper in my heart. Certainly, the physical and hormonal changes coursing through my body naturally compelled me to want to be found beautiful, to attract a man with whom I would spend the rest of my life, to present myself as desirable, as engaging, as what the Vietnamese call *hấp dẫn.* But certainly, none of this was meant to be. After all, who would desire a woman with a tragic past, with buffalo-hide skin, and with the inability to conceive? (Doctors had warned me of the eventuality, anyway; who was I to question them?)

For now, at age ten, living in a skeleton of a house in Trang Bang, enduring devastating pain that most days leveled me flat, trying my best to manage both the heat inside my body and the outside air's average of ninety-five sweltering degrees, all I knew for sure was that I no longer was golden, and I no longer was happy. I did not care for the Kim Phuc I had become, even as I would soon be asked to fight for her life yet again.

GETTING OUT

24 APRIL 1975

The napalm bombs that burned me had been dropped just after I had completed the third grade, and my ensuing hospital visit swallowed every last bit of what should have been my fourth-grade year. Upon my return home, all of the children in my village were preparing for the coming school year, when my peers would be entering the fifth grade. I was woefully unprepared to join them, even as I determined in my heart to do so. I sought out Number 2, our family's resident schoolteacher, and pled my case. "If you will help tutor me," I said to Hai, "then I know I can keep up. Please, do not allow them to put me into the fourth grade. I wish to stay with my class."

It told me everything I needed to know about my sister's confidence in me that she barely deliberated at all. "I will help you, My," she said. "Of course! Let us begin working even now." The fall of 1973, all of 1974, the winter and early spring of 1975—that twenty-month period sits in my recollection still today as my "catch-up season," a time when my sole focus was regaining at least some of what had been lost. I doubled up on my school assignments. I listened carefully, imploring my brain to work harder, as Hai explained the basics of algebra. I pushed past my pain as best I could, intent on completing my work. And in the end, my focused effort paid off. I completed both the fourth and fifth grades in one school year, a shock to everyone, including me.

In the same way that I tried to regain ground at school, Ma and Dad worked diligently at home. Ma still had her shop to run, but anytime she had a spare hour, she joined Dad in his attempt to rebuild our home. While I had been in the hospital, I learned that the war had returned to our village a full four times. My parents would get one part of our home reconstructed, only to suffer even graver losses the next time destruction rained down. By the time I was back home, things in our immediate vicinity had settled down, but a dark cloud still loomed: *Will there be a fifth time? Will Trang Bang become a hot zone again?*

The answer to both, unfortunately, was yes.

Nearly three years after I sustained my burns, my family and I were pushed permanently from our home by the war. The bombs that erupted around us were different this time around. "Mortar bombs," they were called, so named for the mortar projectiles fired from the device's barrel. These bombs did not fall straight down from a plane in the sky, as napalm bombs had, but rather were propelled upward from a tripod on the ground, hitting their target only after making a high, tight arc in the air.

At the beginning of 1975, two years after the United States had pulled out of our war and one year into my country's government-sanctioned ceasefire with our enemy, South Vietnamese and communist forces stirred up their hatred toward each other once more, and for Viet Cong fighters, anyway, the weapon of choice was the mortar bomb. There was a distinctive dual-pitched whistle when a mortar shell exploded, most likely caused by the metal fragments flying through the air. Even now, whenever I hear a sound that resembles that tone, a reflexive shiver runs up my spine.

I remember being on a bus not too many years ago, innocently crossing town in the course of my normal daily routine, when I found myself emotionally sideswiped. A military man boarded, and the combination of his army-issued fatigues and the whistle of the bus's air brakes as the driver resumed his route threw me into such a state of panic that I had to turn my back to the man and force myself to breathe. The man, of course, meant me no harm. But that singular sight, that terrible sound . . . the memories came rushing back.

Back in my village of Trang Bang in April 1975, I did not know what lay ahead for me. I knew only that both inside myself and outside, in my world, I was struggling. So *deeply* was I struggling, and yet there was no time to wallow in despair, as my family's very lives were on the line. Those mortar bomb whistles were sounding with such frequency in and around our village that it might as well have been one long, sustained cry, and sensing the very worst, my ma ushered us kids out of our home again.

Here I was, twelve years old; just a girl, still, not even a teen. But oh, how much life I had seen already—how much pain and how much fear. "Run, children! Run!" Ma pleaded, even as mortars erupted overhead. We headed back to our temple, which had been spared during the napalm attack that began mere feet from its front door, this time to the main sanctuary. If ever we needed some god to smile on us, we needed divine intervention now. Our world was being detonated from the inside out. We just knew we were goners this time.

From the safety of the temple's inner sanctum, I stared with wide eyes at the world outside. Finding a window tucked at the very back of the ornate room, I silently raised the decorative covering to find mortar shrapnel flying through the air. I knew that is what I would see when I peeked, for I had heard that whistle's shriek. But to see the devastation left behind in its wake? Jolting, so very terrifying to watch.

"It was a big one," I whispered to my brother, who had joined me at the lookout spot.

After spending the night at our temple, Ma decided that we needed to go farther, that we were not at all safe in this spot. And so we ran to a smaller temple on the other side of the village. Our temple was considered a "father temple," and our destination was called a "mother temple," but this pair of parents was not at all closely wedded; by foot, it would take us a half-hour to get from one to the other.

We ran along unpaved paths that were canopied by full-grown trees, which meant that as soon as we built up speed, we became targets for helicopters overhead. Those aircrafts were being piloted by South Vietnamese soldiers who never would have purposefully harmed their own, but because the forest was dense and our feet were swiftly moving, they took us for Viet Cong. And what they did when they spotted these South Vietnamese dissidents was fire, and fire, and fire. Bullets whizzed past our ankles, which only caused us to forge ahead with greater determination and speed.

I would later learn about the rules of war, about avoiding what is ridiculously called "friendly fire," as though any "fire" can be friendly, as though there is ever something cheerful to be seen in war. But the rule is this: Whenever active battle is occurring around you, never—I mean *never*—run. Instead, plant your feet as the planes or helicopters make their way past your position, craning your head skyward and holding still. Then they will know you are harmless, that you are mere citizens fighting for life.

Still, I am here to tell you: When bombs are being fired from the ground on which you stand and opposing troops are contesting those bombs with bullets shot from the air, there is no way whatsoever to counteract your natural impulses to *run, run, run* with everything you have got. Stay *still*? Look *skyward*? Remain *calm*, as though all is okay? Forget about it! It is impossible. To stay alive, you must at least try to run.

Eventually, we did make it to the mother temple, my ma, my siblings, and me. My dad was in town once again that day, resuming his usual wartime routine. When we arrived at that secondary shelter, scores of neighbors had already beat us there. My grandmother was there already also, as were two of my aunts with their children in tow. So many of us had descended on that place and exhausted its resources that by day two, we were desperate for food. Two CaoDai temples in as many days, a chorus of pleading prayers for divine help, and yet not one of the myriad gods we revered seemed to be able to get us out of this mess.

—⁓—

Midafternoon on the second day of our stay at the mother temple, one of my ma's cousins named Lieu pulled up in the truck that he used for his forestry business and announced that he and his family were bound for Tay Ninh, the capital city of our entire province, which was also named Tay Ninh. His words were clipped and his tone urgent as he asked if any of us wanted to make the fifty-kilometer journey with them. It was understood that we would have to pay him a fee for the transportation, and I watched closely as my dad, who had been reunited with us earlier that morning, exchanged quick words and rapid-fire nods with my ma, landing on a decision in a matter of seconds. *Yes. Yes, our family will go.*

Lieu turned out to be a very good driver, which was a great benefit to the thirty of us who had climbed aboard, given the skill required to navigate the rutted roads, avoid direct hits from gunfire overhead, and swerve out of the way of the shrapnel that was exploding all around. I have seen video games that pale by comparison to the wild ride my family experienced that day.

As a young child, I was too distracted by idyllic circumstances to fear war. But now? I was older now. I knew well to be afraid. And yet how good and right it felt to leave Trang Bang, the hot seat of these latest battles. In Tay Ninh, we would find replenished resources. In Tay Ninh, we would find the Holy See, our religion's grandest, greatest temple. In Tay Ninh, we would find help and hope and the fresh start we deeply desired. If only we could make it to Tay Ninh, life could begin again.

THE END OF WAR, AT LAST

LAST DAYS OF APRIL 1975

Ma's cousin Lieu went as far as the roads could take us, eventually coming to an abrupt halt at a section of Route 1 that had been barricaded by soldiers from South Vietnam. "You must not go any farther," one of the military men advised Lieu. "The fighting is too heavy for you and your passengers," he cautioned. "Also, the way is paved with landmines. You will not make it to Tay Ninh alive."

Lieu nodded his head in understanding. We could not go forward, but also, we could not go back. Trang Bang was being pummeled by Viet Cong attacks as well; what were we to do? With no other course of action available to us, Lieu put his heavy vehicle in reverse, backed away from the cordon, and backtracked along the road we had just traveled. The artillery fire was so intense for several minutes that Lieu removed his white shirt and began to wave it out the driver-side window, a signal of surrender he hoped would keep his truck from being targeted.

A kilometer or so along the path, Lieu took the turnoff for the hamlet of Gieng-gieng, where my ma's great-uncle and his family happened to live. Pulling up to someone's home unannounced was not a typical occurrence, but this was not a typical day. As soon as Lieu located the correct house, Ma jumped down from the truck and strode confidently toward the front entrance.

"We must ask you for help," she said to Uncle Thieu, who answered the door. To his everlasting credit, my great-great-uncle agreed to share what was left of his food rations with thirty hungry passersby, most of whom he had never met. He opened the two storage sheds on his property to us, allowing us all to bed down not for one night, but for four.

Those days crept by, slow as thick mud after a torrential rainstorm longing for the bottom of the hill, but at least we were safe. Or we enjoyed the *perception* of safety, I should say. We kids ran and played in Uncle Thieu's fields while the adults talked quietly about what to do, where to go, and how to secure food for their families. The piercing sounds of mortar bombs exploding in midair, of return gunfire ricocheting off the ground, made for an unnerving soundtrack during our time in Gieng-gieng, but there was a certain distance to the noise. It did not feel as though the explosions were right on top of us, as it had seemed while we were still in Trang Bang. We had removed ourselves from the epicenter of the turmoil, it seemed—that is, until that epicenter shifted and found us once again.

Just after dawn on April 30, Ma nudged me awake and said that we were continuing on to Tay Ninh. We had run out of food, we had run out of options, and there seemed to be a break in the bombings' rhythm sufficient for us to make our move. I was not at all sure how we would get past the military barricade that had forced us to Gieng-gieng in the first place, but I knew better than to give questions any voice. I gathered my few belongings, helped Ma herd my siblings, and found seats for us inside the truck.

None of our traveling companions remained in Gieng-gieng, agreeing with Ma that now was our chance. Uncle Thieu also came along, choosing to drive his own van rather than risk overloading Lieu's already burdened truck. The two vehicles caravanned along Route 1 successfully for quite some time, but just as we began to believe we might have actually made it out of harm's way, artillery fire exploded on all sides.

"Nooo!" Lieu hollered at the atmosphere, now thick with shrapnel and shells. He slammed on the brakes and then immediately smashed his foot down on the gas pedal, swerving and kicking up dust. He did not want to stay, but he did not want to go—such a predicament we all were in.

Lieu sped ahead, Uncle Thieu just behind him, until he reached a lush stand of tall trees. He barreled up a walking path, coming to a jolting stop half a kilometer in. His heart was racing. My heart was racing. Everyone's heart was racing, I think. We waited there in the forest for what felt like hours, all of us now piled into Uncle Thieu's vehicle until we knew what we would do next. At last, sensing a shift in the environment, Uncle Thieu pushed his transistor radio closer to his ear and heard something that caught his attention. "Shhh!" he nearly spat at us kids. "Quiet!"

We immediately complied. Uncle Thieu's eyes widened in disbelief over the broadcaster's news: The war, just like that, was over. South Vietnam was being ordered to lay down their weapons at once, for the North had overtaken Saigon. We all were communists now.

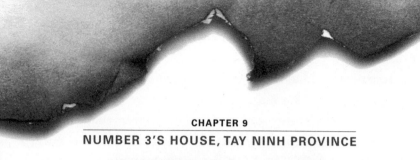

BEGINNING AGAIN

01 MAY 1975

"All soldiers, return," South Vietnamese President Duong Van Minh said via the airwaves during his final broadcast all across a weary country. "You must surrender. The war is over."

Most did surrender and conceded to the new regime. But some refused to turn in their weapons, turning those weapons on themselves instead. They would rather perish too soon than capitulate to the very people they had been fighting moments before. For my part, I bubbled over with enthusiasm and renewed energy. No more war! No more bombs! No more running in terror while gunfire peppered our path! I was elated. Life would be returned to me at last. As would laughter. Oh, how we all needed a good laugh.

In actuality, there had been moments of levity along the way. As is always the case, even the most treacherous situations have humorous interludes here and there, and our experience with war was no different. For example, when Ma was corralling us kids so that we could run from one temple to another to escape those dreadful mortar bombs, she began counting little bodies to be sure we all were there. My oldest sister and brother were already out of the house by then, married and engaged to be married, respectively, so there were six of us children left.

"*Một, hai, ba, bốn, nam . . .*" Ma counted but five. She counted us and counted us again, growing more anxious by the second. "Where is the baby?" she hollered at those of us who were present and accounted for, more accusation than question. For a moment it was silent, and then one of my siblings said quietly, "Ma, you are holding him on your hip."

Later, when we were rushing along the footpath to get to the mother temple, I caught sight of one of the handmade outdoor altars that Caodaists often erect in front of their homes, both to welcome the blessing of the gods and also to ward off any harmful spirits. Inside the altar, which looked to me like a modified self-standing bird feeder, was a pile of incense, a bouquet of flowers and fronds, and a bunch of ripe bananas. Without breaking stride, I ran directly to that altar, grabbed the entire bunch of bananas, plucked one from its companions and peeled it, then shoved the entire fruit into my mouth. A banana has never tasted so good, I must say.

I thought back on those moments and laughed and laughed. It had felt very good to feel something akin to happiness for once, and now, here in Tay Ninh with the war behind us, I expected more of the same in days to come.

—⁂—

Six of us—my father, my brother Number 5, my family's three youngest children, and I—overtook my older brother's home, which sat on CaoDai property and which my ma had purchased for him with profits from her shop a year or so after he was married. Ma had been tempted to come with us but knew that our family's only hope for survival was income from the noodle shop in Trang Bang. She made the tough decision to return and remain there.

Like so many young men his age, my brother Number 3 had successfully dodged the South Vietnamese draft by taking shelter at the CaoDai temple in Tay Ninh, the Holy See. In exchange for food to eat and a small stipend, he provided custodial and managerial services to the temple. My brother—Ngoc is his given name, but we call him "Ba," meaning "three"—would find safety among that group, as we all would following the war.

Ba and his wife had young twin girls, and with ten people crammed into a house meant for four, things were a little tight. There was no extra space. There was no indoor plumbing. There was very little food. And the illusion of safety and predictability we initially enjoyed—walking to school; keeping the home neat; coming together for a family meal; resting peacefully on bamboo mats through the night—was soon enough dismantled. Now, three and a half years after the war ended, we were caught by the escalation of Cambodia's atrocious genocidal movement across the country's shared border with Tay Ninh, a response to Vietnam's Christmas Day 1978 attack on Kampuchea, Cambodia's communist name.

It was interesting: The Vietnamese and the Kampucheans originally had banded together in an attempt to wipe out any and all anti-communist sympathizers, but as is so often the case with wrongdoers, they wind up turning on each other. Those in Cambodia eventually came to fear Vietnam's motives and decided to dismantle them before the Vietnamese could rise up and take over for good.

By the start of 1979, "normal daily life" was replaced by one terror-filled moment after another, with all of us residents fearing the worst. For several years, my typical routine involved getting myself to school, staying after hours to volunteer help in cleaning or straightening the classrooms, getting myself back to my brother's house in order to complete my homework, walking to the temple for various worship services, and assisting my sister-in-law in caring for her twin girls. But as mortar-bomb launches became more frequent—now occurring not only at night, but also in broad daylight—even ordinary comings and goings were now seen as risks too great to take.

Clambering into our homemade bomb shelters brought little relief, since (a) they were hardly big enough to hold everyone, and (b) snakes also took shelter in there. I was afraid of the bombs. I was afraid of the snakes. I was afraid of everyday life. So much had shifted for me between ages eight and fifteen. I liked life a lot better when I was younger.

To assist with the incessant need to feed our family, my dad would take the bus back to Trang Bang each weekend to pick up a large bag of rice from Ma. For many years, Ma would live at her noodle shop, sleeping on a rolled-out bamboo mat on the restaurant floor.

Days after our trek to Tay Ninh, Ma had gone back to Trang Bang to survey the state of our property. She found a massive pile of rubble where our house once stood. Farm animals lay decapitated. Pieces of soldiers' bloodied bodies dotted the landscape. Shrapnel covered the ground. A thick layer of dust and debris filled the air. "It is no more," she said aloud, shaking her head in disbelief.

Once we kids were settled in Tay Ninh, Dad returned to Trang Bang to help Ma sort through those remains, in hopes of finding even one treasure among so much trash, but there was nothing to be found. It had all been blown to bits. Our official CaoDai worship garments, a prayer book, and my records from the Barsky—those were the only things that remained, and those, only because my dad had had the foresight to stash them in Ma's shop.

And so, in order to keep us all alive, Ma would work her fingers nearly to the bone each week, setting aside a portion of her profits and her excess rice. Dad would return to Tay Ninh with rations in hand, prepared for another week of service to his children as primary caretaker and cook. Yes, I had always loved my father's cooking, but with only a few sparse ingredients available to him, his once-delicious meals now left much to be desired.

—⁂—

In terms of my inner world, as weeks gave way to months and months turned into years, certain themes began to emerge, imprisoning me with a sense of despair. I was hurting, for one; physically, my pain was great. Each day, my father or one of my siblings would try to help me reach areas on my neck and back I could not reach myself, pounding my flesh with all their might. But the relief was momentary at best. As soon as their fists stopped pounding, my pain prevailed again.

Most days, I came home from school, found a quiet corner, and cried and cried and cried. *When will this torture end for me? When will I feel happy and whole?*

And then there was the distance from my ma. A young girl entering womanhood needs her attentive mother close by. And yet mine was living in another village, which may as well have been another planet.

Practically, I understood why Ma had to remain in Trang Bang. She was no less than *famous* there—or her noodle soup was, at least. That crunchy pork and those slow-cooked vegetables, which she laboriously swaddled with homemade rice papers and sent swimming in scallion-studded broth—Ma had been perfecting her recipe for *forty years*. People traveled from far and wide for that delicious food, each one willing to pay a handsome sum. We would have been foolish to demand that she relocate to Tay Ninh with us, where nobody knew her or her soup.

But emotionally, it was a different story. I was just a girl who longed for her ma.

On occasion, the distance would be too great for Ma to bear as well, and on those days, she would change clothes immediately after closing her shop, step onto the bus headed for Tay Ninh, and reunite with us, eager for the familiarity of home. During the summer, I would sometimes take the bus southward to visit her. I wanted with all my heart to relish those visits, but the accommodations were unkind to me. Ma's shop was right on Route 1, and between the night's incessant traffic sounds—honking horns, the roar of truck engines, young Vietnamese men shouting—the discomfort of Ma's thin bamboo mat, and the flapping of the mosquito net on my easily irritated skin, even on days when I was "dog tired," as they say, there was no sleep to be had.

Poor Ma. It would have been much better for her to have lived with my grandma, whose home was within walking distance of Ma's shop. But my two aunts were living there already, and because so much of Grandma's home had been blown to bits by bombs, my ma would have needed her bamboo mat there as well. No, this was the right arrangement for us. I just did not like the arrangement at all.

Another challenge for me was that I had no friends—or at least none with whom I was as intimate as I had been with Hanh. The terrible scars I bore had turned a sweet, shy girl into an insecure, self-conscious recluse who was fearful of reaching out. What would people think of me once they saw my wretched skin?

Honestly, I did not want to find out. It was safer to be alone. "Why do you not wear short sleeves?" girls from school would sometimes ask me. Oh, if they only knew.

And so the pretty girls, the girls in short sleeves, the girls who had soaring self-esteem, would walk past me in chatty little clumps, tending to relationships I would know nothing of. And the handsome boys would zoom past on their bicycles and motorbikes, having no idea how much I loved them. And the world would keep on spinning, even as I was stuck in a quicksand of self-doubt.

Having nowhere else to turn to soothe the ache that

pounded in my chest every day of every week, every week of every month, I looked to my studies to provide some sort of proof that I was "making it" in life. I had been a very competitive little girl who loved the challenge of schoolwork, but after I sustained my burns, I found it very difficult to concentrate. What took my classmates a half-hour or forty-five minutes to complete took me at least two hours, sometimes more.

"You do not have to be the best!" my brother and sister-in-law continuously assured me. "We are happy you are alive! Do not be so hard on yourself, Phuc. Learn what you can, and enjoy your schooling. People will understand if you cannot be the best."

I despised their patronage. I wanted to be the best.

During my time at the Barsky, I was so moved by the staff that tended to me every morning and every night that I resolved in my heart to become a doctor myself. I could not labor in a restaurant like my ma. To be on my feet all day long was not an option, and I had no desire to be that close to fire. But medicine? Perhaps that was the path for me. I wanted to help people in the same way that I had been helped. And so I worked and worked and worked, completing math assignments, carefully learning anatomy, pasting a smile on my face for my teachers, even as my insides held oceans of tears.

In addition to applying myself at school, I resolved to thrive in my religion as well. I flung myself wholeheartedly at CaoDai, in exchange for garnering all the divine support the faith could provide. CaoDai looked down on gossip, and so I refused to chatter like other girls. CaoDai expected periods of vegetarianism, and so for one very long decade I eschewed all meat—not only during the required ten days per month, but every day. CaoDai required a whole host of prayers as part of one's moral purification, and so before entering a religious meeting, and before listening to a religious talk, and at the conclusion of a religious meeting, and upon returning home from my day's activities, and before going to bed each evening, and each morning upon rising from sleep, and before sitting down to study, and before placing food in my mouth at a meal, and upon completing breakfast or lunch or dinner, and upon the passing of a loved one, and upon facing some new form of suffering, and on what seemed to be ten thousand other occasions, I would pray the expected prayer. To *whom* I was praying, I was not entirely sure. But I was faithful to speak the words.

CaoDai held four services daily: at midnight, what is called the Hour of the Mouse; at six in the morning, the Hour of the Cat; at noon, the Hour of the Horse; and at sunset, the Hour of the Rooster. And so on exactly four occasions each day, I made my way to the giant Tay Ninh temple, the empire, really, of our faith. In advance of each of those worship services, I would carefully dress in my white worship garments and prepare my mind for what was to come.

There would be the ritual ringing of the ceremonial gong; the official opening chants; the bowing in deference to other worshipers who had gathered; and the rise of music, which filled the room. I would fix my gaze on the Divine Eye, the symbol of our faith, as all of the divinities were welcomed by clarinet, bassoon, drums, cymbals, and buffalo horn, into the majestic place. I would kneel when told to kneel, rise when told to stand, lift my hand to shoulder or forehead when instructed along such lines, fully attentive, fully engaged, fully expecting whatever benefits should come to one as fully devoted as me. I would listen carefully as the ceremonial leader closed each service with the offerings to the deities of wine and flowers and tea, and I would speak clearly as the congregation recited the Five Pledges before departing. And then I would exit the temple, feeling in my inner person every bit as tumultuous as I had felt ninety minutes earlier.

Perhaps it would just take time and greater devotion, so I worked toward both of these aims, telling myself, "Give it time, My. Apply yourself with more heart. Do not give up. This is your only hope!" But by age sixteen, I had to face the truth of the matter, which was that no amount of devotion was going to yield the level of peace I desperately sought. Sure, there were glimpses of happiness tucked inside the tumult—such as when I rode my bicycle through the trees en route to the temple, singing songs to feathered friends flitting overhead. But those glimpses were fleeting, both figuratively and in the case of that bicycle, literally. Thieves robbed my brother's house one night, taking every last possession we had, my bicycle, my hospital records, and the newspaper clippings of my napalm experience included.

No, any prospect of hope for me appeared so infrequently that it could not eclipse the pain I bore.

"When you kneel down," my sister-in-law used to say to me, "your problems look like mountains. But when you stand up tall, the world is at your feet." The philosophy sounded good to me, and so I adopted it as a mantra for life. "Stand up, My. Life will be at your feet!"

And so I would. I would stand up to my problems by leaving them all behind.

LEAVING, FOR GOOD

AUGUST 1979

I was sixteen years of age, just a second-year high school student, the first time I boarded a boat to escape from Vietnam. For twenty years following the war, especially during 1978 and 1979, more than two million Vietnamese refugees fled our homeland[4] in hopes of resettling in safer lands. They loaded themselves in groups five to ten times more than capacity, onto large round rafts, onto rowboats, onto fishing boats, onto any seaworthy vessel, really, and made for a middle-of-the-night exodus. Like baby Moses floating along the river in that vulnerable basket of reeds, they placed their fate into the hands of a big-hearted princess they trusted would miraculously appear. And yet for a high percentage of those escapees, the voyage would end not in rescue, but in death, either because of swelling sea storms, untreated disease, pirate attacks, starvation, dehydration, or their boat simply not proving strong enough to make the dangerous trip.

Perhaps this is why neither my ma nor my dad ever spoke of escape; they saw what happened to those who tried and figured it was not worth the risk. Or else they could not get past the fact that we did not possess the funds necessary for such a voyage. There were fees required—monies due to the trip organizer, to the boat captain, to the merchants selling survival gear for the journey—and financially we were already pressed on all sides. Only later would I learn that at one time we had plenty of money set aside, that at one time we could have escaped.

Across the years, whenever travelers stopped by Ma's shop for soup, more times than not they asked for local currency, in exchange for the selling of their wares. Figuring those goods would someday be useful, Ma was always willing to trade. Day by day, then, Ma released her stash of Vietnamese *dong* for all manner of valuable things—gold bars, gold jewelry, Cambodian china plates—and then buried those items under a bamboo tree on our property to keep them safe, to keep them *ours*.

What Ma failed to take into account were those Viet Cong tunnels and the digging each of them required. Sometime during my stay in the hospital, my great-uncle went with Ma to the site of that bamboo tree and dug until their hands were sore, only to find the earth giving way underneath their feet and opening up a tunnel where those riches used to be. All Ma's earthly possessions, gone.

But truly, even if my parents had the funds to leave,

would they actually have boarded the boat? Our family was in Vietnam. Our earning potential was in Vietnam. Our *life* was in Vietnam. Where were we to go? For me, at least, the answer was a simple one: The same land that had destroyed me could not help build me back up. If it was true that the best way to take on an opponent was with the same weapons or tactics that that opponent had used against me—"fighting fire with fire," or in my native tongue, *lay độc trị độc*—then I would choose to turn my back on the country that had turned her back on me.

At age sixteen, oh, how I fantasized about that journey onto the South China Sea and then north to Hong Kong or east to the Philippines or south to Malaysia. I did not care where we went; I cared only *that* we went.

I dreamed about the freedoms I would enjoy outside of Vietnam, about the people I would meet, about the new realities I would enjoy. At the time, I said nothing of these fantasies to my ma or dad, knowing that they would put an end to any such plans. Still today, they do not know that I attempted to escape! There will be words, once they read this book.

Part of my secret motivation, I suppose, was that I knew full well how occupied both Ma and Dad were with their respective daily concerns. Ma needed to keep her shop going, and Dad needed his kids to survive. At some level, I figured that my departure would provide some relief—one less mouth to feed. To be sure, I was fearful of leaving my family's province without my parents' knowledge, of the vastness of the ocean, and of what the police would do to my friends and me if they caught us trying to escape, but there was no life for me in my homeland. I had no choice but to escape.

—⁓—

"It will happen tomorrow night," a fellow student whispered to me one day at school. "Please, Phuc, be prepared."

Because the province of Tay Ninh is far from the coast, I would need to take a bus to reach the location where I would then catch the boat. My friend's parents, who also were fleeing Vietnam, had made all of the arrangements for us girls—purchasing our bus fare, organizing the plans—and as my friend stared into my eyes that day in class, I knew what the look conveyed. *This is serious, Phuc. Life or death, to be sure. Bring nothing with you—no clothes but the ones you are wearing, no identification, no handbag, no suitcase, no food. Just yourself, and nothing else. You must leave empty-handed from this land.*

During the worst of times in Vietnam, a common sentiment echoing throughout the myriad provinces was that "if the street lights had feet, even they would leave this place," which explains why so many of us were willing to risk life and limb to get out.

As my friend had instructed me, I arrived at the bus terminal in Tay Ninh at the appointed time, caught the bus headed to the center of Saigon, and disembarked with clammy hands—Where was the man who was supposed to transport me to the beach? "He will be wearing red jeans, a black jacket, and a black hat," was all that I had been told. "He will get you to the boat dock, but that is all that you may know."

I nervously scanned the attire of each person in the terminal, eventually locating the man I needed. "Yes," I whispered upon approaching him, "I am one of your passengers, sir."

The drive from Saigon to the unnamed beach took less than an hour's time, but oh, how those minutes crawled by. I was as scared as I ever had been. *Who can I trust? Who should I talk to? Who will tell me what to do next?*

Within moments of arriving, another stranger rolled something across the sand toward me, whispering urgently, "Go! Get into the tube and into the water. Paddle out to the boat you will see." I had never seen an inner tube before but did as I was told—and quickly, not only because of the risks associated with the experience, but also because the thick black rubber tube absorbed the sun's blazing heat and was nearly too hot for me to touch.

The boat was idling perhaps half a kilometer away, but given the fact that I didn't know how to swim, it might as well have been as far away as Mars. How I wished my friend was at my side for moral support, the one whose parents had arranged this attempt. "Kim, affinity groups must not escape together, for it makes capture more likely still," she had once explained to me. "This is work we must do alone."

Despite the forty or fifty others paddling out to the boat in front of and behind me, I felt completely "alone."

Eventually, I neared the boat, and as I queued there in the water, waiting for my turn to be lifted from my tube, I heard the captain of the vessel shout, "Go back! You must go back!"

Alas, the police had discovered our plan and would surely surround us if we tried to board that boat. We were instructed to head for shore and scatter—in other words, "Run for your life!"

And so the first time I fled, I was forced to disappear into the crowd, make my way to a bus terminal, and use the last few bits of my allowance from Ma to catch a ride back home. The second time I fled, the police discovered that I was up to no good and chased me from the beach, waving metal sticks in the air. And the third time, the captain of my assigned boat was somehow injured. Word spread to those of us planning to board that night that the mission had been aborted and we had to quickly return to our homes. Three strikes, and I was very, very out. Or very *in*, I should say. As it related to Vietnam, it seemed, there was no getting out.

In fact, in the homeland I was trying to flee, it is customary that after you try something and fail three times in a row, you must stop trying to do that thing lest you incite the rage of the gods. Perhaps I should be grateful that my escape did not pan out that first time (or the second or third times either), for the simple fact that based on statistics, I would likely be dead.

And so I set aside my fantasy regarding escaping my country and went back home, deflated, to Tay Ninh. I focused as best I could on my schoolwork, eventually completing my high school requirements and setting my sights on entering university later that year, following in the esteemed footsteps both of my older brother—Number 3—who had studied agricultural science, and my sister—Number 2—who, of course, had studied education. It would take me two (but thankfully not three!) attempts to pass my college entrance exam, but at last, in 1982, I was admitted. Against impossible odds, medical school was now a real possibility for me. I will complete my undergraduate studies, I resolved. I will enter medical school. I will work harder than any other student. I will chart a new course for myself. I will *thrive*.

Part II

A LIFE EXPLOITED

CHAPTER 11

PRE-UNIVERSITY SCHOOL, TIEN GIANG PROVINCE

HOT NEWS

AUGUST 1981

I am nineteen, excited to have graduated from high school and eager to begin university, although I will need to study for a full year in order to retake the entrance exam that I failed the first time around. No matter; I scored a decent grade—even if unacceptable by university standards. With a bit more effort, I can pursue my dream of medical school. I am ready to begin this new chapter of my life. I am ready to help children in the same manner that I was helped.

I am sitting in my preparations class when four men who identify themselves as "officials from Tay Ninh sent by Hanoi" show up. I am immediately pulled from class and told to give these men whatever time they need. I am all too happy to oblige them, their importance making me feel important as well. Hanoi is the site of our country's topmost governmental leaders; people of this caliber want *me*?

They have tracked me down by way of Ma's shop in Trang Bang, they explain. One of my brothers had been working with Ma that day and answered the men's questions regarding the whereabouts of the "napalm girl." Evidently, an old reporter from the war had come across my picture in his files one day and thought, *I wonder whatever happened to that girl.* Such an innocent curiosity. Such dire consequences for me.

"She is studying in Tien Giang," my brother had replied, his motives pure. And with that, the men were off.

"Are you really Kim Phuc?" one of the men asks me now.

"Yes, yes," I say, as I quickly push up my sleeve to reveal my left arm.

"She is the one," another man says to his comrade. "Hanoi will be pleased; she still is alive."

A few weeks later, the four men showed up again, this time to take me away. I went with them without protest. It had been ten full years since the napalm attack, one of the men explained to me, and well-known journalists had been called in from many countries in order to ask me about how I was. I listened to the man's words carefully, thinking, *I am just a nobody. Why would these journalists care what I have to say?*

Little more than an hour after leaving campus, I was ushered into a hotel's main-level meeting room in Saigon, where multiple reporters, photographers, cameramen, an interpreter, and an event overseer had convened. "Yes, yes! Kim Phuc! It is you!" the overseer boomed. "Welcome, Kim Phuc! Please have a seat here."

A flurry of activity ensued: A person directed me to a

chair, another placed a microphone on my tunic, another tested the lighting and sound, and another confirmed the spelling of my name. The first questions were certainly the simplest: How was I doing? How was I feeling? What was I studying in school? But just as I settled into this harmless, congenial conversation, one of the reporters looked at me with a steely gaze and asked, "Kim Phuc, do you hate the Americans for what they did to you as a child?"

I answered as truthfully as I knew how, explaining that the napalm bombs that had injured me had been dropped by South Vietnam's own men, not Americans. But based on the head-nodding and grinning that unfolded all around me in that room, I could see that the translator who had been appointed to me had motives of his own.

Following the interview, I was escorted to the hotel's fifth floor, where a lavish display of culinary delicacies was laid out for all of us. Out of deference to CaoDai, I bypassed the massive piles of meats and also the platters of vegetables I figured had been prepared using animal fats, taking only bread, salt, and a cup of cold water. Still, the sight of that spread stuck with me. My entire family could have eaten for *weeks* on that one meal.

—⁓—

In October of that year, I began my university studies in earnest in Saigon, excited to set off on my journey toward pediatrics, the specialty I had declared. But a mere three weeks into the fall's academic rhythm, I learned that the novel summertime visit from those government officials would spawn subsequent off-campus trips. The ten-year anniversary of my picture was evidently quite a draw for the news media, and now that I had been located, officials were unwilling to let me go. Once a week, and then later, twice weekly, a "minder" or two from Tay Ninh would appear unannounced, demand that I change clothes into a state-issued school uniform, and transport me via rickety van back to their governmental offices, where Western journalists with litanies of questions had already set up shop.

Whenever the meetings with journalists were scheduled early in the morning, I would be picked up at my dormitory in Saigon the night before and make my bed on a reception couch outside some official's office. A poor night's sleep was usually the least of my worries. During those interviews, government-assigned translators continued to convey to the journalists views on the war, on the napalm attack, and on postwar life in South Vietnam, none of which reflected my own. It would be many years before I would learn that they never translated what I *actually* said, choosing instead to parrot the lines they had been given by their higher-ups. I did not hate America. I did not despise Americans. And yet based on all that I "said" in those interviews, you would not know these things to be true.

As the weeks went by and the frequency of these kidnappings increased, life became more unbearable. To make matters worse, I could not confide the truth of my situation to anyone—not my family, not my classmates, not a soul—for fear of government retribution. Each time I returned to class after another forced interview, I would explain my absence to my peers with a dismissive, "I was not feeling well," even though they knew full well what was happening to me. I was being used by tyrannical men with guns; my classmates and I knew better than to speak this truth aloud. And so the minders kept coming, and I, Kim Phuc, kept going. With each absence from school, I kept getting farther behind in my work. Three months into that first semester, I was spending more time in Tay Ninh than in class. Regardless of how hard I tried, I would never be able to catch up.

—⁓—

The loss of my sole dream—that of becoming a pediatrician—struck me with a force deeper than I had ever known. I had accepted certain truths about myself that had become my new reality: *My burns make me different. I will never find love for my heart or peace from my pain. I am nothing more than my scars.* So my only hope for a satisfying life was to find work that ignited my passion and cling to it with all my might. But if I could never get to that work, what then? If I could not attend class, then I could not do well on my exams. If I could not do well on my exams, then I could not graduate from medical school. And if I could not graduate from medical school, then I could not work as a pediatrician.

"You cannot do this to me!" I would shout at the minder, gaining courage each time he came. "You must leave me to complete my studies! I am a student, not a propaganda tool!"

"You are very important now!" the minder would respond through gritted teeth. "Your government needs you, and you must comply." Out of all of those civilians wounded in the Vietnam War, why did I have to be the one they chose to dispense the anti-war, anti-democracy, anti-United States messages they wanted conveyed? As an innocent, ill-experienced nineteen-year-old girl, I may not have been savvy to the ways of the world, but I knew enough to know that *importance* was not my friend.

A handful of months after I began my studies, I was informed by university personnel that my time at their school had "come to an end." Those were the exact words they used, and as the phrase sunk in, my frustration hit an all-time high. University leaders had been instructed by officials from the capital city to force me out, and fearing retribution, they were all too willing to comply. In all candor, I could not blame them. Those same governmental officials had made it plain to me that my continued dissention would result in my parents being imprisoned, or worse. What other choice did I have but to submit? I could think of one choice, anyway. And the longer I considered it, the more perfect I found it to be.

NO MORE

OCTOBER 1982

It was a brilliantly sunny day when I sat down on the wooden bench in my sister's backyard, but my heart was dark, a nine-point-five on a ten-point scale of hopelessness. I was ready to leave this life. I planned to go through a back gate toward the busy street a block away that on a Saturday afternoon was surely bustling with families running their errands, enjoying the stunning weather, filling the road's four lanes. I would wait until the traffic signals turned green, and then I would rush into the center lane and stand perfectly still. I would inhale courage to stay standing, inviting the cars to hit and kill me.

I played out this scenario time and again in my mind, imagining that while the pain of those cars careening into me, launching me like a missile into the air, breaking my body in two, would be severe, it could not possibly be worse than the agony I had already endured. The searing fire that penetrated my body; the ensuing burn baths; the dry and itchy skin; the inability to sweat, which turned my flesh into an oven in Vietnam's sweltering heat. The lack of pain pills, the lack of ice, the lack of acceptance, the lack of love. The killing of my only remaining dream, the killing of my hope—what could hurt worse than these hurts? Yes, this was the only fitting end to my story. I would write the final chapter myself.

I was as alone as a person can be. Had I a friend, a confidant, someone I could stop by and visit from time to time, perhaps my dire straits could have been avoided. Perhaps I could have been refilled with hope. But to whom could I turn? My sister, now remarried, still grieved the loss of her first husband, Nang, who died while fighting for the South. What is more, she was raising her teenage son while still working full time. My ma was overwhelmed with the demands of keeping not only my family but also a variety of aunts, uncles, and cousins afloat financially—too much, certainly, for one woman to bear. Communist rule had unfolded all throughout South Vietnam, and those in charge were fining my ma unjustly, forcing her to pay the government ever-increasing sums—mysterious "license fees," baseless taxes, and the like—just to keep her business alive. How could I expect her to devote time and energy to me?

I could not turn to a friend, for nobody wished to befriend me. And truly, who could blame them? Being my friend put a person in jeopardy of surveillance by the very government that kept stealing me away. I was toxic, and everyone knew it. To be near me was to be near hardship. Wise people stayed far away.

I could also not turn to the gods. After years of unanswered prayers, it was clear to me that either they were nonexistent or they did not care to lend a hand.

And so I sat in isolation, which is a thousand miles separated from solitude. I was alone without wanting to be alone. Alone, atop a mountain of rage. Why did those bombs have to come for me? Why was I made to wear these awful scars? Why had I been thrown to an evil and opportunistic regime, like raw meat to a lion's open jaws?

I grew up hearing this proverb: A tree wants to be alone, but the wind always whips it here and there. That was me: a wind-whipped tree. And while all I had wanted for so many years was to be left alone—to have outside forces withdraw from blowing me down—now that I was alone in the worst possible sense of the word, I feared I would never stand upright again.

—⁓⁓—

Several weeks before that miserable Saturday afternoon, I found myself crouched down inside Saigon's central library, pulling Vietnamese books of religion down from the lowest shelf with my index finger, one by one. I was hiding from the government, truth be told. It had been two full days since a minder had come for me, which meant that one would surely be coming today. They had eyes in the back of their heads, but perhaps they would not think to look here in the library, beside a section tucked away at the back.

The stack in front of me on the floor included a book

on Bahai. A book on Buddhism. A book on Hinduism. A book on Islam. A book on another form of CaoDai I had not explored very much. And also a copy of the New Testament from the Bible of the Christian faith. I was familiar with all of these religions, for I had at some level worshiped their gods. But I had never truly looked into the faith systems. I knew little apart from the names.

I thumbed through several before pulling the New Testament into my lap. What was this "Christianity" all about, anyway? I hoped to find out.

An hour later, I had picked my way through the Gospels, logging question after question in my mind, fearing that if I wrote them down on paper, I would surely be found out. I wound up in the book of John, and at least two themes had become abundantly clear. First, despite all that I had learned through CaoDai—that there were many gods, that there were many paths to holiness, that so much of my "success" in religion rested atop my own weary, slumped shoulders—Jesus presented himself as *the* way, *the* truth, and *the* life.[5] His entire ministry, it seemed, pointed to one straightforward claim: *I am the way you get to God; there is no other way but me.* At this assertion, I reflexively shook my head. *What!* I said to myself. *How can this be so?* There are *thousands* of ways to get to God; everyone knows this fact. What a brash position Jesus had taken, that of being the one and only way.

My hands were trembling as I shut the book at once, overcome by confusion and fear. If it was accurate that this Jesus was uniquely able to connect me to God, to truth, to nothing short of *life*, then I had spent nineteen years worshiping the wrong gods, devoting myself fully to a cause that could never soothe the ache I felt deep in my soul. What was I to do now?

The question lingered in my mind as I considered the second of the two themes I had found. This Jesus, he had *suffered* in defense of his claim. He had been mocked. And tortured. And killed. *Why would he do these things*, I wondered, *if he were not, in fact, God?* His pain *must* have been for a purpose, I reasoned, or else he could not have so faithfully endured strife.

I had never been exposed to this side of Jesus—the wounded one, the one who bore scars. In CaoDai, Jesus was presented to me as one of a whole host of prophets—a good man, yes, but certainly not a man who was God. I turned over this new information in my mind as a gem in my hand, relishing the light that was cast from all sides. If this Jesus was indeed who he said he was, and if he had truly endured all he said he had endured, then perhaps he could help me make sense of my pain and at last come to terms with my scars.

I was living with my sister Loan and her family, when I learned that her son required surgery and would be hospitalized for nearly two weeks. A cousin of Loan's first husband, a man named Anh, who served as an associate pastor at a nearby Christian church, showed up each of those twelve days—to pray with Loan and then to head to the hospital to visit my nephew in his recovery room. He came back on a weekly basis for many weeks afterward to be sure Loan was faring well. When I learned of his vocation, I perked up. *I do have many questions. Perhaps this man can help.*

As soon as I met Anh, I began throwing at him the thick, hard bricks of rationalization I had used to erect my wall of disbelief. "Why must Jesus be the only way to God?" I said incredulously. "What about all the other gods? And what is this talk of simple belief yielding something as valuable as heaven? Must we not prove our sincere devotion by doing worthwhile things?"

On and on I went, pelting this poor Christ follower with my litany of library questions, eager for an immediate answer to each one. Anh hailed from a village that had been influenced toward Christianity since long before he was born. Missionaries from the United States and England made a practice of coming to his village, delivering Bibles translated into Vietnamese, and explaining to villagers how to have a personal relationship with Jesus and how to grow in that relationship by reading Scripture. Anh knew nothing of my CaoDai faith, save for what my questions revealed about the assumptions that ran my life. And yet day after day, conversation after conversation, with boundless patience and grace, Anh took my questions in stride, slowly turning the pages of his well-worn Bible, locating for me words of truth.

"It is only by having a relationship with Jesus Christ that you may have access to God," Anh said. "He is the only way."[6]

"Then what is it I must do?" I replied. "In my religion, I have done it *all*, and still, it has not worked."

"Faith comes by hearing," Anh said to me, "and hearing by the word of the Lord."[7] He said that if I would confess with my mouth Jesus as Lord and believe in my heart that God had raised him from the dead, then I would be saved.[8]

"I must only *say* that I believe?" I asked, my thoughts swirling with the lunacy of it all.

Anh quoted from memory about grace coming by faith and not by works, and about good works being God's lifestyle plan for us *after* salvation, instead of his expectation of us before it.[9]

"Phuc," this wise man then said to me, "good deeds are the *response* to salvation, not the path by which it is earned."

I was not sure I could believe this news from Anh, even as something inside of me recognized the truth of his words. Still, there was a more pressing issue I needed to discuss with Anh, perhaps the most important one of all.

"But Anh, what about the napalm attack and these wretched burns I was made to endure? Where was this 'God' when I was left for dead? Why did he not spare me from years of pain, either by giving me a better life to live or by simply allowing me to die?"

Tears sprang to my eyes. "Anh, how does your Jesus justify such tragedy in the life of an innocent little girl?"

Anh studied my pleading expression for a moment and then smiled a knowing smile. "I think you now must go to church."

—⁓—

Anh had rightly detected a certain readiness, an openness to the things of God—not little-g "god," as in the myriad gods I had been taught to worship as a child, but rather big-G God, the God of creation, Jehovah God.

The first time I entered Anh's church, I was struck by the differences I saw. Instead of the white worship garments of CaoDai, people wore tunic blouses and long slacks of every conceivable color—comfortable clothes, clothes they might wear to work or to school. Gone were the bowing, kneeling, and rising on command multiple times throughout each ceremony; worshipers sat relaxed on padded benches, standing only when it was time to sing. Gone were the four-times-daily ceremony options; here, I learned, formal worship happened but once per week.

Then a man—Pastor Ho Hieu Ha—rose and opened his Bible and began talking about how husbands are called to love their wives in the same way that Jesus Christ loves his church.[10] "We are the bride of Christ," the pastor said to us that day, a phrase that I found as sweet as sugar to my soul.

For a moment, childhood memories came flooding back. *Hanh*, I thought, *remember when we played bride and groom with those cobs of corn, eagerly anticipating the day when we would find the men of our dreams? Oh, the marriage celebrations we were to have!* As I sat wide-eyed in Anh's church that Sunday, the image of myself in a beautiful white wedding gown lingered in my mind's eye. Could it be true that Jesus wanted *me* for his bride? How I loved the idea that I was being pursued in that manner, that this "Prince of Peace," as Anh had said the prophet Isaiah called him, could be the prince I had longed for all my life.

For five straight weekends—the resulting duration of Anh's visits to Loan's—I woke early on Sunday mornings and made the half-kilometer walk to church with Anh. And for five straight Sundays, I treasured an idea in my heart—that I could be loved by one so holy as Jesus Christ himself.

But then my nephew recovered, Anh moved on to more pressing crises, and with his departure my visits to church were less frequent. I would find it difficult to hold fast to the idea that I was "beloved" or "worth pursuing," choosing instead to melt back into the darkness that told me I was worthless, hopeless, and alone. The minders would continue to come for me, and my schoolwork, now relegated to simple language studies at a private night school I enrolled in, would continue to suffer neglect. My pain would continue to overtake me, both of my skin and of my soul.

Across those weeks, the pressure mounted, both from outside forces and from within, and eventually I found myself at the precipice of despair. Everything in me shouted, "No more!" I *had* to find a way out. A person could not live like this—abused, forsaken, and alone.

On the wooden bench in my sister's backyard, I looked skyward. I stared at the blueness of the sky, so bright it almost appeared white, and I shook my head over the futility of it all. *What good is this beautiful day when my life is this ugly and bleak?*

I began to sob uncontrollably. And then I began to yell uncontrollably. "God! Where are you? Do you even exist at all? Why am I made to suffer like this? Why will you not come to my aid?"

I wept until I was spent, until I had no more tears to cry, until I had expended every last burst of energy, until I was weak and quiet and still. And it was then that I made a deal with God. "If you will just give me a friend," I said to the heavens, "just one person who knows you and who can help me know you, then I will agree not to take my life."

I gave God twenty-four hours to uphold his end of the deal. Then I rose from the bench and walked inside.

That Saturday night, I did not sleep well. I would drift off, my eyelids heavy with weariness, but as soon as I relaxed, I would jolt awake, my mind captivated with whether God would do what I had asked him to do. I suppose I was testing God. I laid out my ultimatum, and I hoped that he would not let me down.

Sunday morning, I slipped early out of bed and dressed quickly for church. *If God is going to fulfill my wish, the most likely place to do so would be in a Christian church*, I thought. During the twenty-minute walk from my sister's house, I pictured the friend I would meet. She would be Vietnamese, kind, and sitting alone in the middle of the church. That would be my signal, I decided, that this was the person God had sent.

I arrived at church thirty minutes before the worship service was set to begin and entered through the building's front door. A few people were milling about in the foyer, but I headed to the doors of the sanctuary. As I wrapped my right hand around the handle of one of the doors and pulled it, I exhaled my anxiety with an audible *whew* and set foot inside the room.

Oh, God, please do not let me down.
Please, oh please, oh please.

I scanned the room in a matter of seconds—there was a woman, seated alone, in the sanctuary's centermost pew. The skin on my arms puckered and pricked in what I now know are goose bumps. Honestly, I thought the woman was an apparition. In CaoDai, ghosts are frequently mentioned, and as I took my first few steps down the aisle toward the woman, everything in me said she was not real. *She's a figment of my imagination, conjured up in my mind's eye.*

My steps were slow but full of intention, and at last, I was standing beside her pew. I could now see her face, her hands, her chest rising and falling. She was not a ghost at all, but rather a living, breathing human being. My *friend.* God had sent me a friend.

I stood at the end of her pew for a moment, awkwardly staring at her face. Sensing my presence, she swiveled her head ever so slightly and smiled. "Good morning," she said in Vietnamese. "I am Thuy. Have you come to worship today?"

Her voice was as soft as a whisper, her presence angelic and sweet. "Yes," I said, "that is why I have come. I am new to Christianity. I come from a different faith."

Thuy invited me to sit down beside her, and for the twenty minutes that remained until the service began, she and I got acquainted. She was seven years my senior and had been following Jesus most of her life. She had risen early that morning to come to church to pray for her mother, who was very ill. "I am so happy that I found you here today," I said with a wide smile, not disclosing the reason why.

Sunday after Sunday, Thuy and I met at the church before the morning service so we could discuss the things of God. The other six days of the week were still desperately lonely for me, but I knew that if Thuy and I met anywhere else in public, the government would have her surveilled from then on. I did not want to see her harmed in the same way I was being harmed, and so I was guarded in sharing details of my life with her, relegating our relationship almost exclusively to Sunday-morning conversations when I came armed with my most pressing spiritual questions from the week. (There was one time when I accepted Thuy's invitation to come to her house for tea one afternoon, but even as I walked home, I knew that I had overstepped a silent rule. "I must not put her in jeopardy this way," I vowed to myself. I declined her kind invitations from that point on.)

Quietly, patiently, thoroughly, Thuy answered each question as honestly as she could. She taught me how to investigate topics for myself, by using reference pages found in my Bible. She explained how to connect one verse in Scripture to another—cross-referencing, it was called—so that I could obtain a fuller picture of what the text meant, especially Jesus' fulfillment of Old Testament prophecy.

But perhaps the most valuable lesson I learned from Thuy was how to pray. She taught me how to converse with God, how to invite his guidance into my days, something that saved my life each time I left Thuy's presence. From the church to my sister's house, I had to walk along the same bustling street that I had contemplated using for my exit from this world. For a few moments during each of those walks, some dark force would overtake my thoughts, tempting me to step off the curb, to end it all. My thoughts would tumble down on top of each other, leaving a sinking feeling inside of my chest. *You cannot choose faith in Jesus, Phuc! Your family will disown you at once! What is more, why would God ever want you, given how you blasphemed him all of your life? The wrongs you have committed against his name can never be set right. You are hopeless, Phuc. Life is worthless. You must simply end it here at once.*

"You can take your thoughts captive," Thuy taught me, "and God can help you point them in a different direction." Thuy also encouraged me to pray Scripture back to God, such as a psalm.

"Simply take the words and use them as a request of the Lord," my friend advised. And so I would try: "Heavenly Father, please help me to walk in integrity as I head home from church. Please show me mercy for my past wrongs and put my feet on an even place as I step into my future. Please help me to *bless* you and not curse you in all that I think, say, and do."[11]

At first, this very personal and intimate interaction with the Lord felt extremely awkward, so different from what I had practiced as a child. To me, "religion" meant complete deference to the gods with no expectation whatsoever that any dialogue between them and me would ensue. They were distant. Dead. And in my experience, anyway, dispirited regarding my needs. But the more I practiced this Christianity, the more comfortable things began to feel. Still, there was one painful truth that I knew awaited me: In pledging my allegiance to Jesus alone, I would, in fact, be disowned by my family.

CHAPTER 13

TAY NINH PROVINCE,
MY BROTHER'S HOME

GOING TO MY NEW GOD

JANUARY 1983

I was on my way from Saigon to Tay Ninh, where my entire family was gathering to attend the worship ceremony for Tet, the morning of the first day of the Lunar New Year. Ma was traveling from Trang Bang along with many of our extended relatives. I was eager to see my loved ones, even though I knew this visit would be different from all the others.

As was customary during my visits home, I was expected to attend temple, and as part of that experience, to don the official worship garments, the ceremonial white *ao dai*. What my family did not know until I arrived home that day was that I no longer followed Caodaism—I had given my life to the Lord Jesus Christ.

My salvation experience had happened just a few weeks before, fittingly enough on Christmas Eve. I attended a special worship service at church, and there, on the night before the world would celebrate the birth of the Messiah—a baby born in a manger in a tiny, forgotten town—I invited him, Jesus, the One and Only, into my heart. I had spent several months studying the Scriptures, choosing to use the rare moments I had enjoyed away from my minder to devour the plentiful promises of God. And oh, how they had gone down like thick chunks of guava, the delicious fruit I had enjoyed as a child.

The more I read, the more I came to believe that God—Jehovah God, the God of the Scriptures—really was who he said he was, that he really had done what he said he had done, and that, most important to me, he really would do all that he had promised in his Word. How I prayed those promises were true: Peace! And joy! Abundance and true life! If it really was so, that I could possess these things, I would surrender one *thousand* hearts to this Jesus, had I that many hearts to give.

On Christmas Eve, Pastor Ho Hieu Ha began his remarks to the congregation with a question. "What year is it?" he asked. We glanced at each other uneasily, knowing the obvious answer but believing it must be a trick question.

"What year is it?" he asked again, this time with a hearty laugh, motioning with his hands as if to say "Come on, tell me!" "Nineteen eighty-two!" one bold soul finally shouted out. "Nineteen eighty-two! Nineteen eighty-two!" we all joined in.

"Yes!" Pastor Ho Hieu Ha said. "Correct. Now, tell me this: Why is it 1982?"

We were sure this was another trick. Nobody said a word.

Pastor Ho Hieu Ha thankfully let us off the hook. "It is 1982," he said, "because nineteen hundred and eighty-two years have passed since the Messiah came to earth. The whole reason we even have a thing called *years* is that God chose to send his beloved Son to us. That event—the *Incarnation*—was so significant an occurrence that humankind decided to mark time according to it. Each time you write the date—on a check, on correspondence, on your day's calendar—you are acknowledging that point in history when Jesus Christ came to dwell among us. You are honoring the event that quite literally *split time*."[12]

Pastor Ho Hieu Ha continued. "This Christmas occasion is not about the gifts we carefully wrap and give to each other as much as it is about one Gift in particular, who was wrapped in human flesh and given from God to us. The Gift is Jesus, his only Son. He is our greatest Gift."

I listened carefully to the pastor, knowing in my heart that something was shifting inside of me. I had read the entire Holy Bible, and Thuy had answered my most pressing questions. I had faithfully worshiped with other believers in Jesus. And now I was ready to follow God.

At the conclusion of Pastor Ho Hieu Ha's sermon, he said, "If you are here among us this evening and you have never invited Jesus Christ to be Lord of your life, I would like for you to consider doing so here and now. The Bible says that baby Jesus grew up and lived a perfect life. The Bible says that he then willingly died on a Roman cross, serving as a sacrifice for your sin and mine. The Bible says that Jesus rose from the dead three days later, proving his power over death. And the Bible says that the only thing we need to do in order to obtain full, unencumbered, and eternal access to the One True God is to confess with our mouths and believe in our hearts that Jesus Christ is Lord. If anyone sitting here today shall open his or her heart to this Jesus, then Jesus will come to you, and bring you peace, and remove all burdens from your life."

This was exactly what I had gleaned from my reading of the Holy Scriptures too! *Yes!*

I nearly jumped out of my seat then and there. How desperately I needed peace. How ready I was for love and joy. *I have so much hatred in my heart*, I thought. *This burden of bitterness is too heavy to bear.* I wanted forgiveness for my transgressions. I wanted to let go of all my pain. I wanted to pursue life instead of holding fast to fantasies of death. I wanted this Jesus.

When Pastor Ho Hieu Ha finished speaking, I had already stood up, stepped out into the aisle, and made my way to the front of the sanctuary to say yes to Jesus Christ. "Yes, you are my Savior now! You are my Father, and I am your child." Thuy was still standing in the row where we had been sitting next to each other, and when she lifted her head from prayer and opened her eyes, she noticed that I had disappeared. Scanning the room, she located me at the altar. "Yes! You did it!" she mouthed, her fists joyously pumping the air. After the service, Thuy and I were reunited, and as she reached for both of my hands, I met her gaze with tears. "Thuy," I said, "thank you for praying for me and for loving me. You are a great, great blessing in my life."

"You will always know peace now," Thuy said to me, as she wrapped me up in a hug.

When I woke up on Christmas morning 1982, I

experienced my first-ever *heartfelt* celebration of the birth of Jesus Christ.

If only my ma could see my side of the story. *Ma, I am finally at peace!*

During that Tet celebration, I felt out of place in the temple for the first time in my life. While everyone else was dressed in their white *ao dai*, I was wearing street clothes. Each time I was presented with ceremonial food honoring the CaoDai gods, I shook my head and declined.

The people who had been teaching me about God indicated that by engaging in practices that honor idols, I could not only put myself in spiritual jeopardy, but also I could wrongly influence others who might otherwise come to the saving knowledge of faith in Jesus Christ.[13] As I passed trays piled high with delicious candied fruits, steamed square cakes, sticky rice, and boiled chicken, I considered each step an act of faith—of my new faith in Jesus Christ. He would find a different way to nourish me, a way that did not involve consuming tainted foods.

My actions got my ma's attention. She approached me and whispered passionately, "*Phuc!* You must eat *something!*"

"It is not for me now, Ma," I said. "My new faith disallows such foods!"

"Then you are no longer my daughter," she spat her words at me, her religious devotion fueling her rage.

I was already on my way out of the building as those words came out of my ma's mouth, hot tears stinging my eyes. "I am ashamed to call you my child!" Ma shouted. "You will pay for this, Phuc!" she screamed.

I could not blame my ma for being angry. Exactly one year before, Ma had observed me making my declaration to follow CaoDai all my life. Ma was part of the official ceremony in the Trang Bang temple that signified my intentions. As I lay facedown on the marble-tiled floor, seeing every scratch and streak I had memorized more than a decade before, Ma initiated the vow of allegiance I repeated, pledging myself fully and completely to the religion of my grandparents and my parents. When the formalities were concluded, Ma's face boasted the widest of smiles. So much had changed in my heart in a year's time. Ma was mystified by my decision, believing I was far smarter than this.

—⁓—

I walked around Tay Ninh while the rest of the ceremony was conducted at the temple, but as night fell, I headed to my brother's home, where my family was gathered for Tet's first-evening feast. Ma was calmer, probably hoping that I had come to my senses and was ready to return to her, to family, to CaoDai. But this was not the case. Again I declined the Tet foods, and again, Ma was incensed.

"Phuc, you have never been a bad child to us, but this . . . this is *worse* than bad. It is the worst thing you could possibly do. Should you continue to deny CaoDai, you will ruin not only your life here on earth but also your opportunity to be in heaven with us.

"We must stay together, Phuc!" Ma implored me. "Do you not see how important that is?"

"I do, Ma! I do!" I said to her. "This is why I pray to Jesus that you, too, will be saved!"

It was as if I had raised a loaded gun to Ma's aching heart and pulled the trigger at point-blank range.

"Phuc!" she cried out, enraged. "This God of yours? You go to him now. You go get your rice from *him*."

I left immediately, knowing I was now considered a dissident, and dissidents *never* returned. In CaoDai, they were treated as dead. I boarded the bus headed for Saigon, having no idea how I now would survive. Ma had always supported me financially, but she had made her position crystal clear. I could no longer come to her for food, for clothing, for books. She would no longer pay my tuition fees at the language school. She would no longer pay my hospital bills whenever I became ill. Within twenty-four hours, my father and my siblings, the neighbors in Tay Ninh, and friends and family back in Trang Bang would know from Ma that I had gone from being one beloved to one banished. I was "no longer" in their eyes.

As the bus ambled along Route 1, I thought briefly about Jesus' reminder to his disciples that their allegiance to him would often involve letting other allegiances fall—even to loved ones, even to dads and moms.[14] I was momentarily comforted by that and then the practical reality gripped me. The bus fare had cost me thirty-thousand dong. I still had a little bit of money from Ma's most recent stipend, but it would only last me so long. *Oh, Jesus, you must help me!* I prayed silently, there in my seat. Looking back on the experience now, I like to imagine him grinning and nodding his head. "I see your faith, my child, Kim Phuc, and though it is small, it is sufficient and real. You remain beloved to me and will always be such. I will care for you each of your days."

How I hoped he would be true to his word.

PERILS LEFT AND RIGHT

SPRINGTIME 1983

For many weeks following that disastrous trip to Tay Ninh, I repeated the phrase from Scripture, "Take therefore no thought for the morrow: for the morrow shall take thought for the things of itself,"[15] as though each time I said it, life would somehow find its balance, its stride. And yet nothing of the sort occurred.

I was hungry, with nothing to eat until my peers kindly gave me bread and milk. Within four months of my return, the church I had been attending was shut down by the communist government, and Pastor Ho Hieu Ha was imprisoned for six years until American president George H. W. Bush signed a letter demanding his release; the gaping wound created by the argument between my ma and me seemed to expand; and the government continued to abuse me, forcing me to miss language class in order to sit for interviews that misrepresented my views.

To be honest, I was cracking under the weight of so much ongoing struggle and strife. Had not Anh taught me that God was "a very present help in trouble" and "a refuge for the oppressed" and the one who upholds me with his righteous right hand?[16] If these promises were so, then why on earth was I enduring such unrelenting pain? *Why are you abandoning me, Lord?*

I realized that I could no longer afford even the one class I was taking. Besides, given the government's frequent interference with my studies, what was the point of staying in school anyway? I dropped the class, figuring it was more important for me to sort out my new faith and secure a steady source of food. Whenever I was not under the control of my minders, I would lose myself in the pages of Scripture, focusing intently on stories such as that of the apostle Paul, who wrote candidly about everything he suffered as a believer in Jesus the Messiah.[17] Poor Paul! His story made my own seem tame. And yet my suffering was very real. I needed a dose of hope, some sort of supernatural signal that God had not lost sight of me.

By spring, the worldwide media was focused on the tenth anniversary of the Paris cease-fire accords, which had prompted the US withdrawal from the war. The public attention to my story escalated, as droves of journalists now wanted articles that "looked back."

Now, instead of arranging one-on-one interviews with

reporters, my minders held large press conferences. Often these media events were held in Tay Ninh, the province that still maintained official jurisdiction over my citizenship.

On one such occasion, I concluded my remarks and then was introduced to the government's media-relations photographer, whose name was Minh. Mister Minh had been given permission to escort me to a nearby state-run daycare center, where children played for hours each day while their parents worked.

"I would like to take pictures of you smiling and laughing with children around you," he explained, "to show that you are doing all right."

I knew there was no use protesting. "All right," I said. "Let us go, then."

When we entered the daycare, Mister Minh spotted a lovely little shiny-haired girl on the other side of the room and ushered me to her side. "Here," he said, hoisting the girl toward me. "You hold her in your arms and just talk sweetly to her."

For a moment, I lost myself in the sheer joy of holding a baby girl. *How wonderful to be a mother someday.* That simple act of holding a tiny baby in my arms, her countenance brightening as I cooed and sang to her, caused all of the medical input regarding my sure infertility resulting from my burns to momentarily slip away. But as quickly as the hope-filled thought of ever becoming a ma entered my mind, I evicted it. *Who will ever want me for a wife?* Without a husband, there would be no child.

I smiled enthusiastically for Mister Minh's camera, genuinely enjoying the few minutes basking in the tender innocence of a child, and then I was whisked away for whatever was next on the agenda.

Days later, one of the photos that had been snapped during my daycare-center visit appeared in the national newspaper of Vietnam, which came as no surprise to me. What did catch me off guard was the caption that accompanied it: "A decade later: Kim Phuc and her baby girl."

When I read those words, I was angry, experiencing something rising up from a deep place in my soul. "What have they done to me!" I silently cried. "*Now* what will become of me?"

It was true that with my wretched scars and my painfully slow recovery, I had very low expectations for one day marrying and bearing a child. But I had not given up hope *entirely*; that is, not until now. Everyone in my country would see that photo and its caption, and then think, *Oh, Kim Phuc has found a husband, and look—they have had a baby girl.* Any prospective husband would avoid pursuing me altogether.

Mister Minh had not requested the caption that ran alongside his staged photograph; in fact, he had no knowledge of the misrepresentation until I pointed it out. I did not blame him, but oh, how I wished he had never arranged for that shot. Within hours of its publication, the image and the words circulated all throughout Vietnam, taking with it the final glimmer of hopefulness that I would ever find true love.

—⁂—

One of the journalists who surfaced during those tenth-anniversary-celebration days was a German man named Perry Kretz. I had first met Mister Kretz in my hometown of Trang Bang, shortly after I returned from the hospital and during his visit to Vietnam to file a report on the Paris peace accords. My country's government had denied him entry and placed him under house arrest, most likely because he published a photograph he took of a South Vietnamese soldier asleep at his machine-gun post, a disparagement the South would not soon forget.

In 1973, while Mister Kretz was holed up in a hotel awaiting the next flight from Saigon to his native Hamburg, he bribed his minder with American currency to allow him to go visit the Associated Press office nearby. "I cannot get out of here for another three days," he mentioned to a colleague there. "Any ideas on how I should spend my time?"

"You should consider checking in on Kim Phuc."

Mister Kretz replied, "Who is Kim Phuc?"

"Surely you remember the napalm girl!" the colleague said, which prompted Mister Kretz's visit later that afternoon to Trang Bang.

I had been wandering around at my grandmother's hip for hours when the long, black car pulled up in front of my parents' home from which Mister Kretz emerged. My father, who was out front, escorted the journalist to me, explaining that I was wanted for a news story regarding my burns. Mister Kretz was warm, friendly, and very patient as I explained my experiences through the interpreter who had made the trip with him. At the journalist's request, I showed him all around what remained of our family home. I led him over to the CaoDai temple and told of how the other neighborhood children and I had been chasing a black bird all over the place when the soldiers ordered us to run for our lives. And I escorted him all the way up Route 1, retracing the steps I had taken fourteen months prior, as wild, hot flames licked my heels.

I had not spent any time around reporters at that point in time, save for the moment with the ones on Route 1 who offered me a drink and doused my blazing-hot skin with water, but I knew instinctively that this man possessed a rare level of compassion. He looked at me and truly saw; he listened to me and truly heard. I trusted him almost instantly.

Now back in Saigon for the first time since that visit with me nearly a decade before, Mister Kretz found himself reliving his times in Vietnam and longing for how the South once was. The communists had changed street names and city names, altered business models and lifestyle norms, and strangled whatever beauty and liberty we had once enjoyed, in favor of "reeducating" us in their ways, none of which was lost on Mister Kretz.

When he returned home to his native Hamburg, perhaps in an effort to revive his fond memories of "old Saigon," Mister Kretz rummaged through his file drawers until he found copies of the photographs he had taken during wartime all those years ago, coming across the handful of images he had snapped in and around my parents' home. He was the reporter who had wondered "whatever happened to that girl," and while his decision to find me would bring me into the public eye and thus present wild complications for me for years to come, it also may have saved my life.

Mister Kretz submitted the necessary paperwork and secured the required permission to return to Vietnam and interview me for himself. After greeting me with a great big hug, he asked me how I was doing. I had to trot out the lies I had been trained to trot out: "I am very well! I am studying in Saigon to be a doctor. I am enjoying my studies very much!"

I thought that I had been convincing to Mister Kretz, but either I was not as persuasive as I had hoped, or else his years as a human-interest reporter made him keenly astute. He returned to Germany haunted by my countenance. *Something is not right with her*, he thought. *She is not doing as well as she says.*

Later, Mister Kretz would explain to me that he simply would not have been able to live with himself, had he not at least tried to help get me out of Saigon.

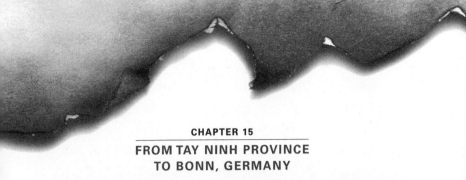

HELP WHEN I NEEDED IT MOST

JULY 1984

Not long after that reunion with Mister Kretz in the spring
of 1983, I had mustered the courage to write him a letter,
explaining that I was out of options—and also money. *Did
he have any ideas for me?* I wondered. Little did I know that
he had been working on a plan since we met in Saigon. It
would take fifteen full months, focused and persistent effort,
and wads of bureaucratic red tape to get it done, but by the
summer of 1984, Mister Kretz had turned that far-fetched
plan into reality, and I was sitting across the table from him
in a governmental office in Tay Ninh. He had made arrangements to escort me to West Germany's premier burn clinic
for what would be my seventeenth, and hopefully final, skin-
graft surgery. Taking me, Kim Phuc, Vietnam's token propaganda tool, out of the country seemed about as simple and

straightforward as removing a juicy bone from a ravenous dog's jaws.

But Mister Kretz was undeterred. "This is the one way I can help this young woman," he had said to his wife before making the trip. "I must do this one thing I can do."

Also at the meeting were my parents, with whom I now shared a civil, yet strained, relationship; my usual minder, Tam; and an interpreter to facilitate communications between Mister Kretz and me. Within moments of the exchange getting started, I learned the details of Mister Kretz's plan and quickly surmised it was doomed to fail.

"You may not simply take Kim Phuc out of our country!" Tam hollered at Mister Kretz.

I could not believe the next words out of Mister Kretz's mouth. "I am here with the permission of *your* government, sir, and for the purpose of helping one of your *own*."

Oh, what a relief. Mister Kretz had done his homework! He had cleared his plan with Hanoi's foreign-affairs office already, a fact that Tam was just learning now. Tam knew if he protested and upset his superiors in the capital, he risked having them remove me from Tay Ninh province officially and making me one of their own. Tam and his fellow Tay Ninh officials could not stand to lose such a valuable media resource.

"If you can help her," Tam said gruffly, his eyes icy cold, "then you may. You may leave now to your stated locale."

—⚬—

Family members and friends, curious spectators, and a crowd of reporters gathered at the airport to see me off to West

Germany, all of whom were elated that at last I was getting out. This is no small feat, where communist countries are concerned. Of course, both Mister Kretz and I had been required to sign various papers that guaranteed my safe and relatively prompt return to Vietnam, but others had signed similar papers, only to get out and never return. Strange things sometimes happened; I secretly hoped they would happen to me.

Mister Kretz took advantage of our layover in Bangkok, Thailand, to take me on a whirlwind shopping spree, purchasing several beautiful garments for me—white long-sleeved blouses; dark, wide-legged trousers; a smart-looking rattan hat; and a proper suitcase for carrying them all. More than a half-day's journey later, we arrived in the lovely Rhine River–straddling town of Bonn, West Germany. I had made it! Vietnam was officially in my past—for this handful of weeks, anyway.

I was a wide-eyed girl of twenty-one, all alone in a distant land, save for the oversight of a relative stranger. For me, it was a glimpse of the fuller freedom I hoped would someday come. No minders, no abductions, no forced interviews, no misrepresentations or hunger or pain. I had landed in a place of plenty—plentiful food, plentiful medicine, plentiful care. I needed more of these realities in my life, and that trip to Germany would prove a pivotal first step.

As Mister Kretz helped me get settled in my lavish hotel room, through a series of hand gestures, pantomimes, and English words I had only slightly started to understand, he gave me instructions regarding answering the door. "You hear knock? No open! Look through hole!" he conveyed, pointing to the peephole. "You see a person? Not me? *Do not* open the door!" I nodded, relieved to have understood him completely.

That first night I sat on the edge of the bed and whispered my gratitude to God. "I know what has happened here, Father," I said to the Lord. "It is *you* who brought me out of Vietnam." What a wonderful, long-awaited gift.

The following morning, a government-appointed translator named Hang showed up. Hang would help me navigate each conversation and also would become my friend. I liked Hang immediately, perhaps because one of the first things she said to me was, "Kim Phuc, the hotel's chef has offered to cook whatever you would like to eat. You tell him what you would enjoy each day, and those things, he will prepare." What an offer! I would indeed try Germany's best fare—specialty cheeses and pastries and coffees—even as my stomach eventually insisted that I return to rice and vegetables, the simple foods I had always loved.

—∿—

The primary reason I was in Bonn—to undergo my seventeenth skin graft—involved two routine surgeries at a clinic to release bands of scar tissue, which gave me more mobility. Everything went well, and in three weeks I was discharged from the clinic to recover before flying back to Vietnam. Mister Kretz was not returning with me, so he bid me goodbye over lunch and ice cream.

The leaders of my country were quite nervous about my traveling home alone from liberated West Germany, believing I would certainly escape their clutches, so they insisted

MY LIFE WAS CHANGED FOREVER BY ONE PICTURE.

The world did not know me before my photo was taken on a Vietnamese village road. How I wish I had family pictures from my childhood that would show you how happy I was growing up, but unfortunately there are none left. This accounts for the gap in time of the following photos. Hopefully, the words of my story will help fill in what's missing in your mind's eye.

On June 8, 1972, everything I loved about my home in Trang Bang was destroyed by the napalm-fueled inferno.

Vietnamese prime minister Pham Van Dong and I were as close as family. I called him Bac Dong, meaning "beloved uncle."

How could anyone love me with my horrible scars?

I tried to pretend they were not a problem, but instead they reminded me that I was different.

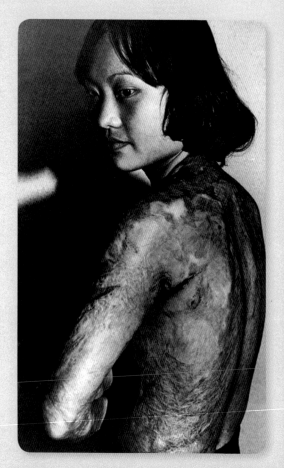

No one believed

*I would ever be physically able to
bear children. Thomas's arrival
in 1994 proved them wrong!*

Dec. 1992
Scarborough - canada.

Toan and I quickly discovered that Canadian winters are nothing like winters in Vietnam.

Dec. 1992
Scarborough - Canada.

Canada

"Mom Nancy" Pocock (left) with Thomas and me in 1994. Nancy was our family's first "angel" in Canada—

a true friend of refugees.

I am grateful Toan decided to pursue freedom with me. Here we are celebrating becoming Canadian citizens.

During a visit to my homeland in 2005, I visited my aunt Anh, who had lost two sons—Danh and Cuong—due to the napalm bombs and was badly burned herself on that fateful day in 1972.

Vietnam

My brother, Number 8 (left), and my cousins, Bon and Tinh (right), stand with me in the spot where four decades earlier Uncle Ut had snapped our picture. Sadly brother Number 5, who was ahead of me in the famous photo, had died before this new picture was taken.

The CaoDai temple in Trang Bang where we ran for sanctuary. When the village was attacked, we fled through the large doors onto Route 1 where the bombs were dropped.

Walking down Route 1 toward the CaoDai temple with my sons, Stephen (left) and Thomas (right), on their first trip to Trang Bang.

Revisiting Cuba

For our twenty-first wedding anniversary, Toan and I took our sons with us to Cuba. We wanted Thomas and Stephen to see the place where God had brought their parents together.

My trip to Cuba was not complete until I reunited with the Diaz family. Manuel and Nuria were Papi and Mami to me when I was attending school in Havana. Their love and concern made me think of them as "Jesus with skin."

This is my favorite picture from our trip to Cuba because it shows the joy that is inside me all the time. Although I was scared to swim, I decided to be adventurous and went snorkeling—with a helpful guide by my side.

This is one of my happiest days—in my home in Canada making muffins for the first time for Ma and Dad.

Summer 06

God's Gifts to Me

My two sons, Thomas and Stephen, have outstanding character and big hearts, which makes me extremely proud.

This photo was taken in November 2016 when I had just arrived home from another laser treatment for my burns. Holding my new grandson, Kalel, helped ease my pain.

I cannot express how grateful I am to God for bringing Doctor Jill Waibel and me together. Her specialized laser treatments over the last two years have reduced my pain considerably. She celebrated my birthday with me in San Diego on April 6, 2017.

MY LIFE WAS CHANGED FOREVER BY THESE TWO MEN.

If it were not for photographer Nick Ut (left), the world might never have known about the tragedy he captured on film. And dearest Toan (right) captured my heart with his great love and has never let go.

that someone from the Vietnamese embassy in East Berlin pick me up and drive me six hours back to their state, where I would stay until departing from there. Instead of flying to Saigon, I would be rerouted to Hanoi. They could keep better tabs on me in the North's capital city, and given how much press coverage they expected my return to generate, they were determined to keep me close.

I had been treated like royalty during my time in West Germany, but throughout my week-long stay in East Berlin, while I awaited my flight back to Hanoi, I was viewed with suspicion and even disdain. One woman in particular who had been deployed to keep an eye on me was so ugly toward me that even the driver, a kind man named Quang who had been responsible for carting me around Bonn and had escorted me to Berlin, took note.

"I have a friend in Hanoi you can stay with," he said to me. "Staying where your government assigns you will be as bad as staying where they have assigned you here." I breathed a sigh of relief. Finally, someone who understood my plight.

The night of that conversation, I stood on the little patio at the embassy and looked at the night sky, a vast blanket of twinkling lights. *Oh, God*, I prayed silently, *how desperately I long to be free—as free as these stars I see dancing above.*

CHAPTER 16

HANOI, CAPITAL CITY OF FORMER NORTH VIETNAM

BELOVED BAC DONG

SEPTEMBER 1984

When I arrived in Vietnam, I was greeted by a thick onslaught of foreign reporters and photographers, all of whom wanted to know how my surgery had gone, how I was feeling since recovering, and what it had been like to have finally "gotten out." I answered each question in turn, marveling over all of this attention and wondering where it all would lead.

I stayed in Hanoi for three full weeks and was actually pleased when my trip got extended not once, but twice, by government officials who wanted me to sit for still more interviews with journalists. I had nothing, really, to return home to. Resuming life in Saigon meant resuming destitution. I had no schooling to speak of since I had dropped my language course prior to departing for Germany with Mister Kretz, no intimate relationships beckoning me, no pursuits save for securing food and shelter: Why would I be eager to return?

For part of my time in Hanoi, I took Quang up on his kind offer to stay with his friend—it was actually his friend's mother, the middle-aged widow of a North Vietnamese army official. Upon learning of my treatment in West Germany, she petitioned for, and received, funding from Hanoi to treat me to delicious meals each day. The gesture was nice, but as my ultimate departure date from Hanoi neared, the contrast between that reality and the reality I would face upon returning home caused me to feel even more despondent over my situation. "I need help," I said to myself. "But to whom am I expected to turn?"

And then a most obvious solution occurred to me, centered on the man who was ushering me in and out of each interview, my previous acquaintance Mister Minh.

"I have something to say to you," I told Mister Minh discreetly at a dessert reception held in my honor that night. I had taken to calling him "Uncle Minh," a sign in my culture of deference and respect. I hoped he would prove himself worthy of my faith in him.

Members of the foreign press had been invited to the gathering, and while my country's officials played the part of kindhearted hosts well, in truth most of them had no interest in honoring me. They only wished to profit from my story, my pain. Except for Uncle Minh. Prior to my trip to Germany, I had detected in Uncle Minh a different sort of tone, a certain compassion, a tenderness I could trust.

He leaned in toward me now, his attention trained on my words. "What is it, Kim Phuc?" he asked.

"For the past two years, your government has robbed me

of a higher education," I said. "They have taken me from my school and studies, and forced me to speak statements to journalists from far and wide, statements I myself do not believe. And now, with this latest photograph of me published for all the world to see, saying that I am a mother to that little girl, it will be utterly impossible for me to find a husband and marry for real! My life is in ruins, Uncle Minh! What am I to do?"

Uncle Minh's eyes grew wide. "What is this you are saying?" he said, dropping the sugared rice ball that he had just picked up with chopsticks onto his plate. "This cannot be true!"

He himself had bought into his own staff's propaganda—an irony lost on neither of us.

"It is true!" I whispered with urgency. "What I am saying is what has happened to me . . . what is happening to me *still*."

"This must not stand," Uncle Minh said to me. "I will do all I can to assist you, Kim Phuc. You are a national treasure. You must be protected from such mistreatment as this."

Uncle Minh asked me to write down my story in the form of a letter that he could deliver to his boss. I complied immediately, and within two days I had received a reply. It was a dinner invitation from the office of Uncle Minh's boss, one Pham Van Dong. I had been invited to the residential villa of the prime minister of Vietnam.

Without hesitation, and with arrowed prayers shot heavenward for outright miracles to abound, I agreed to go.

—∞—

"Kim Phuc," Pham Van Dong said to me upon my arrival, "I would be honored to hear your story. Please, do sit down."

I told the prime minister everything, leaving no critical

detail out. There could be no greater ally for me than my country's senior-most leader, this powerful patron who had miraculously befriended me, and I would never forgive myself if I left something unsaid, one important turn of events or another that could possibly sway him to my side. I had brought along the newspaper article that implied I had taken a husband and bore a daughter, and as I reached the present-day goings on in my life, I unfolded the paper and laid the scandalous image before him.

"Perhaps the very worst part of my mistreatment is *this*," I said, tears springing to my eyes. "It is so unfair! I will be alone forever now, because men will think that I am already married."

Prime Minister Dong took a long look at the article and its accompanying photograph, then he sat back in his chair and began to laugh. He laughed and laughed and laughed for so long that I thought he surely must not have understood what I said. Had I not been clear in my explanation? I knew that I had. I stared at the prime minister incredulously, saying nothing, silenced by outright shock.

Eventually, the prime minister's laughter died down, and he composed himself once more. "Ah, Kim Phuc," he said, his words stitched together with fatherly love, "you need not worry. Pay this no attention. Things will work out for you."

I was not so sure that I should believe this man, high position or not. What did he know of tragedy and loss? Of suffering and deepest pain?

He knew much of these things, I would soon discover, for the prime minister had his own tale to tell.

Several hours later, I was still with the prime minister. After eating a meal together, he asked to see my scars. I would have hesitated, but I realized by his tone that he wanted to sit with me in my pain, not gawk. "Of course," I said to him, raising the arm of my shirt.

I watched the prime minister's face as he slowly and methodically took in the entirety of my wounds. Gently and with great care, he then raised his hand toward my arm, his fingertips grazing my bumpy skin with the slightest touch. "Oh, child," he said, "the troubles you have known."

Prime Minister Dong placed his hands in his lap and he wept. With tenderness, he cried for my situation and for my scars.

"You," he said, looking at me, "you are my daughter now. I will care for you as a child."

It was then that I learned about the prime minister's family, his one and only son, who at that time was more than twice my age; his wife, who was suffering from mental illness; his lifetime spent longing for a daughter. I would be as a daughter to him. From this moment on, I would address him as Bac Dong, meaning, "beloved uncle" or "great-uncle" or "grandfather."

"I care for my wife every single day," Bac Dong explained to me, "and so I, too, understand great pain. There is no cure for what ails her, but I do all that I can do."

Bac Dong talked with me at length about his wife's grave condition, about the medicines and treatments he administered day by day, about his hopes for her healing, about the toll it had taken on his heart. "I simply want you to know that I also walk a challenging path," he said to me just before

I left, "and that I will help you, my fellow sufferer, in any way that I can." Over the year, Bac Dong and I kept in touch and would meet twenty-five or thirty more times. And each time was like reuniting with a treasured family member. I believe God himself had brought us together, providing me with a safe, sure advocate whose power was a catalyst for meaningful change in my life.

The first change Bac Dong orchestrated was arranging for me to go back to school. From 1984 to 1985, my school year unfolded largely uninterrupted. Yes, minders did continue to show up from time to time, but the situation *had* improved. At last, I had completed an entire year of school with decent marks.

I opted to study English instead of medicine, figuring that it would be an easier degree to secure, and as that freshman experience came to a close, I remember looking with great anticipation toward the summertime months and my second year of school. But that plan would not come to pass—in Vietnam, anyway.

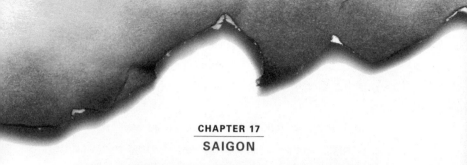

AN UNWELCOME TANGENT

APRIL 1985

It was near the end of Saigon's hottest month of the year—April—when my English professor came to me and said, "Phuc, the youth conference is seeking confirmations for this year's festival, but I cannot send in your registration until you complete this form." As I looked at him, a resentment burned inside me that rivaled the blistering conditions outside.

The conference he was referring to was an international recruitment and reeducation gathering for students held every four years by the Revolutionary Communist Youth League. The "form" would be my official consent not only to attend the festival but also to join the organization and support its cause.

"But sir," I explained, "I do not wish to be part of the

Communist Youth League. And I do not wish to go to the conference."

"Kim Phuc," he said, his expression grave. "If you do not take these steps—completing your formal registration, attending the conference, agreeing to this cause—then you may not continue your studies. Your schooling will end. What is more, you are not just wanted as an attendee but also as a participant. You are to speak on a panel against war."

I wanted to be known as an excellent student, which meant I must pledge allegiance to communist methods. Well, if that is what was required, then that is what I would do—on the outside, anyway. In my heart? I still abhorred that way of life.

In Russia's capital city, I joined delegates from more than one hundred countries, all of whom had come together under the banner of socialism, disarmament, and peace. My days were filled to overflowing with speaking sessions, one-on-one interviews, and panel discussions regarding war and its effects. Following each encounter, people applauded my remarks, came forward to meet me, and asked for my autograph. In those moments, I felt like a superstar.

I could not help but flash back in my mind's eye to a conversation I had had in Saigon just a week before with a small group of classmates I knew fairly well. We were sitting in the classroom, but when our professor did not show up, we went outside to a grassy area and began to chat.

"Nobody will ever want to be his girlfriend," one of the girls in the group was saying, to which the others giggled and shook their heads.

"No way!" the others agreed.

"Who are you speaking of?" I asked the first girl.

"Oh, Vu. You know, the boy with the scar."

Vu was a handsome, intelligent young man in our class. The first time I had met him, I immediately noticed a scar on his right hand—we are always quick to spot in others those things that trouble us most, are we not? It was the smallest of scars—from a pocket knife, I surmised. But there it was, permanent proof of his imperfection, a lasting flaw that marred all else about him that was right.

"Who would ever want to hold that hand?" the girl was saying, even as I drifted far, far away, lost in tormenting thoughts. *Oh, if she only knew of my own scars. What would she say about me?*

For three days after that conversation, I could not eat. I could not study. I could not sleep. I could not talk. I could not smile. Even though I was a Christian, I was not mature enough in my faith to understand how to stand up against feelings such as these. Nobody would ever reach out to me. Nobody would ever care. Nobody would ever find me beautiful. I was hopeless, and helpless, and cursed.

Who would want to hold his hand, with that terrible scar?— I replayed that comment again and again in my mind, changing the pronoun and multiplying the scar.

Who would want to hold her hand, with those terrible scars?
Who would want to hold her hand, with those terrible scars?
Who would want to hold her hand, with those terrible scars?

The words were a lyric I could not get out of my head, no matter how hard I tried. Each time the dirge floated through my consciousness, it was joined by my mother's well-intentioned advice to me: "My, you must devote yourself fully to CaoDai, to our religion, if you hope to live apart from lone-liness. It is to be your only companion, my child, for you will never marry in life."

Will I ever make peace with my wounds?

As the festival came to a close, the organizer informed me that I had been officially invited to remain in Moscow for four weeks longer—"a vacation, of sorts," I was told. That monthlong extension gave way to another, and then another after that. During those months, I was carted all over the country, stopping in no fewer than fifteen states—Vladimir and Ryazan, Tula and Bryansk, Orel and Lipetsk and Kursk—in order to sit for television and radio interviews with Russian broadcasters, journalists, and photographers, all of whom were greatly intrigued with my tale.

To this day, I have no idea what I *actually* said in those sessions. I did not understand a single syllable of Russian, my translator was stone-faced at best, and although the entire experience was cloaked in hugs and smiles, pats on the back and post-interview feasts, the one and only reason I was there was for the sake of propaganda. These people were cut from the very same cloth as the leaders back in my homeland. I knew better than to believe their motives were pure.

This went on for seven full months, with one lengthy interruption. As winter came to Moscow, my scars began to wail, a setback that caused my Russian minders to take action. "We shall temporarily move you to Sochi for rehabilitation."

The following day, I boarded a flight bound for Sochi, one thousand miles from Moscow, where I would remain for the next eight weeks.

The accommodations at the rehabilitation center were even more elaborate than those in Bonn. This was no medical facility; it was a hotel, a spa, a *resort*. Flanked on the east by the Black Sea and on the west by the Caucasus Mountains, Sochi was part of the Caucasian Riviera, one of the few places in Russia with a subtropical climate. I was sure I had found utopia.

My days in Sochi ran like clockwork, a rhythm I came to adore. Each morning, I would be treated to a breakfast of pastries and a bottomless pot of tea. A driver would arrive and take me up the mountain to the hospital for my daily sulfur bath. The sulfur smelled awful, but it was effective. I would emerge from those baths, and attendants would slather medicated cream all over my wounds. Then I would be driven to a restaurant for an indulgent afternoon meal before returning to my hotel room for a two-hour nap. Dinner was another elaborate affair before I retired for the night.

Two things happened during those two months in Sochi: My scars temporarily stopped aching, and my body got *fat*. Eventually, the only thing that fit me was the hotel-issued robe! Thankfully, the Russian government generously offered to buy whatever I needed, and I added to my wardrobe from the nearby shops.

Today, being sequestered for seven months in a foreign country for politically self-serving purposes would be considered by many as outright abduction, but for me, back then, nobody seemed to mind. Who was going to stand up to the whims of the communist government? Who would risk their own livelihood to intervene? I figured that upon my eventual return to Vietnam, I would just pick up my schooling where

I had left off. For now, I had to admit: This treatment was pretty nice.

—⁓—

When I finally returned to Saigon, I had missed four months of school; my classmates were preparing to enter the second semester of our sophomore year. I knew it would take a lot of hard work on my part to catch up with them, but I was up to the task. My professors were not convinced, threatening to kick me out of school.

"You have missed too much, Kim Phuc," they said to me. "It is hopeless for you. You may not come back."

Holding back the tears that were rising up from deep within, I said, "But I *must* come back. How else am I to survive?"

It was true. I relied on my student status. Everyone enrolled in university in Vietnam received weekly coupons for rice, and without that aid, I would have nothing to eat. Although student housing was available, I made arrangements to stay with my "adopted" aunt, Sau Huong, who had been taken in by our family during the war so many years ago.

"We will see what is possible," my professors said, securing a special dispensation for me to re-enroll in school. "But you will have to begin again as a freshman," they clarified. I was not pleased with that change, but at least I was still a student. I would befriend this inferior plan. And it *did* work, for two undeterred months. But then Tay Ninh came calling again, this time with unbelievable news. "You are going to go to the United States, Kim Phuc. We have work for you to do there."

Fear and frustration tangled themselves into a knot in my

stomach. "The United States!" I shouted at him, without thinking how this powerful man could easily ruin my life at that moment. "I do not know what this 'work' is that you speak of, but I will *not* be going on this trip." I was so angry that I spat my words.

It seemed my Russian publicity tour had been so successful that Vietnam wanted to raise the stakes. *If my story generated such high interest in Europe*, they reasoned, *just imagine the response in the United States!* The Vietnam Veterans Memorial in America's capital had been dedicated less than three years prior, and it was as if the nearly sixty thousand names etched into its granite wall beckoned another entire generation toward confusion and embitterment over their country's seemingly senseless involvement in our civil war. By trotting me out as a childhood victim of war, communist leaders in Vietnam could leverage those feelings of discontent and garner greater support for their way of life. The Communist Youth League did not need to be relegated to eastern countries; why not recruit members in the West? I was the best magnet to draw others to their cause. They knew this, and so did I.

My mind raced. *I am so weary of being manipulated. But I did enjoy being treated as a celebrity in Russia.* I was a bundle of contradictions indeed.

In the end, I knew what I needed to do. With fresh resolve, I looked at the Tay Ninh official and said, "Sir, please understand what I am saying to you. I cannot fulfill this request to visit America because I need to finish my school. I am already far behind, and each week that I am away from Saigon sets me back even more."

The official looked at me with a weary expression. "Kim

Phuc," he said, "you are different. Do you not understand this by now? Your scars make you different. You are the only one who can do this work. You must obey your government at once."

—⟋⟍—

My "work order" had originated in Hanoi, and as soon as Tay Ninh's provincial officials completed and submitted my paperwork to the capital, I would be on my way. I did not know how long I had—perhaps a few weeks at most. It was the only time I can remember wishing for my country's bureaucratic red tape to be multiplied instead of reduced.

"More days, Lord," I prayed during the next three sleepless nights. "Give me more time. And please, show me the path to take."

I stewed for those three days before the thought hit me: I had an ally on the inside—Bac Dong. Although he and I had never discussed politics during our many lengthy and deep conversations, the time had come for me to beg his assistance in escaping the clutches of his minions' tight grip. I reached for pen and paper and began crafting my heartfelt plea.

"I have only one wish," I told him, "which is to study and thus create a future for myself, so that I can succeed, so that I can live free." And in order to do that, I explained, I needed space. I needed a quiet space without distractions.

I decided to deliver the letter myself, to make sure my request reached him.

The following morning, an acquaintance told me that a low-level official from Hanoi had flown into town to pick up a ministry vehicle and drive it back to the capital.

I got in touch with the official and boldly asked if I could ride along with him. "I have no money," I explained, "but I do have important business in Hanoi." *Would he have mercy on me?* In the end, he took not just me, but two other passengers as well, neither of whom I knew.

The trip took a full week. We only traveled during the day, when the driver could see and navigate the rutted, war-torn roads. The car had no air conditioning, so when temperatures soared above ninety degrees, we stopped to sit in the shade, dip our feet in a nearby stream, and catch our breath.

During those roadside conversations, I was cordial but did not give my companions any details about why I was going to the capital. *The less they know, the better.* I wanted neither to put their lives in jeopardy nor sabotage my own mission. I never knew the reasons those fellow sojourners were making the trip either.

I do remember those long hours staring out the backseat window of the car, watching Vietnam's beautiful countryside pass by. Under any other circumstances, I would have lost myself in those purple-flowered hills.

Within an hour of our arrival in Hanoi, I contacted one of Bac Dong's aides, handed over the letter, and expressed its urgency. "Please," I said to the aide, "please make this task a priority."

By midafternoon, I received an invitation to the prime minister's residence for dinner. My request had reached his ears.

I greeted Bac Dong with a warm embrace and asked after

his family and himself. He invited me to sit down. "Kim Phuc," he said, "who helped you to write the missive I received?"

"Nobody helped me!" I answered him truthfully. "I prayed about what to say and then labored over every word myself!"

He eyed me with fatherly pride. "Well, it was *very* well done, my child. Every one of my staff members who read your letter cried. I cried as well. I wish to help you, Phuc. We will find a way."

For ten days, I waited in Hanoi for an answer from Bac Dong. What "way" would he be able to find for me? How would he help me fulfill my dream?

Evidently, word of my upcoming trip to the United States had reached administrators at several universities in New York, each of whom stated via the press that if I would like to attend their schools, they would welcome me, free of charge. Oh, how my heart soared over this news! If I could attend school—at no cost to me—I would happily travel to the States.

When Bac Dong finally called me in to reveal his plan for my immediate future, I was still elated. "*Three* universities!" I beamed. "Might I give one of them a try?"

Bac Dong still oversaw a communist operation, and to release me to a free land would be something he would never live down. "Kim Phuc," he said, dismissing my idea with a wave of his hand through the air, "I have already determined a way for you both to leave Vietnam *and* to continue your studies."

I perked up. I was *leaving*—leaving Vietnam for good? I could become a full-time student again? My dream . . . it was coming true?

"Your plane will leave in the morning. You will resume your schooling in Cuba, my child."

I had no idea where Cuba was, but based on Bac Dong's information, it was located outside of Vietnam. Truly, that was all I needed to know.

NOTHING LEFT FOR ME HERE

SEPTEMBER 1986

There was one person I needed to visit before leaving the country. Ma was still living in Trang Bang, and despite the emotional gulf between us, I needed for her to know my plans. A mother should always know where her children are in this world.

Not surprisingly, I found her working in the noodle shop. Within moments of Ma seeing me, she asked, "Have you decided to return to CaoDai?" Her eyes barely made contact with mine.

I suppose it was proof of some level of Christian transformation already taking root in me that instead of lashing back at my ma with defensiveness or rage, I responded with gentleness, with tears.

"Oh, Ma," I said, barely above a whisper. "No, Ma . . . no."

Ma's gaze bored into me, effectively saying, *Well, then why have you come?*

In her inner person, my ma possessed a beautiful, laudable faith—that much was easy for me to see. It is just that her faith had been pointed from birth toward the wrong god, a truth also plain to see. As she stood before me, eyebrows stitched together, consternation etched on her face, I envisioned her spiritually transformed, redirecting her faithfulness toward Jesus. For a moment, I could *see* it; yes, this would someday occur. *How I covet this peace for you, Ma.*

I was compelled to tread carefully here, to measure my words and guard my tone.

"Ma," I said, thinking through each syllable, each phrase. "I love you. And I know that you love me. I know that I hurt you very deeply when I left our family's faith to follow Jesus. I understand that you were very angry, very upset. I am your daughter! Your own flesh and blood."

My ma was listening with great interest to everything I was saying. *Oh, Father, please help me to say words that are useful here. Please do not let me hurt my ma.*

"Ma," I continued, "all those years that I was suffering so deeply—my burns, my scars, my agony, my pain—you would have done anything to make me feel better, I know, but all you could do was cry. You could not provide joy for me. Or peace. Or comfort at the level of my soul. You could only shed tears for me and offer me CaoDai, which in the end was no comfort at all.

"But Ma, when I encountered Jesus, the joy and peace I

had been searching for came to me *just like that.* I was comforted from deep within. It is only in Jesus that true peace is found, Ma. How could I turn my back on him, when he gave me this critical thing?"

My ma said nothing in reply. Truly, what could she possibly say? She knew that the words I had spoken were true; during my worst days—when the pain was greatest and the medicines were hard to come by and no amount of massaging could console my angry skin—she could hold me and she could cry with me, but she could not make things okay. In Jesus, I had come to understand that all things really do work together for good for those who love him and are called according to his purpose,[18] and while I could not yet see precisely what that "good" would entail, simply knowing it was promised was enough to help me hang on.

Jesus can help you, Ma! I wanted to cry out to her, even though I knew the prompting to accept him had to come from God, not me. *Oh, how he would help you, the moment you invite him to step into your life.*

I knew Ma struggled with an impoverished self-image from the time she was a little girl. Instead of going to school, she cooked soup to sell to schoolchildren. Ma would peek through the classroom windows for hours upon hours, desperate to learn her letters, her numbers, her shapes. That poverty could be transformed into something beautiful in Jesus. In God, Ma would see the plot twists not as turns to be despised, but rather as part of the route that would lead her straight to him.

I left Trang Bang thinking about my ma, and about Jesus, and about my old friend Thuy. I had lost touch with Thuy while I was in Russia and when I returned to Vietnam, I asked about Thuy and her family. Most people I spoke to believed they had relocated to Belgium.

I thought about Thuy's lessons regarding prayer: "The more we cry, the more we pray," she used to say. And oh, did I know a thing or two about tears! As streams of sadness coursed down my cheeks en route to Hanoi, where I would board my flight to Havana, I weighed the truth of Thuy's statement. *Yes, we pray more not through laughter, but tears.* It was then that I began pleading with God to save my ma.

On that bus ride to Hanoi, and on countless occasions since, I thanked God for my good friend Thuy. She demonstrated the gentle spirit I have aspired to ever since. She taught me the value of bringing peace into all situations. She taught me to listen well, to speak carefully, to pray faithfully, and to bear pain with great faith. She taught me to embrace wisdom, not shun it, counting wisdom a friend all the days of my life.

Even now, as I write these words, my eyes pool with tears. What a gift Thuy was to me! What a lifesaver when I was adrift at sea. Oh, Thuy, should you ever discover these pages, may you know what a treasure you are. When I had nobody else to turn to, you appeared to me as love, levelheadedness, and light. Oh, that we all would have such impact in other people's lives, drawing them to Jesus by the way we listen and learn and love.

THIS IS PROGRESS?

OCTOBER 1986

Before my first full day on Cuban soil had elapsed, I had to be rushed to the hospital designated for foreign visitors. That is when I realized that while Havana's climate was moderate compared with Vietnam's nearly year-round sweltering heat, it was not stable, and my scars protested immediately. Being an island, Cuba is subject to the whims of the wind, and how fickle Atlantic winds could be!

This trade-off—milder temperatures in Cuba for predictable wind patterns in Vietnam—was one I was not sure I wanted to make. But here I was, beginning a new chapter in a new city, with new opportunities awaiting me. I wanted to make the best of things—once I got out of the hospital, anyway.

My weeks-long hospital stay was problematic for several

reasons, not the least of which was I did not speak Spanish. This came as a terrible shock to me. When I was flying to Cuba, I had studied the fold-out airline map en route, surprised by how close I would be to the United States. Naturally, I assumed that Cubans spoke English. I did not know English very well either, but I knew it better than I knew Spanish. Now, not only would I need to settle back into a rhythm of studying, attending classes, and taking exams, but I would need to master an entirely new language. And these things could only happen once I was released from the hospital.

More than anything, I did not want to be seen as a troublemaker by the Vietnamese embassy officials who had taken charge of me when I arrived in Cuba. What if they determined that I was unfit to manage this new life and shipped me back to Vietnam? I could not allow that to happen. I had to get well, get stronger, become sturdier.

The whole reason I had come to Havana was to pursue the education I deeply desired. I had not had the chance to attend even a single class before being hospitalized for observation and rest. This was hardly the path to take if I ever hoped to get where I wanted to be.

Although Bac Dong had assured me that I would be free from oppressive "minding" by Vietnamese officials in Cuba, an embassy man named Hoa had been assigned to me from the start, visiting me in the hospital almost daily, checking in on my goings-on, gathering details to take back to his superiors. I feared that life for me in this new locale would fall into the same pattern I had grown accustomed to back home, one marked by distractions, abuses, and false starts.

When I finally was released from the hospital into the

bustling city streets of Havana, my enthusiasm was short-lived. Hoa, the only person I had met so far who spoke fluent Vietnamese, took me to my new home, a small room shared with seven other girls. The room was located on the fourth floor of a giant building containing university offices and student housing. My floor housed twenty-four girls, with one washroom for all of us, which contained one shower, one toilet, and one sink.

Due to water rations throughout the country, water only flowed through the tap for an hour each day, and it was never the same hour two days in a row. Hopefully during that hour someone on the floor was home to hear the flow of water gurgling through the pipes, turn on the tap, and capture as much as possible in the fourth floor's large, metal cistern.

It was critical to wake early in the morning to brush your teeth or wash your face before the cistern ran dry. When nobody was available during the hour when the tap was flowing, my fellow residents and I were relegated to carrying pre-purchased pails down to the first floor and outside the building to beg water off of the Cuban residents who lived nearby and whose taps ran more often than ours.

I doubt that Bac Dong knew about these conditions when he relocated me to Cuba or the challenges I would face. It was imperative for me to shower every day. My scars demanded to be soothed. But I was always stressed, thinking, *Is the water on? Is the cistern full? Is my pail handy? Will someone take pity on me? I must shower—there is no other option.*

These moment-by-moment considerations were a heavy burden, but they were not the weightiest part of my grief. During that last conversation with Bac Dong, I had felt relief, believing once I left Vietnam, I would be able to grow spiritually. I would experience the joy of being *transformed*. I assumed I would have more discretionary time, and I would find a God-honoring church to attend. My assumptions were all wrong. There were no Christian churches in Cuba, no warm, welcoming believers with whom I could learn and serve and grow. There was only me and the Bible that Thuy had given me. That would have to be enough.

Indeed, those first months in Cuba, I felt as though I had been dropped on a deserted island and left to fend for myself. I did not have good health, I did not have good friends, and I was not having a good time at all. I imagined the locals all looking at me in pity, whispering, "Who is this strange person we see?"

—⁂—

I attended class each morning at the yearlong language institute in which I had been enrolled (*still*, I was not in "real" school), and paid attention as best I could, trusting that over time I would sort out the meanings of key words—*escucha, trabajo, examen* . . . listen, work, exam—and from there, perhaps, sort out my life. That was easier said than done.

Between my studies, my attempt to get the sleep my body required each night to promote healing for my wounds, the issues surrounding personal hygiene, and the requirement for us students to be at the bus stop an hour before morning classes began, I never had time for breakfast—not once in my six years in Cuba.

My classmates and I would attend classes until two-thirty each afternoon and then finally eat. And even when I was *able* to eat, I had trouble choking the food down. To go from the mildness of rice, vegetables, and fresh fruit to spicy Cuban cuisine was quite a jolt indeed. Still, I did my best, realizing that it was that or nothing. I had had enough of nothing. "Come on, tummy!" I would encourage my stomach. "You can do this! You *must* do this for me."

Those meals were few and far between, with the portions ever shrinking, as more stringent governmental rations were enforced. So my willpower to get the spicy food down only went so far. I was always hungry—dreadfully ravenous.

One day, a classmate of mine suggested that we venture into Havana proper and get ice cream at Coppelia. Coppelia was named after the famous nineteenth-century comedy ballet, which was why the ice cream shop's logo featured a dancing ballerina. It was one of the most popular places in Havana, and people stood in line for hours. We were no exception.

By the time we reached the counter to place our order, I was so hot and famished that I asked for ten full bowls of ice cream. "*Si, me gustaría diez bolas de helado, por favor,*" I said confidently, as I handed over the five pesos that it cost. I selected chocolate, mango, walnut, vanilla, strawberry, malted crème, pineapple glacé, caramel, guava, and banana. I carefully balanced the small glass dishes on my tray, keeping them from clinking against each other as I made my way to the patio where my classmate was sitting at a table. My classmate, who had ordered half the amount I had, sat in shock as I proceeded to eat every last bite in a matter of minutes, a very foolish thing for me to do. In fact, it was nearly fatal.

Leading up to that ice-cream-eating extravaganza, I had

had very little food—nothing for breakfast, a few bites of beans and tortilla for lunch, maybe another half-cup of beans and some onions for dinner. The following morning, having eaten all of that sugar and milk at once, I got horribly ill and had to be taken to the hospital. The doctor at the hospital that afternoon told me in no uncertain terms to lay off the sugar—"You have diabetes!" he said with a stern expression.

"I was just so *hungry*," I explained, to which he replied, "Hungry enough to land yourself here?"

Ah, he had a point.

For a week, I remained in an in-patient clinic, where nurses could monitor my blood sugar and nutritionists could provide education regarding how to manage this *diabetes* I did not know I had. "You need animal protein!" I remember them saying time and again. I did not tell them how long I had been a rigorous vegetarian. Oh, the trouble that truth would have caused!

No, I simply did as I was told: I took my daily pill, I incorporated meat into my diet whenever it was available, and I never again looked Coppelia's way.

—∽∾—

In Cuba, the government had two priorities: education and healthcare. This meant that the university and a visit to the hospital were both free. Once those two benefits were extended to a person, there was no additional aid to be found. For a long time, the Soviet Union and several of the Eastern Bloc countries supported Cuba's economy, but after the Soviet Union fell, that support quickly dried up. Cuba no longer could fund its own well-being. Degradation was bound to occur.

Tourists who frequented the island enjoyed every modern convenience, but for those of us who called the place home, it was a despairing, impoverished existence at best. Water and electricity were not guaranteed, food was taxed out of reach, roads in dire need of repair were never fixed, and gasoline for the buses that took us to school could dry up in a flash.

I distinctly remember Fidel Castro ordering thousands upon thousands of bicycles for students to ride to and from school when many of the buses no longer ran. This may seem like a noble effort, but none of my classmates knew how to ride a bicycle, and so time and again, a student would fall from a bicycle into the crush of traffic and be killed on the spot. When a bus was available, it was overflowing with people, with others simply jumping onto the side of the bus as it took off, holding on for dear life as it jerked and swerved through crowded streets.

—⁂—

As hard as it was to believe, I wound up feeling more controlled, more handled, in Cuba than I had in Vietnam. Certainly, fewer people in Cuba knew who I was, what I had endured, or why my story mattered to the media, but I was still required to report my every coming and going daily to the Vietnamese embassy in Cuba.

"Where have you been today?" Hoa would ask me each afternoon. "Class," I would reply every time, hoping to keep our conversation brief. "Until tomorrow, then," Hoa would say, expressionless.

"Someday, we will have no 'tomorrow,'" I wanted to tell Hoa, determined to spring free of his grip, even though I would never in a million years verbalize that thought. What was it Thuy had said to me? "Let wisdom be your friend."

I look back on my time in Cuba and see a bird in my mind's eye, a bird who had flitted from one cage only to land in another. One evening I sat on the tiny balcony of my dorm building with the tattered pages of my Bible in my hands, rereading the account of my friend the apostle Paul's suffering.

I looked at the waters below me as the sun sank deep into the inky abyss, and I wept. A scene that should have been stunning to me was not, due to the plain fact that I was still living inside communism's cage. During my years in Cuba, I witnessed students jumping from that same balcony into the waters below, their despondency too much to bear. What a tragic ending to life; how such an ending must grieve the heart of God. "No, Kim," I would tell myself between sobs. "You must not give up on this life. There has to be a better way."

I had been in that place before, and I had found the better way. I simply had to choose God, moment by moment.

For the next six years that I lived in Havana, I was challenged almost to the point of despondence every day. But I determined to choose God, which meant seizing every spare moment to read his Scriptures, letting him put his law into my heart.[19] As I sat with my Bible and allowed its truth to penetrate my flared-up defenses; as I let my shoulders fall, my breathing slow, my fists unclench; as I anticipated experiencing the same innocent joy I had known over reading *The Monkey King* as a child to show up here and now; although nothing about my situation was altered, I was made brand-new. The peace I began to discover preserved me from outright despair. While I was in Cuba, the terrible circumstances I faced taught me to more fully trust and obey God. I would read and reread the apostle Paul's explanation of how he had trained himself to be content with whatever he had or did not have.[20]

"Oh, Father," I would pray through tears, "please teach me to be content like Paul. Teach me this special secret of living so that I am not overtaken by despair."

It was not long before people began to call me "the girl who is always smiling!"—further proof that something supernatural was underway. No, I had not stumbled upon freedom that the world could detect—freedom from communism, freedom from oppression, freedom from pain. But inside—on the level of my soul—I was settling into a type of contentment that paid little mind to external things.

One of the passages that never failed to comfort me when I was feeling especially down was the list of blessings Jesus proclaimed to his disciples in the Sermon on the Mount. There he says, "Blessed are they which do hunger and thirst after righteousness: for they shall be filled."[21] I would run my finger along those phrases, wondering if those words could really be true. *If I pursue your ways, God, will you really satisfy that which is hungry in me?*

What, exactly, did I hunger for back then? That which we all crave, I suppose: safety and security; provision and unshakable peace; hope in the quietest of moments; the sense of family, so far from home. Partway through my first year in Havana, God's blessings in my life shifted from being frightening leaps of faith to visible, tangible gifts. At the top of that gift list was my being invited to move from my campus dorm into a quiet, apartment-style home on the west side of Havana that was much closer to the language institute, where I would report for classes for another five months.

My Spanish professor was the one who saw plainly that the challenging living conditions on campus were less then helpful for me, given my health issues. With thousands of students residing in one tight block of dormitories, the setting was always bustling, chaotic, loud. And so when a student moved out of the West Havana home, freeing up a slot in one of the bedrooms, I was encouraged to take the spot. I would have constant access to water, I could use the shower whenever my itchy skin needed it, and I would enjoy a break from the noise of dorm life.

Adjacent to the apartment was a small dorm that held perhaps one hundred students, and university officials told me to feel free to join those residents for meals anytime I wished. On my first day in that *comedor*, I met another language-school student, Yami Diaz, a native Cuban studying German in hopes of landing a job in Germany someday. Yami and I were fast friends, a welcome shift from the isolation I had felt for so long, and soon enough, she was inviting me to accompany her home on the weekends to enjoy time with her ma and dad.

After a few weeks of visits, Yami's parents said I was welcome to call them *Mami* and *Papi*—Mom and Dad. It had been months since I had received a letter from my own parents, so Nuria and Manuel Diaz's gesture carried great significance for me. Soon after, when I received my father's update from Vietnam, I could feel the distance between us. I had hurt my parents so deeply by leaving my family's religion that I feared in coming days this Cuban couple might be the only mother and father I would be able to claim as my own.

Mami and Papi were, practically speaking, Jesus with skin to me. I still am unsure of where they stand spiritually. But in terms of accepting me for who I was and promoting my growth and development toward becoming all I was meant to be, they loved me about as well as a person could be loved. All those evenings spent with the entire family gathered together, as Papi gently rubbed cream into my scars. All those lengthy discussions with Mami regarding boys and marriage. All those rides to and from school with Yami, basking together in the joys of young womanhood. The Diaz family did not just accept me—they embraced me. They enveloped me with care. And because they valued me so highly, I was compelled to start valuing myself.

I would part ways with Yami following our year in language school, but her family's imprint on my life and heart I carry with me to this day. In fact, it was their influence back in the late 1980s that singlehandedly carved out in me a greater capacity for chasing my dreams. Certainly, I had determined by this point that a career in medicine would be too rigorous an educational path to take—it was for this reason that I had landed on English as my chosen degree. But then I began thinking. *Maybe I could find a compromise, something that still helped people with health issues but was not as taxing for me. Pharmacology!* If I could not oversee diagnoses or surgeries, interventions or therapies, at least I could send ailing ones on their way with medicines to assuage their pain. This course correction meant a move back to student housing, but I figured it was worth it if it meant a meaningful career in life.

So in October 1988, I gathered up my belongings and headed back to the heart of Havana, excited to enter school in earnest, ready to study and learn.

—⁓—

Of course, returning to student housing had its downsides. There were frequent brownouts, for example, and on those occasions, no taps flowed—at any hour of the day. All of the dorm residents, including myself, had to take our individual pails to the ground floor of the building and have them filled by an emergency generator that was pumping water. To make the long, laborious process even worse was the fact that without electricity, the elevators could not run. For me, no elevators meant trudging up six flights of stairs lugging a heavy pail of water. Because of my scars, the entire left side of my body was weak, and relying solely on my right side proved too difficult for my back. I should have foreseen the folly in attempting such a feat, but I was young and believed myself to be up to the task.

Sadly, I was not.

A few hours later, I was laid up in a hospital bed again, writhing in pain. Suddenly, the overseer of the Vietnamese students at my school dropped by for a visit—a "courtesy call," he explained. "The next time you need water hauled up six flights of stairs," he said to me with sincerity and gentleness in his eyes, "an assistant will be present to help."

I was the only female Vietnamese student at the university,

so I do not know if the man's motivation was pity or chivalry, but within the hour, four of the male Vietnamese students, all hailing from the North, had been assembled and informed that from that day forward, they would rotate as my assistants, always available to meet my needs. I would conclude my classes each day and find one of the four of them waiting—to carry water for me, to drive me someplace, or simply to keep me company. What a gift this was to me.

On day four of the arrangement, I stepped into the *comedor* in my building following my morning classes to get something to eat. I selected rice and beans, and when I turned to find a seat, I noticed a very handsome Vietnamese man seated at a table nearby. *Oh, this must be the fourth one in the rotation,* I reasoned, approaching him and asking to sit down.

"*Vâng, xin!*" he said, his eyes brightening. Yes, please! And then he rose to pull out my chair.

I could tell from his accent that he was from the North, which confirmed to me that he had been assigned to help me. But from that first moment of introduction—"Kim Phuc!" he had beamed. "So good to meet you! I am Toan."—I considered him not a helper, but a friend. Toan possessed an impossibly charming style and knew nothing of pretense or pride. He was a gentle, big-hearted lover of life who bubbled over with selfless questions and generous observations.

"Your smile is so beautiful!" he said to me in those first few moments together. He laughed then, as did I. Who cared that Toan was from the North? All I cared about was that he was here, before me, now.

Toan and I talked about feeling homesick for Vietnam, even as neither of us liked what was becoming of her. "Well, at least now we have each other," he said. "I will help you in any way I can."

Toan offered to take my tray following that innocent lunchtime meal, and I let him. I hoped it was the first of a million kind gestures I would be able to enjoy in years to come.

Beginning that afternoon, Toan and I would see each other nearly every day for four years, which is how I came to know and be drawn to his laudable character. "My family suffered greatly during the war too," he explained to me during one of a hundred walks we took around town. "This is why my education is so important to me. It is my only way out of the poverty I know so well." Toan had already earned his bachelor's in English and had been offered an advanced degree in computer programming by the university because of his high marks and diligent work.

"It is how I view my own education as well," I had told him then. "But my story there . . . it is complex."

For many weeks our conversations only deepened, until the plain facts stood tall before us: Yes, Toan and I were dear friends, but also, we were falling in love. One afternoon Toan came to me with unexpected news. "A woman from my homeland—she is in Hanoi . . . she is awaiting my return from university, Kim, so that she and I can marry." I was stunned.

As Toan's words penetrated my consciousness, all the old fears returned. *You are different, Kim. You are unlovable. Your scars . . . they are your curse. You will never find love. You will never marry. You will always be alone.* In the same way that a victim of trauma blocks out unsavory recollections, I cannot remember my response to Toan. *My first true love, now gone.* Really, what was there to say?

"Kim, *Kim*," Toan said, jolting me out of my free fall toward self-pity and pain. "Kim, you do not understand. I am telling you this only to explain why I wrote her a letter this week. I told her of you, Kim . . . and of *us*. I told her that she and I are no more."

"Oh, Toan!" I beamed at him. "You are my true, true love."

I loved Toan deeply, and yet I had to admit to myself that things were imperfect between us. It was his drinking, his smoking, and his blatant disregard for the things of God that caused me to decline his first marriage proposal.

"Kim," he would say to me, "I cannot believe this virgin lady had a child and that that child is supposed to be God. It is impossible!" Or, "Kim, if this Jesus could save people, then why did he not save himself when he was hanging there on a cross?" Or, "Kim, you and your Bible stories. Please, no more stories like that."

I would just shake my head in disappointment, thinking, *Yes, I was in your boat once too.*

There was also the conspicuous lack of response from my parents after Toan sent them a heartfelt letter. "Kim and I would like to be husband and wife," he had written to them. "Would you please give us your blessing for this union?"

"You are a *Northerner*," I reminded him, attempting to explain my parents' silence over the matter. "It would violate everything a South Vietnamese family stands for to openly welcome one who is North Vietnamese into our fold."

"But you are okay with me being from the North?" Toan then asked, even as he knew full well my response.

"It is just geography," I told him for the hundredth time.

Part of my relaxed attitude toward the division that had

defined my childhood—"We are from the South; our enemy is from the North," I was incessantly reminded when I was a child—surely is attributable to the Western adage, "Out of sight, out of mind." I had been in Cuba awhile, where that line of demarcation was nowhere to be found. And for quite some time I had observed Toan with his North Vietnamese buddies at school, all of whom warmly befriended me. In the same way that a Bostonian may find a Southern drawl from Charleston, Atlanta, or Baton Rouge attractive, Toan was charmed by my dialect, which is softer, gentler than his.

"It is as though you are singing each time you speak," he often said to me.

Given the estrangement from my kin back home, I needed to build a new family. And despite any reservations I harbored regarding Toan's lifestyle choices, I wanted that family to begin with him. Still, I hesitated.

One night in late August 1992, when Toan and I were relaxing with our circle of friends, the subject of marriage came up again, and the group gave me an ultimatum: I had three days to decide whether I would marry Toan. I agreed to make it a matter of prayer.

For the next three days, I did just that. My prayers were fervent, reminiscent of a month earlier, when I had implored God to open up a door for me to leave Cuba forever. In a bold move, I asked the Vietnamese ambassador if I could take a three-week holiday in Mexico, and I was granted permission. *Freedom would never be closer,* I thought, *just over the border to the United States.*

But my plans were not God's plans. I was more controlled

by my minders in Mexico than in Cuba. As much as I prayed for a way to escape, nothing materialized. Yes, I was disappointed, but I never questioned God's wisdom, never asked why he did not make a way. While I walked in faith, he was putting the pieces together, and one big missing piece was waiting for me in Cuba—dear Toan.

Now, as I prayed about whether my future would include him, I asked God to direct my heart and give me peace about this important decision. After three days, I knew what my answer would be.

"I will," I said to Toan upon his second marriage proposal. "My answer, Toan, is *yes*."

———

With my decision made, our friends celebrated by immediately going into action, pulling together all the wedding details in ten days. One friend found a beautiful gown for me and another took care of Toan's tuxedo. The flowers, decorations, and food were covered. Just before my second year of studies ended at the University of Havana, Bui Huy Toan and I exchanged vows with borrowed rings before a large crowd of college friends in the home of the Vietnamese ambassador to Cuba. Neither of us had family there, and so during the traditional ceremony, the ambassador represented Toan's family, and the highest military official spoke on my behalf. Despite the fact that it rained cats and dogs all afternoon long, it was the most beautiful day of my life.

We were from different worlds—he from North Vietnam, I from South; he from the political religion of communism, I a devoted follower of Jesus Christ. But his tenderness toward the pain I had suffered, his selfless love that enveloped me daily—I knew he was the man for me.

"But, Toan!" his family had protested via their letter written in response to his news. "Why would you wish to marry a burned, disabled girl when there are so many strong and beautiful girls from which to choose?"

"Because Kim Phuc," he had replied without a hint of defensiveness, "she is the one I adore."

Indeed, "adored" is just how I felt. That wedding day was the first time my lips had met Toan's. Throughout our days of courtship, I longed for purity—but not just for spiritual reasons, although that was certainly part of it. The emotional reasons were far weightier—I was *terrified*. Terrified of what Toan would think when he saw my uncovered skin, terrified of how my scars would feel to his touch, terrified of the eventual rejection that I knew in my heart would occur. And so, for months and months after we began dating, he would only hold my hand, kiss my cheek, and lose himself in my wide smile. As things progressed from the innocence of friendship to intimacy neither of us could deny, I showed him the entirety of my left arm. I did not allow him to touch the skin, only to see it. Still, in baring my scars for him, I was saying, "I trust you, Toan. I love you. This is me."

Toan knew these things. He understood the gravity of what I was showing him. And he allowed that rare, close proximity to be enough.

I knew that Jesus suffered greatly during his earthly life and the fact that he could sympathize with our pain was one of the most profound truths I saw reflected in Toan's total acceptance of me—weaknesses and all. "The more I touch your scars," he said to me once, after we had been husband and wife for many months, "the more I love you. In your scars, I see your suffering. I see that both are deep."

I knew that my winding and woeful journey to Cuba had been for the purpose of meeting and marrying Toan. According to Vietnamese custom, rain on one's wedding day means good fortune, a superstition that in our case has proven to be true. Even today, I regard my decision to marry Toan as the second-best decision I have ever made, placed just below my choice to follow Christ.

The moment I married my husband, I said, "I love you so much, Toan!" and I have not stopped saying that since. He always laughs and sighs and says with his heart full, "Thank you, Kim!" Then, after a few beats, he adds, "I love you, too."

Due to the embassy's restrictions on both Toan and me, our honeymoon destination could only be in a communist country. We did not want to return to Vietnam, for fear that we would never again be able to leave. Staying in Cuba did not sound appealing. The Middle East held no allure for us. And so, by way of elimination, we chose Russia.

One of the most amusing recollections I hold from those days of deliberation is hearing the student supervisor in charge of our plans say to me, "Toan may travel to Moscow, but you, Kim Phuc, must stay here. You have already been out of the country this year when you went to Mexico. You cannot leave again."

"You expect my husband to go on his honeymoon *alone?*" I nearly doubled over in laughter.

The student supervisor, reassessing his declaration in light of my incredulity, raked his fingers through his hair, and without even meeting my gaze said, "Fine. Then you both will go."

What I hoped for, but did not know for sure, was that Toan's and my departure for Russia would not be a round trip. If I got my way, Toan and I would never reside in Cuba again.

Part III

A PEACE PURSUED

THE HONEYMOON IS OVER

OCTOBER 1992

I am a married woman, twenty-nine years old, holding hands with Toan, my husband of three weeks. I have proven my fate wrong, the doomsday prediction that even my own ma made, that my scars were my death sentence, preventing me from marriage. "Look, Mommy!" I want to cry out. "Look! I have found true love!"

True love. What odds I have overcome to land in this place, this place of acceptance and intimate care. Yes, Toan and I are meant to be—of this, I am completely sure. The only question that remains is whether Toan will see things that way, once I confide in him this scheme of mine, this plan that must soon be told.

Moscow was not the most charming of honeymoon destinations, but we knew that would be the case. It was not just the frigid weather and the cloud of communism that were off-putting, but also the "minor" detail that I was never once alone with Toan. At every turn—in our hotel, during outings, at every evening meal—minders from Russia's Vietnamese embassy were present, monitoring each syllable that was said. Furthermore, we had to report to that embassy each night of our sixteen-night stay, informing them of our next day's plans. I would not have been surprised in the least to learn that even our hotel room had been bugged. Toan and I behaved as though it were; to act otherwise would be too large a risk.

"This is why we must be faithful to complete our schooling," Toan whispered to me. "Graduating from university is our only hope." I acknowledged his sensibility, even though it did not mesh with what I had planned.

I had heard rumors of Cuban students who studied in Europe for a semester and then "never quite made it home," choosing instead to defect to Canada. *Maybe this plan could work for Toan and me*, I reasoned to myself, once I discovered we would be honeymooning in a far-off land. Yet whenever I would try and bring up the subject with Toan here and there during our trip—while enjoying a lengthy group tour of Red Square; while dining together over large plates piled high with too-rich beef stroganoff; while wandering through Moscow's shopping marts—I realized that my husband did not wish to defect at all.

"What if we were to simply remain in Canada?" I whispered to Toan, as he stood holding the blue jeans and Walkman cassette players he intended to resell back in Cuba. "How would that be, do you think?"

Toan responded not with words but with laughter. That should have told me all I needed to know. I decided to keep silent. At least, until we were heading home.

On an otherwise uneventful afternoon, Toan and I boarded a flight out of Moscow bound for Havana. I knew we had a seven-and-a-half-hour plane ride ahead before we needed to refuel at Gander International Airport in Newfoundland, Canada. We would be there for a short layover before the final leg of the trip. Throughout that lengthy flight, I carefully broached the subject with Toan again: I could not live in bondage any longer; defection was in my sights. I was unsure who was seated around us, and for whom those people worked, and so I never raised my voice above a murmur in Toan's ear.

"I am not going back to Cuba. If you must return, I understand, but I cannot go."

I thought my husband might faint in his seat. I had pledged my unyielding loyalty and love to him just weeks before, and now I could see his utter shock and confusion regarding my apparent infidelity. I was the one person he had come to love more than any other person in the world. And yet I was choosing my freedom over him.

"We *have* to go back to Cuba," he said to me, his jaw slack in disbelief. "We *live* there. That is our *home*. All of our things are there."

Yes, all of our possessions were in Havana or else on the plane. When Toan was shopping in the Russian markets, he had insisted on buying many expensive items. Since I was already formulating my plan, I tried to talk him out of those purchases, saying how little room we had in our new apartment to store such things. But my argument did not dissuade him. I felt badly that he had wasted all of that money, especially given how little money we had had to begin with.

"Toan, I am sorry that I allowed you to throw away all of that money on those electronics and trinkets and clothes, but my decision is made."

"The *money*, Kim?" Toan said to me. "Losing the money is the least of my concerns. How do I bear losing *you*?"

As he continued to absorb the weight of my words, Toan attempted one final argument. "Think of my family, Kim! And also of yours." Surely I was not serious about endangering not only our own lives, but also the lives of our families back in Vietnam, who would certainly be punished for our "misstep." We could not just *defect*.

"Yes, I know, Toan," I whispered in response. "But I am thinking of *our* family as well, of the children that *we* will have someday. You know how terribly I have suffered, Toan. I do not want them to suffer as well."

At Gander, everyone on our flight deplaned. As instructed by the flight attendant, Toan and I left all of our belongings on the aircraft, save for my handbag. We entered the international terminal and found seats at a nearby gate. I felt so sure about my plan, I half expected someone to come right then, put a hand on my shoulder, and quietly offer to help us, but it did not happen.

I could not sit still, and told Toan I was heading to the washroom and would be back soon. I walked around the concourse, eventually ending up in the washroom. I hid in a locked stall, trying to calm down and think what to do next. I had seen Canadian police officers in the hallways and wanted to say something, but I did not know if I could trust them. When I left the washroom, I glanced at a clock in the terminal. Only twenty-five minutes before we would need to reboard the plane.

I began to panic and then I heard a small voice say, "Pray, Kim."

With eyes closed, I whispered, "Dear Lord, I need your help. I want to stay in Canada. Show me how to do that."

When I opened my eyes, I saw a door that I had not noticed before. It led to a hallway, and I could see through the door's little window that seven passengers from our flight, a Cuban man and his daughter, a Cuban family of three, and two Cuban university students, were standing in the hallway.

My heart began to race. *They are planning to defect!* I *knew* this must be the case. I opened the door and when I asked them in Spanish what they were doing, they confirmed my suspicions. They told me exactly what I needed to do next.

Energized by what seemed to me to be a clear path of escape, I headed back to the waiting area and quickly found Toan. "Please hand me your passport," I said, which was a weighty request indeed. Once our passports were handed over to the officials, the defection would be set in motion and there would be no going back. In my husband's gaze was keen understanding of this fact. And yet, as the stakes rose higher and higher with each passing second, Toan came through for me. With soberness in his voice, he quietly replied, "Okay."

Years later, Toan would explain to me that in the midst of the incredulous situation I had placed him in, he had a flash of insight, a method for navigating the treacherous waters all around: "Do whatever she says to do," the idea went. "Do whatever you have to do *in order not to lose this girl.*"

I do not know if such an insight equates to true love or to outright insanity but thankfully, my husband complied.

Toan may have surprised himself with that answer, but I was not the least bit surprised. From the first time we met, Toan resolved in his heart to be faithful to me, even when I was not sure I could completely trust him. I was the one being unfaithful when I forced him to choose between the life he knew and loved, and me.

Oh, Toan, I am sorry to have put you in that awful spot. *Thank you, Toan, for choosing me now—again.*

When it was time to reboard the plane bound for Havana, my Toan and I were safely in another waiting room with a window that overlooked the tarmac. As we clasped hands, I watched the line of passengers go up the portable stairs into our plane getting ready to depart for Cuba.

Toan and I exchanged a knowing look, and I could not keep from smiling. The customs agent's first words when I handed him our passports kept replaying in my mind: "Welcome to Canada."

MIRACLE UPON MIRACLE

OCTOBER 1992

What Toan and I did not know was that our defection coincided with a brief time in Canadian history when the government was fulfilling a mandate to diversify the country's population. For months, all international refugees had been welcomed warmly, regardless of why they wanted to defect. After indicating to the agent inside the room that we did not wish to return to Havana, we were asked only three questions: (1) What is your name? (2) Where are you from? and, (3) Why do you want to live here?

"Phan Thi Kim Phuc and Bui Huy Toan; Vietnam; we wish to be Canadian now." It was the easiest and most abbreviated test we had ever taken.

Less than an hour later, a government official from the airport transported us to the Fox Moth Motel in Gander,

Newfoundland, where we would stay for the next two weeks until our paperwork could be processed. Once we were checked in, our temporary host directed us to a café, where we enjoyed a delicious meal. He then settled us into a comfortable room and gave us extra quantities of toiletries and a little money to purchase the things we needed in order to feel "at home." Despite my husband's obvious reservations, which he wore like a suffocating mask, for the first time in my life I felt like a bird uncaged. Other than my stay at the Sochi spa, it was the best treatment I had ever received. This *freedom*—yes, it suited me well.

During those first few days, I made no fewer than five collect calls to Nick Ut—Uncle Ut—who was living in Los Angeles, California—an entire world away, admittedly, but a world closer than it had ever been before. After Uncle Ut drove me to the hospital at Cu Chi that fateful day in 1972, he and I would not see each other again until 1989, when he was in Cuba on a business trip with the Associated Press.

The AP arranged everything—Nick's and the accompanying journalist's travel expenses, as well as securing permission from the American embassy in Cuba for our reunion to take place. At the appointed time, I was taken to the famed Habana Riviera hotel in Havana, where I waited for what felt like hours for Uncle Ut to show up. Finally a large, black vehicle pulled up, and moments later, my favorite photographer emerged. The minder who was at my side—of course, my country's government could not trust my motives here—took in the scene and said, "There is Nick Ut, the one wearing the white polo shirt and jeans."

Uncle Ut was much shorter than I remembered—shorter even than me. My breath hitched as I watched Uncle Ut make his way toward me. Before I knew it, I got up, started walking toward him, and then flat out *ran* to get to this important man. I reached Uncle Ut and collided into his arms, clutching him as tightly as I possibly could.

Uncle Ut pulled back slightly from our embrace, and I could see that he was too overcome with emotion to speak. *I will hang onto this sacred hush then*, I told myself. Sometimes silence says more than words can.

During my reunion with Uncle Ut, he reminded me that we had, in fact, seen each other on one other occasion since the bombing. "I came to see your family in Trang Bang, you recall? Just after you returned from the burn clinic?"

At that time, Uncle Ut had given my ma and dad a large print of my picture, the photograph that in 1973 won Uncle a very important award, the Pulitzer Prize for Spot News (now called "Breaking News") Photography. The AP had named the photograph "The Terror of War"—a fitting title, indeed, not only because of the picture's subject matter, but also because the photograph itself would be reduced to shreds by a mortar bomb that hit my parents' home shortly after Uncle's trip.

What is more, while Uncle Ut was making his way to my parents' house, he himself was struck by mortar fire, which left holes not only in his leg, but also in his beloved camera. A South Vietnamese soldier dragged Uncle away from imminent danger, a fellow AP photographer made sure that Uncle got to a hospital, and soon enough, Nick Ut would be snapping pictures once more. But the experience had changed him. He had had it with Vietnam and decided then and there to head to the West.

Weeks later, Uncle arrived in southern California and sought asylum at Camp Pendleton, eventually moving to Los Angeles, where he has lived ever since. Uncle married, had two children, and became an American citizen, even though to this day he *still* cannot grasp English-language ways. "Uncle!" I would jokingly reprimand him. "You live in that country but cannot communicate with your countrymen!" To which he would grin and say simply—in Vietnamese, of course—"Yes, but I take very good pictures still."[22]

Uncle Ut and I spent the next three hours enjoying a marvelous lunch of fish and rice inside the hotel's lovely dining room, replaying the scenes from South Vietnam in 1972. Sadly, I did not recall that visit to Trang Bang that Uncle Ut had made. "I wish I could remember that time!" I said to him. My mind had likely been busy dealing with so much change, so much transition, so much pain.

This visit will matter all the more to me. I will hang on Uncle Ut's every word, I thought.

"Oh, Uncle Ut," I said from time to time that afternoon, "I cannot believe you are here with me. Are you sure it is really you?" To which Uncle Ut simply boasted his winning smile. "It is so good to see you, too."

Those who had been assigned to keep tabs on Uncle and me that day were brazen. They were not sitting close by in the dining room—they were sitting at our table! I was so irritated that I wanted to shout at them, but I knew better than to resort to that tactic. Instead, I looked at Uncle Ut with pleading eyes and said, "You rescued me, Uncle. I thank you for rescuing me."

Uncle Ut nodded and grinned and said, "Of course, Kim Phuc, of course."

There was more to my gaze than mere thanks, and Uncle Ut knew it. I kept repeating the sentiment—"You rescued me . . . you rescued me . . . you rescued me . . ."—subtly changing one word as I went on: "You rescued me . . . rescued me . . . rescue me . . . rescue me." *Please, will you not rescue me now?*

When I was nine years old, Uncle Ut's quick, decisive, and selfless action in Trang Bang had saved my life. But how would he be able to rescue me now, when my every move was monitored? I knew that he would have done anything to help me. But there was nothing to be done, and we both knew it. I was in communism's grip and would return to the very same bondage the moment Uncle Ut left, the suffering I had been experiencing since day one in Cuba.

Back in the Canadian hotel, I picked up the phone in the hotel room and began to press the numbers to connect me to Uncle Ut.

Please answer, Uncle Ut. Please pick up the phone.

He didn't answer on my first try. Hours later, at Toan's urging, I called again. Toan and I were both desperate for some glimmer of hope, so I waited a while and called a third time, and then a fourth, and then a fifth.

To my shock and deep dismay, despite my whispered, impassioned pleas—"Uncle Ut! Where could you be? I have no one else to contact. You are my only way out!"—my one-time rescuer was not available to rescue me this time around. I was devastated. And disappointed in my own lack of preparation. How could I ask Toan to go through with this defection when I had no plan for getting us on our feet? What had I gotten us into? I did feel very glum that day.

Well, what I did not know at the time was that Uncle Ut's unresponsiveness was a blessing in disguise. If Uncle Ut had answered my calls, his strong sense of journalistic integrity would have compelled him to inform his associates of the big news of my defection and my whereabouts. That was the exact opposite of what I wanted, what we needed.

I wondered what on earth Toan and I would do. We had no clothing, save for what we were wearing. We had a little money for essentials, but not enough to purchase a new wardrobe. The cold, humid weather was wreaking havoc on my scars, and we had no access to medicine that would ease my pain. We knew nobody, we had nothing, and we were completely naïve about life in this foreign place. These worries flashed through my mind, threatening to pull me under, and yet still, my resolve was firm. *God has allowed us to make it this far*, I reasoned. *Surely he will get us out of this mess.*

During those days, Toan would observe my enthusiasm and listen to my stubborn insistence that all would work out fine, and say, "Kim, I haven't slept in many nights, fretting about how we will survive here. What will happen if Vietnamese officials learn that we have left the communist way of life? And yet, I watch you sleep soundly, hour by hour, *snoring* even, from sleeping so hard. How is this possible? How are you able to feel happy when all around us is sad?"

I would laugh in response—the answer was so obvious to me! "Because, dear husband," I tried to explain, "we are *free*, and God is good. He will provide everything we need."

———

During our stay in Gander, Toan and I became friends with a Cuban man named Ricardo and his wife, Holga, who were our suitemates at the hotel. As we got to know each other, I asked the couple about their plans. *Maybe their plans will inspire ideas for our plans*, I thought. The first few times I asked the question, Ricardo simply shrugged his shoulders and kept his mouth shut. But something told me he knew exactly where he and his wife were headed. Ricardo just did not trust me enough to divulge where that was.

Still I persisted, always asking the question politely, even teasingly. Eventually, my wide smile and winsome ways must have worn Ricardo down because one morning when I asked, "Ricardo, where will you go from here?" he sighed, paused, and then said with a hint of resignation, "Toronto."

Toronto? What was Toronto? It sounded like *toronja*, Spanish for "grapefruit." *I love grapefruit!* Perhaps this was a sign from heaven! If so, I did not want to miss it.

In a matter of moments, Toan and I were huddled over a map of Canada with Ricardo and Holga, listening to the Cubans' words. Toronto was a major city, had a moderate climate, plentiful job opportunities, and was known to be friendly toward immigrants. "Toan," I whispered excitedly, "we must get to Toronto. This is the perfect place for us!"

At twelve hundred miles away, Toronto was the farthest place on the list of designated cities that the Canadian government would provide free transportation to; anywhere else, we had to shell out the money ourselves. I did not know this when I begged Toan for us to head to Toronto, but God certainly did.

Once the decision was made, Toan and I felt a sense of relief. However, there was still the question of what we would do once we arrived in Toronto. We would truly be on our own then. Someone gave us the phone number for the Vietnamese Association in Toronto (VAT), a volunteer-based service agency established to support Vietnamese natives who had immigrated to Canada. Certainly they would be able to give us advice on how we could successfully integrate into everyday life. As Toan and I each leaned an ear toward the receiver, we felt sure we would be warmly embraced. God's favor had carried us this far, and I had no reason to believe he would let us flounder now.

After three or four rings, a VAT representative picked up, prompting Toan to nod at me as if to say, "*You* talk."

"Yes," I started, speaking in Vietnamese, "my husband and I have defected to Canada. We are in Newfoundland now but are planning to come to Toronto soon. We are wondering if . . ."

Before I could say another word, the representative shouted so loudly that I pulled the receiver away from our ears. "You have escaped? You have to go back! You must go home! There is nothing we can do for you. You have made a very poor choice indeed!"

Toan and I were so jarred and terrified by the explosive response that we abruptly hung up the phone. Were we not in a free country now, and yet *this* is how we were treated? Were the members of the Vietnamese association not our own countrymen? And *that* is how they chose to act? Now who were we supposed to trust?

Several days later, during a morning prayer time with just my heavenly Father and me, God all but whispered to me, "Kim, I want you to look to *me* for your provision, not to another human being. I will take care of you. Please, when you find yourself in need, come and talk with me first."

I rose from that quiet time with God with a germ of an idea running through my mind. Inside my purse, I had the business card of a woman who lived in New York. A few years earlier, she had come to Cuba for an initial meeting in preparation for my making a trip to the United States. In the end, communist officials prohibited me from going.

I was not even sure what organization the woman worked for, but suddenly, as though I had been struck by lightning, I remembered that I had kept her card. *Find that card! Perhaps she can help.*

I rummaged through my purse until I found the card. Then I picked up the phone in our hotel room and dialed the operator to place a collect call to New York, as I inhaled an anxious breath.

"Hello, this is Merle," I heard a woman's voice answer, to which I blurted out, "Merle! This is Kim Phuc. Do you remember me? I have defected to Canada from Cuba, and now my husband and I—we need help! We want to go to Toronto to live . . . can you help us find a way?"

I heard Merle sigh on the other end of the line, which I

suppose was a perfectly appropriate response, given the grenade I had just dropped in her lap. She knew what I was also aware of: Any help she offered me could endanger her own well-being. But the fact remained that before Toan and I would be allowed to travel to Toronto on the government's dime, we needed to provide our immigration officer with a permanent address and a valid phone number of someone in Toronto who would claim responsibility for us.

"Please, Merle," I said softly. "Will you please help us today?"

Several seconds passed before Merle spoke, but even then her tone was guarded. "Kim," she said, "I have a friend in Montreal I can connect you with . . ."

"No! No, Merle!" I interjected. "Toan and I cannot go to Montreal. We do not know French. We know at least a little English. Toronto is the place for us. We know that Toronto is it."

Merle gathered a little more information from me, carefully weighed her thoughts, and ended our phone call with the grace I could only hope for. "Give me two days," she said with certainty. "In two days, I'll call you back."

True to her word, Merle got back to Toan and me two days later, and with wonderful news, no less. "Kim, I am putting you in touch with Ms. Nancy Pocock of Toronto," Merle announced, explaining that Nancy was known as the "friend of refugees" across the region and that she had a soft spot in her heart for Vietnamese immigrants. "She has worked with people just like you for thirty years, Kim, people who are in need of practical resources so that they can begin their lives anew."

When I hung up the phone with Merle, my hands were shaking. I had to force them to be still long enough to dial Nancy's number—collect, of course. This was the answer Toan and I had prayed for! A compassionate Toronto-based person willing to help us get on our feet? I was beside myself with excitement while Toan shook his head in disbelief. God's favor had prevailed again.

The first few minutes of my conversation with Nancy were awkward since I was not fluent in English and she did not speak Vietnamese. Fortunately, she had a full-time Spanish translator on her staff who joined our conversation and relayed my words from Spanish to English. I conveyed my thanks to Nancy in Spanish for agreeing to host Toan and me, and then we began to go over the specific travel plans. We had been drowning in a vast ocean, but then a rescue boat appeared. Nancy was captaining that marvelous vessel; I could not *wait* to give her a big hug.

And yet when I phoned Nancy over the next few days prior to our departure for the final details, no one answered. "Toan," I said reassuringly, staying as calm as I possibly could, "even though we have no one to receive us, we are headed for Toronto." With that, we were on our way.

As it turned out, God's solution to our problem of not knowing where to go once we arrived in Toronto began to unfold en route. This was no quick excursion, but rather a multi-vehicle, multi-day affair. In Gander, Toan and I boarded the bus that took us to the ferry for the first part of the trip to

New Brunswick. There, we would travel by train for three days, passing through Quebec City and Montreal before reaching our final destination.

It would have made sense for us to keep to ourselves, to simply sit quietly, not causing a stir. We did not know whom to trust, and we did not speak the local language.

And yet at the beginning of that trip, I felt emboldened by the adventure of it all. I knew this escape from communism was going to succeed. So, on the ferry, I found myself engaging a kind-faced woman who happened to be seated nearby.

"You go to Toronto, too?" I asked, to which she nodded vigorously.

"*Dah*! Yes, yes!" she said.

"Oh! You are from Russia?" I then asked, to which she nodded vigorously once again.

Through a series of warm smiles, one-syllable answers, and a makeshift version of sign language I hoped she could understand, I conveyed our story to the woman. She nodded, saying that she, too, had left her homeland to build a better future in Toronto. It took a half-hour or so to piece together the major parts of our sagas. Finally, I communicated to her that Toan and I were in dire straits. We had a contact in Toronto, but she was not set up to receive us immediately as guests. We needed food to eat during the day and a place to lay our heads at night.

The Russian woman began digging through her purse, and a moment later pulled out a scrap of paper. "Ah!" she said, beaming. "*Tam!*" Here it is.

Scribbled on the paper was the name and address of a shelter in Scarborough where welfare representatives were available to help immigrants arriving into the city. The woman had been given the information back in Newfoundland and was planning to utilize the service as a first step in her new town. When the ferry docked at Saint John's in New Brunswick, the woman tugged on my sleeve, inviting Toan and me to share her taxi. Off we flew, into the next chapter of our lives.

CHAPTER 22

GO, GOD, GO

NOVEMBER 1992

Toan and I and our new Russian friend arrived at Family Residence, the temporary refugee shelter, just as the taxi's meter clicked over to seventeen dollars, a number that might as well have had multiple zeroes behind it, given how much money we three had to our names. I entertained a few fretful thoughts while I reached for my handbag and prepared to step out of the cab. Then I saw someone from the shelter walk purposefully to the driver's window, give the driver Canadian currency, and wish him an enjoyable day. *This place even pays our way to get to them?* I was astonished.

"To Henry's Motel, eh?" one of the coordinators inside the shelter hollered to Toan and me, after we handed over our completed registration packet. My husband and I both nodded compliantly, having no idea what or where Henry's

Motel was. Soon enough, the staff member from the shelter would hail another cab for Toan and me, give our driver funds to cover our trip, then bid us a cheerful, "Welcome to Canada!" In the flurry of activity, we had lost track of our Russian friend. As we stood waiting for our ride, we looked this way and that, trying to spot the one who had flitted down straight from heaven to help us get here. But she had disappeared, apparently already rerouted to a different hotel than ours.

I breathed a prayer of gratitude. *Oh, thank you, Father. Your favor is evident to me.* We arrived at the motel at six-thirty in the evening and were met by the manager himself, who warmly greeted us, passed us the key to room number two, and told us to report to that front desk each morning in order to retrieve our daily welfare allotment—seventeen dollars per person. We made careful note of that to-do, as we could not afford to goof that up.

We found the way to our room, unlocked the door, stepped inside, and exhaled huge sighs of relief. What a trip it had been! At last, we were here. It was as if the room itself were rejoicing. The apartment-style layout boasted a giant bed, a washroom outfitted with both shower *and* bath, and an in-room kitchen . . . we were undone by the sight of it all.

"Toan!" I beamed. "We can *cook*!" To which Toan grinned and said sheepishly, "But Kim, one small problem: We have no food."

We went back to the hotel manager. Given the long day, we did not feel energetic enough to explore Toronto's grocery-store system quite yet, and so we asked the manager if there were any other options available to us. "Ah, yes!" the manager said, as he reached for a room-service menu. "You may order from this list," he said, "and food will be delivered right to your room."

While we waited for our food to arrive, I turned on the television and had my first glimpse of *I Love Lucy*. I understood precious few words that were said between the women and men on the screen, but their antics got me laughing so hard that I was soon wiping tears from my eyes. I looked over at Toan, who was seated in a nearby chair, to see if he was enjoying the program as much as I was. He was deep in thought, his gaze distant, his arms resting awkwardly on his knees. I shut off the TV and allowed silence to fill the room. After a few moments, I said, "Toan, perhaps we should call Nancy Pocock now to see how she can help us?"

He glanced at the clock and then said, "Her office is surely closed already. Tomorrow morning will have to do."

The brief exchange was enough to bring Toan out of his fear and concern. Half an hour later, plates of grilled chicken, steamed vegetables, fluffy rice, and above-average wonton soup were delivered on trays. We felt immensely grateful to the genius who had conceived this "room service" plan. Toan and I ate and ate and ate, until our bellies poked out of our clothes, and then we got ready for bed.

The following morning, Toan and I woke up in the rickety but warm bed at the motel, astounded that we had actually done it—we had made it to Toronto at last. We dressed in yesterday's clothes, pocketed the small amount of cash we had been given to purchase something to eat, something to wear, and a few toiletries, and headed outside for our new

Canadian life. I still have one of the dresses I bought that first full day in Toronto. The dress and the handbag that made the trip from Cuba with me are precious possessions as well.

After Toan and I got provisions to carry us through our first few days—a razor for Toan and over-the-counter pain medicine for me—we called Nancy Pocock's number again. *Surely someone will pick up the phone during business hours,* I thought. Once again, the Spanish-speaking translator was enlisted so that we could talk with Nancy by phone.

Nancy informed us that she had already secured a lawyer who was eager to talk with us, that she could provide us with any essentials we had neglected to pick up that morning, and that she was available to talk about our first steps. Toan and I eyed the meager remains of our cash stipend and agreed that it was wise to spend a few of those dollars on bus fare to Nancy Pocock's office. We stepped out in faith, believing that our investment would bear fruit for us.

We would miss our bus stop the first time around, since we had no idea how to make the bus driver stop. So we just stayed in our seats, riding the entire route again. Toan and I carefully watched what other passengers did, so we were savvy by the second pass: You must make your way to the exit *before* the driver jerks to a stop, and *then* the doors open for you. Oh, what a metaphor that simple process would be for us, as we established ourselves in this new land.

Mom Nancy, as we came to call her, welcomed us heartily, supplied us with everything from chopsticks to forks and spoons, and assured us that we would not merely survive in Toronto; no, given the persistence she had detected in us, we would absolutely *thrive*. As she laid out packets upon packets of information for us to review, absorb, and sign, her big smile calmed our anxious souls. I exhaled the emotional weight of this complex expedition Toan and I had been on and whispered my heartfelt thanks to God.

I had reached for God when I was nineteen and had reached for him every day since. I had done this because at one time or another I had reached for all other saviors, and none of them had saved me at all. As I thought about my new life in Toronto, I realized how life-changing that choice had been. In my heart, I knew that God would care for me, and also for Toan.

Toan and I quickly settled into a routine at our temporary residence, and I expected that would calm my husband's frayed nerves, but he continued to be gripped by fear. Instead of seeing the blessings that were being given to us, he saw only gaping holes that needed to be filled.

"Kim!" he would say earnestly, his brow furrowed, his palms upturned. "We have only money for a few days at a time. We cannot put together a future this way. The food and the clothes, people to help us . . . do you not see how in need we are?"

I began praying fervently for the Lord to captivate my husband's heart. "Please, Father," I begged him day by day, "please call Toan to your way." I prayed while I was in bed, I prayed while I was in the shower, I prayed while we stood in line at the Scott Mission food bank, where we ate more than a few of our meals. I prayed while we rode the bus from here to there and back again—indeed, I prayed "without ceasing,"[23] as the Bible told me to do. "He is such a good man,

Lord," I reminded God. "But with you? Oh, much better still!"

One afternoon, while Toan and I rested in our room at the motel, two gentlemen rapped on our door. My husband shot me a look that said, "I knew it! We have been found." With blazing-fast speed, Toan had us accosted, deported, and jailed, even as I stepped with certainty toward the door.

"Toan," I said to him, peeking through the little hole as Mister Kretz had once taught me to do, "it is two nice-looking men—that is all. Let us open the door and have a chat with them."

Against his better judgment, Toan agreed, and together we welcomed into our room Pastor Gary La More and one of the deacons from Scarborough's Grace Missionary Baptist Church.

A Cuban man who volunteered with the church's Spanish ministry, which often helped out at Henry's Motel, had tipped off Pastor La More to our whereabouts, explaining that Toan and I had recently defected and had few resources. The pastor seemed genuinely concerned for our welfare, and as he talked with us I felt drawn to him as to a trusted friend.

"Excuse me, Pastor?" I interjected at one point, curious if my confidence in him was well placed or not. "Do you read the Bible—as in, the Christian Scriptures, God's Holy Word?"

Pastor La More laughed good-naturedly and assured me that yes, he did. "Okay, then," I said, "please continue. I would like to hear more about your church."

Thankfully, the deacon who accompanied Pastor La More was from Chile and served as our translator so the pastor could understand us and vice versa. By the end of the conversation, we had been invited to their bilingual church on Sunday, transportation provided.

For the four weeks that Toan and I were living at the motel, Pastor La More or one of his associates would show up on our doorstep each Sunday morning, ready to give us a ride to church. As I look back on those worship experiences, I see how vital they were for Toan.

The first three times, Toan would groan over going to church. "Our days are so stressful, Kim, just trying to fit ourselves into this new life," he would plead with me. "Can we not just sleep in once a week?"

Toan was still drinking too much, still smoking like a chimney, still questioning every syllable of every Bible verse I chose to share. He pushed back against my suggestions to tithe, citing the fact that "Ten percent of nothing is nothing, Kim!" On and on it went.

Despite my inner frustration with Toan's resistance, I made sure never to scold him or shame him for his habits and ways. I did not remind him of our lack of financial resources, I did not roll my eyes over his spiritual stubbornness, and I did not lose my temper even once. No, my response was simply to pray—always just faithful prayer. "Father, if you wish for Toan to change, then you will have to change him," I would say in the quiet of my heart, meaning every syllable of that surrendered plea. I knew that prodding my husband to pick up habits he did not think up himself would only make him bitter and angry. And so I fell quiet, knowing that in God's way and in God's time, he would capture my husband's heart.

On the fourth of our four weekends at the motel—Christmastime 1992—Toan could not fight it anymore. He found himself undeniably drawn to Jesus and he simply *had* to have what I had. "Okay, Kim . . . *fine*," he said with a grin, offering his hands to me in surrender. "I want to know about your God."

The following day was Sunday, and after the morning worship service, Pastor La More and the deacon gave us a ride back to the motel. As we were getting out of the car, I told the pastor of Toan's sudden openness to discussing things of God, to which the pastor offered to answer Toan's questions then and there. Our little group did not even make it inside the hotel before Toan accepted Jesus as Lord.

The very next morning, Toan woke up with fresh determination in his heart. He would no longer drink. He would no longer smoke. He would quit his old ways "cold turkey" and begin to walk by faith. "I do not want to prize anything more than I prize Jesus," he explained to me. Wow, had God captured his heart.

Throughout the years, whenever I traveled through Scarborough and saw the parking lot of Henry's Motel, I would think, *That is where my husband met Jesus.* What a marvelous memory it is.

FORSAKING ALL FEAR

JANUARY 1993

In the early nineties, refugees in Canada who were waiting to become citizens—a two-year process—were not permitted to work. Toan and I begged the government for jobs. We would head to the immigration office each week to inquire through their onsite translators about working—even for a small sum—but time and again we received the same response: "No. You may not work. If you work, you are in violation of the law, and you will have to return to Cuba." We certainly did not want to return to Cuba, and we also did not want to be on the national dole, especially given all that we had seen in Vietnam and in Cuba where societies expected government handouts. But finally we had no choice and applied for welfare.

During that first year, even as we were trying to adjust to

the newness of marriage, we changed residences five times, scrounging together bits of welfare income in order to rent one place after another, going wherever we could think to go in search of safety, security, and, later on, proximity to work. At each transition, I mailed a letter to Ma and Dad back home, desperate for some sense of connection and for them to simply know where I was. But I never received a reply. How my heart ached over that deafening silence.

One rental was located on the second floor, but going up two flights of stairs multiple times proved too challenging for my aching back. Then we rented space in a family's basement, but a few months of listening to the boom-boom-booms of rambunctious kids jumping on the floor above our heads was too much for me. I begged Toan to find us another home.

I had been having nightmares off and on, and in some places we lived, the nightmares escalated. "The soldiers!" I would shout out from the dead of sleep, startling Toan. "They are coming to kill me! They want me dead!"

In my dreams, I was always running, always rushing away from fire. I would wake to the sense of bone-chilled cold, trembling from my head down to my toes. "Kim!" Toan would say, shaking me awake. "Kim, you are in Canada now. You are safe. You will not die."

"Oh, Toan, please hold me," I would cry. "Hold me close and keep me safe."

"It is okay, Kim. What you have been through, you will not suffer again. I will pray over you as you fall back to sleep."

Finding a place to call home that did not trigger my

nightmares became a critical priority for me, even though that goal would not be met for years to come.

In an attempt to feel even more at home in Toronto, we sought out members of the Vietnamese community in our Chinatown neighborhood and cultivated relationships with many of the people we met. It was a far different reception than we had received from Toronto's official Vietnamese association, and we were grateful for that fact. We forged deep relationships with fellow church members, most notable among them our dear friends Kathy and Gary Parkinson, who became family to Toan and me. In fact, some time later, when the Parkinsons decided to transfer their membership to one of the most diverse faith communities in the region, Faithway Baptist Church, Toan and I knew instinctively that we would go too. Nearly every Sunday, we would have lunch at the Parkinsons' home, relishing their companionship, enjoying Kathy's wonderful food, and building memories that stick with us still today.

Although Toan and I could not work, we did volunteer, eventually serving as government-sanctioned translators in Chinatown. We taught English to both Vietnamese and Spanish speakers, while we attended ESL classes ourselves.

I think back on those days of being alone in a foreign land where people spoke a foreign language, attending evening classes at a local high school, and Toan and I trying desperately to survive. I can see how anyone looking at our situation from the outside would see nothing but a giant void: few friends, no stable residence, no educational accomplishments, no employment opportunities, no reliable food sources—in Vietnamese, *so khong, so khong, so khong.*

But despite how it all *looked*, it was a marvelously joyful season of life. We were *free*, after all. And as far as I was concerned, anyway, Jesus was leading the way. What more did a person truly need in order to overcome, in order to thrive? I decided that regardless of what was happening around me, I would choose to be content.

There is a wonderful phrase in the West that perfectly captures how I felt about being "found" in Toronto—"the straw that broke the camel's back." I remember this occasion as though it were yesterday. Toan and I were peeking through the thin curtains of our humble second-floor apartment in Chinatown, watching the two men loitering near the entrance to the building. They were acting suspiciously, looking up every so often at the windows of our unit. How they learned our address I do not know, but there they were, day after day, longing for an interview with, a photograph of, the "girl in the picture," Kim Phuc.

It wasn't the first time we had seen them. In fact, we had felt their presence for a while now—behind us, beside us, across the street—whenever we left our residence for groceries from the street-side stands or went to the government building as translation volunteers.

For so many years I had lived in outright fear, knowing that I was always within two or three days' time of being detained by communist minders. This had been the pattern for so many years of my life that I found myself incapable of shaking the rhythm from my bones. The incessant guardedness left me cynical and exhausted, and to be quite candid, I had simply had enough. Here in Toronto, I determined in my heart that I would no longer live like that, always looking furtively around me, always fretful over what the days might hold, always fearing the worst.

I was *Canadian* now, and Canadians lived free. Yes, there was still paperwork to be finalized before I was legally a citizen, but I resolved to no longer feel afraid. The full support of the Canadian government was coming. Jesus' flawless protection was already here. I had no reason to fear what man might do to me. At last, I could lay my flight tendencies down.

"Just focus on living your life," I told myself. The debilitating nightmares that had been interrupting my sleep would not have power over me any longer.

I went to Toan and explained my decision: that I would no longer live in fear, that I would practice the courage that Jesus promises his followers all throughout Scripture. I recounted several Bible verses, more for my own sake than for Toan's, especially the idea that we are no longer slaves to fear because we have been adopted into the very family of God.[24]

The more I talked, the more excited I became, even as my husband's sense of incredulity grew. He was new to our faith. He did not yet understand how to rid himself of his fears. And oh, how very many fears he faced! He worried about where we would find our next meal. He worried about where we would find our next home. He worried about employment, and about education, and about the family we hoped to start. He was a full-time worry machine, filled to overflowing with that enemy Fear. And yet here I was—his wife—boldly declaring, "I will stop running from my fears, from my picture, from my past. Starting now, I refuse to hide."

I stayed planted inside my home that day until the photographers down below gave up and went home themselves. The following morning, I woke with fresh resolve, determined to simply live my life.

EIGHT POUNDS OF PERFECT

JULY 1994

From the time I had been hospitalized as a child, doctors, surgeons, specialists, nurses, therapists, and my own well-meaning ma all came to the same conclusion: Because of the severity of burns I had sustained, my body was unfit to carry a child. My skin at those burn sites had lost its elasticity, which would be problematic when my pregnant belly decided to "pop." My internal organs, while functionally fine, had endured too much stress from being singed by the napalm and would not fare well during any stage of childbirth. My blood pressure—such a critical marker of health during pregnancy—had all but slowed to a stop and showed no signs of picking up speed. My typical daily pain was already off the charts; how would I cope with still more?

But truly, since those days of playing corn-cob prince and

princess with my childhood friends, I had always seen myself getting married someday and, later, bearing a child. Now my real-life prince, Toan, and I were praying about this very thing. "Lord, are we meant to become parents? And if so, how will that occur?"

The practical considerations before us were great: We had no family here to help us with caring for a baby, and our food and home situation was always fluctuating. And then there were my myriad health problems—did we have any business adding a baby to this mix?

"But Toan," I remember saying to my husband, "if I wait too long to become pregnant, then the risks will only rise . . ." I was now thirty-one, which by gynecological standards at the time meant o-l-d.

With Toan's consent, I sought advice from a naturopath in Chinatown. In Asian culture, one's "pulses" are a big deal, and evidently, my pulses were quiet. My menstrual cycle was irregular, my circulation was not great, and the stress that I had endured for two decades did no favors for my adrenal glands. The practitioner mixed together a variety of herbal remedies and gave me thorough instructions regarding their use. "You come back in ten to twelve weeks," he said. "We check you again at that time."

Nancy Pocock also put me in touch with Doctor Phillips, a Western doctor she knew, so that Toan and I could weigh a professional opinion alongside our own. Looking back, Nancy's introduction to this gynecologist transformed my entire world for the better. In addition to the herbs taking effect, the doctor assured me that I was capable of carrying a baby and proceeded to encourage Toan and me to try for the pregnancy.

—ɱ—

Within six weeks, I was dancing through our tiny kitchen, waving a completed pregnancy test in hand, all but singing the results to Toan. "We did it, Toan! We are pregnant! You are a daddy now, and I am finally a ma!" Toan pulled me into a tight embrace, his smile giving way to laughter, and for what felt like an eternity we simply held each other. Our dream was at last coming true.

Toan and I had been reading the Bible together one morning when we both were struck by a name we saw there: Thomas. We loved it immediately and decided it would be the name of our first baby boy—if it were a boy, that is. We had already chosen the name Rebecca if we had a girl, but there was something about Thomas. I loved it from the start.

The moment we named our child, the abstract idea of a baby—inside *me*!—became very real. I began to draw pictures of my baby, as I imagined him or her: perfectly formed, thriving, *alive*. I sang the same lullabies my grandma had sung to me when I was a child, hopeful that my baby would know my voice. I talked to my baby day and night in a soothing voice. "I love you already, sweet child," I would say. "May you always be healthy and strong." I spoke these things in Vietnamese, in Spanish, and in English, figuring I ought to cover my bases in case he or she ever lived in any of the countries where I had lived, even as I secretly prayed to God in heaven that my child would always stay by my side.

At the time, Toan and I were still enrolled in the ESL class and were studying several hours each evening in order to improve our inflection and pace. I do not remember much of those classes, save for one thing: the smell. A group of immigrants from Africa were also in our class, and although I never pinpointed it, one of the spices they used in their cooking made me sick. Oh, I do remember rushing to the washroom on many an occasion, while our teacher plodded faithfully on.

During those quick walks to the washroom and also whenever I was headed to the subway station or bus terminal, I held my belly carefully, not wanting to jostle him or her to and fro. From the beginning of my pregnancy the baby was big, and kept getting bigger as the months passed. The doctor expressed concern about the baby's size. "If your baby continues to grow at this pace," he said when I was thirty-five weeks along, "you most certainly will require a C-section, which for you is not a good thing."

That was on a Thursday afternoon, during a regularly scheduled appointment, and as Toan and I started to leave, the doctor said, "I think we ought to do another ultrasound, Kim, just to be sure everything in there is all right. Call on Monday, and we'll schedule it."

The next morning my water broke. Toan immediately got up and headed for the door. "I will go get the shopping cart in the alley."

"Toan!" I hollered, barely catching him before he rushed out the door. "What will you do with a shopping cart? My water has broken, Toan. This baby is about to be born."

"Yes, Kim, I know, I know!" he said, a flurry of movement and stress. "This is why I will get you the shopping cart, so that I can transport you to the hospital at once!"

In my husband's defense, we only lived three blocks from the hospital—not a long trip, by any measure. But still, would it be wise for me to make that trip by shopping cart? And did I mention that it was raining?

For several minutes, I rested comfortably on the little couch in our living room, doing my best to calm my pacing husband, who was quickly losing control. "Toan, it is no problem yet," I kept saying to him. "I have zero pain at all."

As I waited, I reviewed in my mind what Toan and I had learned in the Lamaze classes we had taken. *But I have no pain to speak of,* I thought. *I do not need to recall how to manage my pain, until I actually have pain to manage!*

An hour passed before I said to my husband, "I still do not have pain, Toan, but I think I should get to hospital now. I do not want to get an infection. I do not want our baby harmed."

"But how will we go to hospital, Kim? We have nobody to take us there!"

Since Toan and I had never once called a cab service or dialed 911, it never occurred to us to do so now. Instead, we opted for waking our landlord, Andy, who happened to live upstairs. Thankfully, Toan did not ask me to climb the stairs too.

After hearing what was going on, Andy said, "Oh, Toan, I'm so sorry, but my car hasn't run in weeks. I've been taking the bus to work each day."

Toan was resolute. "Andy," he said very quietly, "would you mind trying the car . . . just this once?"

Andy indulged my dear Toan, and the car decided to run.

By 7:00 a.m., Toan and I were nestled in a hospital room, eagerly anticipating all that was to come.

As the hours ticked by, I became more and more aware of my lack of pain. "You will experience ever-increasing discomfort," the kind Lamaze lady had informed the other mothers in my class and me, "culminating with a pain so sharp and severe that if you were holding an iron rod, you'd be certain you could bend it."

Wow, I had thought at the time, now *that* is some kind of pain. Here in my hospital room, I might have considered the anomaly of no pain to be a cause for grave concern—was something wrong with my child?—but I did not. Instead, I treated the entire smooth, peaceful experience like the divine gift I believed it to be.

Just before Thomas arrived, I felt perhaps forty minutes of intense pressure, during which I focused my attention on the image of a beautiful red rose, fully in bloom. Red roses are my favorite flower, and something about that visualization kept me calm. Toan was okay when we arrived at the hospital because he had gotten all of his pacing done when we were at home. And he was okay when I went into labor and when the contractions intensified, reaching for my hand to pray with me. But when the doctor pulled out the forceps to help get Thomas out, due to our son's large head, Toan nearly became unglued. "Stay with us, Toan!" I remember cheering for him, as he braced himself on the edge of my bed.

Once the doctor safely delivered my Thomas, I noticed that my baby did not cry. For several heartbeats there was silence, giving everyone in the room great pause. I glanced at

Toan as the doctor patted Thomas's back, and within seconds my boy was wailing—what a wonderful sound it was! At last, I had birthed a baby. This was not a politically staged photo shoot; this was me, holding my own flesh and blood.

Because he had arrived earlier than my due date, Thomas's birth coincided with our ESL class's final exams. I would fail to graduate once again from school, but I gained something more meaningful instead. "Yes, you all received a diploma," I told my classmates with a wide smile, when I saw them at Toan's graduation ceremony, "but I received a baby. Much better, I think you agree."

I spent three days in the hospital before being discharged; Thomas, who had jaundice, stayed a week longer. All in all, this was for the better, because I was weary and craving rest. As soon as my milk came in, Toan would make four or five trips per day to the hospital to drop off bags of breast-milk for Thomas. Finally, seven days later, my Thomas was healthy . . . and home.

It was during Thomas's extended hospital stay that the driver of a large truck pulled up to the curb outside our apartment building, located Toan and me, and proceeded to unload box after box of baby items. It turns out our beloved family doctor, Paula Williams, had put a note on the bulletin board in her waiting room, explaining that an immigrant couple from Vietnam needed gently used baby goods—anything a little boy might like.

Dozens of families responded with nursery decorations, toys, and clothes. When Toan finished sorting all of the clothes, we realized that Thomas had a complete wardrobe that would last him until age *seven*. What a generous gift from people we did not even know.

I look back on those days in our tiny Chinatown apartment, and I can still feel the love that the three of us shared. We were free at last, finding our way in a brand-new country, nothing but hope and beauty before us. It was picture-perfect! Except that it was not, for the simple reason that I was still at odds with my ma. Since I had never received any responses to letters I had written, I had no idea whether she knew I was in Canada, and that I was never returning to Cuba again. Or even if she knew I was married or had given birth to a child. She did not know so many important things about who I was becoming or about the treasured dreams I now held. And as the years flew by with ever-increasing speed, I wondered if she and I would ever see each other again.

Every day I prayed a simple, straightforward prayer: "Father, please protect Ma while we are apart. And please let this distance between us end soon."

CHAPTER 25

SCARBOROUGH, ONTARIO

HE MAKES A WAY

SUMMERTIME 1996

Around the same time that the Lord was helping me to relinquish long-carried fears and showing me how to minister to my expanding family, we became more deeply involved with our church community and were growing spiritually in rapid fashion. Toan had begun taking the Bible at its word, believing it was not fantasy but trustworthy truth, which was no small thing given the Marxist, evolutionist cloth from which my husband was cut. In addition, Toan had secured and was thriving in a paid position at the University of Toronto as a filing clerk in the admissions office. There he made a new friend, a fellow Christian who was saving money to return to his native Hong Kong and share the gospel with his countrymen. Weeks later, at a missions conference at our church, Toan was so moved by the missionaries' radical testimonies that he wondered if he, too, felt a prompting from God.

"Kim," he said, "this Christian approach to life would benefit so many of my family and friends back in North Vietnam. I think I am supposed to become a missionary so that I can go tell them the Good News about grace."

I shook my head in amazement over all that God had done in Toan's life. The changes were so drastic and happened so fast!

Toan knew the first step in fulfilling that dream was to go to Bible college. It would cost eight thousand dollars for one year. We did not have eight thousand dollars—we barely had *eight* dollars. But I knew that extra zeroes are not obstacles to God. And so, as you might now guess, I prayed. With great fervency, I prayed to God. "Lord, we need money!" I said to him, as though this would come as breaking news. "Toan wishes to attend Bible college, Father, but he cannot go unless he can pay the dues!"

The money wasn't the only issue that seemed to stand in our way. We were still living in Chinatown, located a good hour's drive away from the school Toan had chosen—Faithway Baptist College of Canada—and the only thing we had for transportation was a beat-up 1984 Honda Accord that did not always like to run.

"Father, we need money, and we need a reliable car." I laid our needs before God, their full weight thudding to the floor beneath me. "Lord? You see our needs here, yes?"

Evidently God did see our need, for in a creative collision of events that only he could orchestrate, he combined my decision to stop living in fear with Toan's decision to stop living for himself, and emerged with a truly magnificent plan. This plan involved the media in Canada, an irony that amused both Toan and me.

I had told Mom Nancy that I wanted to work, to help support my family while Toan went to school. "Kim," Mom Nancy had said in reply, "if you want to do *anything* 'out there,' you will have to embrace the picture you have been trying so hard to run from. You will have to endure an onslaught of publicity if you wish to help Toan."

I told Mom Nancy that I had already resolved in my heart to stop living ashamed of my past, of my pain. "I can do this," I said to her. "You arrange everything for me."

Mom Nancy looked at me for a moment, weighing my seriousness. "All right, Kim," she said at last, "if you're sure, then I can help."

Within a matter of days, Mom Nancy had arranged a meeting for Toan and me with entertainment lawyer Michael Levine, who quickly set up a whole series of interviews and opportunities for me. One television reporter who interviewed me subsequently established a trust fund for us, funded by readers' donations. The producer on that story, a brilliant Scottish woman named Anne Bayin, befriended me. We talked each week by phone, and whenever Toan was unable to travel with me to media events, Anne would accompany me. As she and I spent more and more time together, I realized Anne was an answer to my prayer for a friend as close as my childhood friend Hanh.

"How you say *w* in English?" I would ask Auntie Anne.

"It is *wuh*, Kim . . . *w*ater, *w*iggle, *w*onderful," she would patiently coach me.

On a speaking trip to Barcelona, my pain came to me so unexpectedly and with such force before a lavish dinner that I feared I would not be able to make the keynote speech. I looked at Anne, seated at the table next to me and said, "Oh, Auntie Anne, the pain. . . . It is too much for me tonight. I cannot sit still over dinner. I must get up and move."

Auntie Anne rushed over to the event coordinator, whispered a few sentences, motioned for me to get up, and then escorted me into the night air. "Come, Kim," she said with a gentle smile. "Let's walk."

Auntie Anne and I must have circled the center sixteen times that night. After what had to have been a full hour, I stopped, exhaled, and said, "Better. I am ready to go back now."

As we made our way to the head table, I had a few minutes to gather myself before taking the stage. *How lucky I am to have a friend such as this.* Some twenty-plus years later, she is still my dearest friend.

That initial burst of publicity led to another offer, this time from a publishing house that was interested in "my book."

"But I do not have a book," I remember saying to them, to which they replied, "We would like to help you change that."

Would you like to venture a guess as to how much money they wanted to pay me for telling my tale?

Eight thousand dollars, on the nose. *Oh, Father, you are so good.*

As soon as that check for eight thousand dollars arrived, Toan wasted no time in registering for Bible college, and we moved once again, finding housing closer to the college. Toan would not have to worry about a long commute with an unreliable car.

The publisher connected me with a writer, Ms. Denise Chong. The book-writing process was equal parts rigorous and satisfying. The rigor was twofold. First, the only way that Ms. Chong and I could communicate was in English, and I was still pitifully poor on that front. I recall those interview sessions being long and laborious as she and I searched for ways to align intention with words.

The second, and more consequential, challenge I faced was forcing my flagging memory to recall countless details of the life I had lived. What *had* I thought as I was running up Route 1 just after the napalm bombs had dropped? Who *did* come to see me while I was recovering at the Barsky, and what *did* they say to me? When *did* communist minders start forcing me to sit for staged interviews? How *did* I cope with my pain? So many questions Ms. Chong had for me; so few answers readily available. But then, a sliver of remembrance would surface. And like a fragment of light from a cracked door that illuminates an entire room, that sliver would open up my memory in ways I did not think were possible. I would double check my facts with Uncle Ut, or with Mister Kretz, or with news clippings I had compiled, and before long, I cobbled together an entire scene—*yes, yes, this is how things unfolded that day.*

I was grateful that the memories returned, but for me the greater satisfaction in the process of piecing together my past was realizing that I was no longer bitter about the trauma I had experienced. Yes, I still had my terrible, stubborn scars, but the anger I had carried for so many years was gone, left behind. A few of the photographs included in *The Girl in the Picture*, published in 1999, were images I had never seen before. One in particular that Mister Kretz had taken showed me showering outside in Trang Bang. I looked at the photo and thought, *That poor, poor little girl.* It was as though God had distanced me from the agony. I was no longer facing the pain I had endured.

While I was busy on the book, Toan studied hard, preparing himself for the multiple trips he would take to North Vietnam during midterm breaks from school. Emboldened by the protections afforded us as Canadian citizens to travel to our homeland, he visited his family on these trips, holding secret house church services and leading hundreds of people to Christ, including his uncle, a devout communist. Toan's uncle had been gravely ill and did not express any interest in "Toan's God" until my husband's final day of his first trip. When Toan went to bid him farewell, that uncle dissolved into waves of tears and said, "Toan, I wish to be saved! I agree to accept Jesus Christ as my personal Savior!" Six months later, Toan's uncle passed away.

During Toan's second trip to the North, he visited his father, who had fallen ill and was hospitalized. "My father is the firstborn in his family," Toan said to me prior to his departure. "To choose to believe in God would be a terrible betrayal in the eyes of his family. You must pray for me each day I am gone, Kim."

I prayed like I had never prayed before while Toan was at his father's side, and yet the news I received from Toan only worsened day by day. His father was no longer taking food and appeared skinny and frail. The family, assuming the end was near, prepared a coffin and sat quietly, waiting for his death. And yet there knelt Toan beside his father's bed, pleading with heaven for healing, trusting for a miracle to unfold.

On Toan's third day in his father's hospital room, his father opened his eyes, which had been shut for more than twenty-four hours. Then he cupped Toan's chin with his feeble hand and whispered, "Son, I accept Jesus Christ." Toan's father not only righted himself with God, but also made a complete recovery. He is alive and well as I write these words.

Toan and I both counted ourselves among the millions of Christ followers down through the ages who have witnessed God's miraculous faithfulness firsthand. Of course, what I did not know at the time was that God was just getting started—a tsunami of blessings was headed our way.

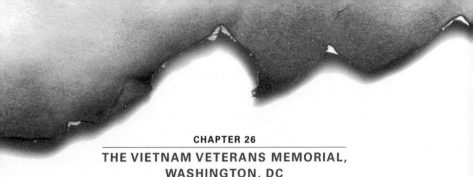

CHAPTER 26

THE VIETNAM VETERANS MEMORIAL, WASHINGTON, DC

A TIME TO FORGIVE

NOVEMBER 1996

On a frigid morning in November 1996, a little more than two years after Thomas was born, I woke up in a Washington, DC, hotel room, eager for the day to begin. I had been asked to speak at the annual Veterans Day ceremony held in front of the Vietnam Veterans Memorial on the famed National Mall, with more than three thousand people expected to attend, and tens of thousands additional viewers watching the televised event.

I believed passionately in the remarks I had prepared and hoped that in some small way I could persuade those listening that regardless of the question, war never is the answer. I had discovered peace and wanted to share it. I had discovered love and knew of its healing balm. What I could not have anticipated was that my lofty theories about these moral ideals was about to be put to the grandest of tests.

Even though I laud the many benefits of knowing my

Jesus, of surrendering to him and submitting to him, of obeying him and seeking to please him, I acknowledge that living for him comes at quite a high cost. For me, the weightiest aspect of remaining in relationship with Jesus was a little thing called forgiveness. I was grateful that God had forgiven me. But extending it to those who had wronged me, I was unsure if I could forgive.

The topic of forgiveness had initially surfaced for me years prior, long before I met Toan, when I had read two short verses of Scripture in the Gospel of Luke. Jesus said to his disciples: "But I say unto you which hear, Love your enemies, do good to them which hate you, Bless them that curse you, and pray for them which despitefully use you."[25]

This cannot be right, I thought. *Maybe I misread it.* I read the verses again, focusing on the last part this time around: "Bless them that curse you, and pray for them which despitefully use you."

Bless them that curse me? Pray for them which despitefully use me? But how could this possibly be done?

I stared at those sentences for a long time and then began to laugh. "Oh, Lord!" I said aloud. "Do you not recall how many enemies I have?"

So I began logging my "enemies list." At the top of the list, of course, were all those involved in the destruction of my country and the dropping of the napalm bombs that forever changed my life. The strategists who drew up war plans, the commanders who ordered air strikes, the pilots who dropped bombs—I was furious with them all. I did not have names for all of these guilty parties, but I reserved places on my list for each one.

Next on my list were communist officials, man after man who had killed my dreams. They had used me for propaganda and had abused me day by day, and by way of recompense, I believed they should pay. If a person hits you one time or twice, perhaps forgiveness may be extended to him. But to suffer blow after blow, day after day, abuse after devastating abuse? That person must not be forgiven. I was surer than sure about that.

I sat with my list for the better part of an hour, adding names or positions as they came to mind, and at the end of the consuming exercise, I shut my Bible with more than a little force, thinking, *Forgive them? Forget it. There is just no way. Christianity is too difficult a thing.*

I struggled with the prospect of accepting and implementing those lofty-sounding instructions. The wrongs that had been done to me were deeply grievous, and I feared that forgiving the wrongdoers would equate to dismissing or even approving of their sins. *How would justice ever be served,* I wondered, *if I myself did not carry my cause?*

And yet, I kept finding other Scriptures about forgiveness.[26] I was being asked to be kind and tenderhearted, to believe that vengeance was God's responsibility, not mine.

I understood what God was asking, but I had many answers for God.

"Father, yes, but you do not understand how severe is my pain!"

"Yes, I know you say to forgive, but the terror, the destruction, the abuse, the scars!"

"Yes, I know that vengeance is to be yours, but all these years that have been taken from me! Is there not justice for me to be paid?"

"Yes, forgiveness is the wise thing to do, but Lord, I cannot ever forgive."

"Yes, but . . ."

"Yes."

"But . . . no."

Even the honest question that Jesus' disciple Peter posed regarding just how many times a godly person is to forgive[27] fueled my fury. "Seven times?" Peter asked, to which Jesus replied, "Seventy times seven." That equals four hundred ninety times. For me, if I factored in well over a decade of tragedy and abuse from those on my list, the total came to four or five *thousand* wrongdoings against me. Why bother with only 10 percent of what was needed for me?

The lunacy of my thinking would not dawn on me until I stood at that point in time and space when I had to decide whether I would travel the road paved with life and peace and joy, or the one marked by suffering and bitterness and rage. Would I hand over my life to the lordship of Jesus or not? Which path would I choose?

Back in Washington, I was shivering when I took the stage at last. "Dear friends," I began with a quivering voice, "I am very happy to be with you today. . . . As you know, I am the little girl who was running to escape from the napalm fire. I do not want to talk about the war because I cannot change history. I only want you to remember the tragedy of war in order to do things to stop fighting and killing around the world. I have suffered a lot from both physical and emotional pain. Sometimes I thought I could not live, but God saved me and gave me faith and hope. Even if I could talk face-to-face with the pilot who dropped the bombs, I would tell him we cannot change history, but we should try to do good things for the present and for the future to promote peace."

As I concluded my remarks and the buglers began to play "Taps," I exhaled the significance of the moment and wiped tears from my cheeks and eyes. The ensuing moments were a blur of activity, as hosts led me quickly from the stage to a police cruiser that was waiting to take me back to my hotel. I did my best to greet those who were waiting to shake my hand or give me a hug, even as I sensed the coordinator's urgency in leaving the scene. And in the crush of people was someone who needed my forgiveness.

Captain John Plummer was a US Vietnam veteran who had seen my story recounted on a television show, *Where Are They Now?* Seeing Nick Ut's photo brought back horrific war memories for the army captain. When I met him that Veterans Day, he identified himself as the person who coordinated dropping the napalm bombs that day on Route 1 in Trang Bang. Now a pastor, Reverend Plummer said, "Kim, I am sorry. I am so very, very sorry. Will you forgive me for what I have done?"[28]

When Reverend Plummer asked me that question on Veterans Day, I reached for his hands, I looked deep into his eyes, and I said, "It is okay. I forgive. I forgive!"

I was thankful I could offer forgiveness to one person, but what about the others? How could I possibly extend forgiveness to them when, in some cases, I did not even know who the people were? Yes, I knew they were part of a certain military group, or that they were from a particular part of this country or that, but how was I to go to them to forgive them when I did not know their names?

I had memorized a lovely verse written by an Old Testament prophet that describes God's promise to those who love him: "Call unto me, and I will answer thee, and show thee great and mighty things, which thou knowest not."[29] And so I did just that. I would wake in the morning and sense a familiar bitterness eclipsing my thoughts and prayers, and so I would simply pause and take a deep breath and call unto the Lord. "Oh, God," I would say aloud, there in my bed, "please show me things I do not yet know about how to truly forgive those I presently despise. They have harmed me so deeply, Father, that I cannot think straight, and yet I know that your Word asks me to forgive—and even bless—them. Please explain to me how I am supposed to get that done."

I never received a clear answer from the Lord in response to those myriad requests, but do you know what happened to me? Over time, as I begged God for wisdom I noticed that instead of muttering curses toward my enemies, toward those who had wronged me, I began praying for them. A certain journalist would come to mind, for example, one who had written falsehoods about my life, and instead of bristling in my spirit toward that person, I would say, "Father, please protect him. Please prosper him according to your will. Help him to do excellent work today. Please, would you give him your peace?"

I would move from there into a time of prayer for all the leaders of communist regimes, the same governmental structure that had ruined so much of my life. "God, please enlighten those men today with your presence and power. Give them spiritual eyes with which to see."

I would pray in this way for everyone who was involved in the Vietnam War, for those who had marginalized me because of my unsightly scars, for those who had misunderstood me, or neglected to help me, or failed to treat me as a human being who had real feelings . . . for them all, for every last one on my list.

The more I prayed, the better I felt, and the better I felt, the lighter my spirits were. At some point—two or three months into this practice, perhaps—I looked along the lines of my prayer journal and realized that the people I had been fervently praying for were the same ones who used to be on my list of enemies! *Wow*, I remember thinking, *my heart must surely be changing, for the very people I wanted to murder I now feel nothing but love.*

My heart was no longer angry. I no longer looked for revenge. My enemy list had become my prayer list, and my fury had declared a cease-fire.

When I saw all of those names etched on the wall of the Vietnam Veterans Memorial something stirred up inside me—a calling, I think it was. Yes, I grieved for all of the men and women who had lost their lives because of the war. But equally true, I grieved for all the children who had been wounded during wars, young boys and girls who had nobody to fight for them, nobody to help them put the pieces of their lives back together again. I knew the predicament they faced! I was one of them too.

Following the Veterans Day event, I took steps to establish what is now known as The KIM Foundation International, a nonprofit organization that helps fund groups already actively involved in providing relief for the world's more than six million children severely injured or permanently disabled in wars during the past decade alone. These groups provide prosthetic limbs and orthopedic devices, medication and wheelchairs, rehabilitation services and counseling, and they help integrate wounded kids back into the communities in which they live.

Of great importance to me is our work in Uganda, where we funded the development of the Nakyessa Day and Boarding School. Throughout that country, more than 90 percent of kids fail to complete high school requirements, which means they are at risk of not finding employment as young adults. The reason for this dropout rate comes down to a lack of facilities. There is no money to build buildings, and without school buildings, there cannot be school.

In conjunction with one of our partners, High Adventure Gospel Communication Ministries, we were able to build classrooms, an administration building, and residential rooms—facilities that today support more than seven hundred kids, ranging in age from five to seventeen. I have been to the school. I have hugged those children. I have told them that I understand how devastating it feels to be told you cannot complete your education. And I have seen the hope in their eyes as they were invited back to school.

Each time I receive an update from my team regarding another child who has been served well, there at Nakyessa or at any of our other projects, I cannot help but pump my fists into the air. "Yes! Our efforts are making a difference." That truly is enough for me.

As my calendar flipped from November to December, I received the greatest Christmas present I could imagine: I learned that I was pregnant with Toan's and my second child. I told the news to Toan and Thomas together. "Guess what, Thomas? Daddy and I are preparing a best friend for you! You will never have to play alone again."

Once again, Toan and I consulted the Bible for possible names. We held over "Rebecca" for a daughter, and for a son we decided on Stephen, after the faithful man in the Bible martyred for his spiritual courage and strength. I rubbed my belly in eager anticipation, ready for that little germ of a baby to start to grow, ready for the next nine months to unfold. I had been down this road before and knew it was a lovely, enjoyable ride. *Here we go!* I cheered to my midsection, hoping my little one could already detect my voice.

Unfortunately, my second pregnancy was not quite as smooth as my pregnancy with Thomas had been: For the first five months, I was so sick that I could not keep even a single bite of food down; strong smells made me queasy; and I became so weak that I wondered if I would make it through. But then little two-year-old Thomas would come barreling into the room, bury his face in my belly, begin chatting to his sibling, and all my concerns would melt away.

I was under the care of the same marvelous doctor who had seen me through my first pregnancy, which gave me tremendous peace. "You are doing just fine, Kim," Doctor Phillips said to me during those terribly sick months. "Many women experience morning sickness such as yours."

I was relieved. All the years I had spent receiving negative medical reports from white-jacketed "people in the know" had caused me to be immediately fearful whenever I entered any doctor's office. "Ahh, finally, a good report!" I said to Doctor Phillips. "I believe you! I will be fine."

Nine months later, in the wee hours, I called Kathy Parkinson, my friend from church, and said, "Kathy! I know that it is two-thirty in the morning, but I am having my baby soon! Can you babysit Thomas while Toan and I go to hospital?"

Thankfully, Kathy and Gary lived only five minutes away from us. Four minutes later, there was a soft knock on our front door. Kathy was standing there, still in her pajamas. Oh, the blessing of a faithful friend.

In the end, we welcomed Stephen, a perfectly formed, perfectly healthy baby boy, and my husband proved far steadier on his feet than he had upon Thomas's entrance into the world. Once again, God was showing us that he is always up to something good.

All of the initial publicity of my story brought about a fortuitous result. An executive film producer discovered my story and contacted me. "I would like to turn your story into a documentary," he explained to me, "with you serving as a creative partner, of course." The moment I agreed to participate, a line producer, Shelley Saywell, was assigned to the project and we began the process of mapping out key scenes to tell my story.

Kim's Story premiered in Canada in 1997. Soon after, a gentleman from Montreal was so touched by all that had happened to me that he offered to make arrangements for my family and me to be reunited with my parents. It would be the answer to a decades-long prayer. *What are you up to, God?* I wondered.

"I cannot divulge that information just yet," I imagined God replying. "But I think you will like what unfolds."

So many years ago, my heart was filled to the brim with bitterness, darkness, and rage, like a cup running over with thick, sludgy coffee, so dark that it swallows all light. I had suffered so much and lost so much that I saw no reason to live. Everything was awful, everyone was awful, life itself was awful, and quite candidly, I just wanted out.

For too long, I carried around that black sludge, let it slosh up the sides of my inner world and splash out onto innocent passersby. Darkness is heavy to carry, and I looked every bit the part. I was burdened. I was weighed down. I was sinking under the load I'd allowed. But thankfully, I did not remain there forever. God himself chose to speak into my pain. "Kim," the Lord whispered to me one day, "you simply must pour the black sludge out. Day by day, a bit at a time, until there is no more darkness there."

That instruction felt impossible to carry out, given the volume of sludge inside. But then I would remember the instructions I had been given: a bit at a time. I wondered if I could do that.

I started with my list, choosing simply to pray blessing over one person instead of cursing his or her name. I then began to pray for two, and then for three, and then for the entire list. The more frequently and fervently I prayed in this way, the more sludge I was able to pour out. Of course, it was not I who did the pouring, but God. He is the only de-sludger there is!

Sometimes, in a moment of weakness, I would befriend my bitterness again, and like a river raging over a broken dam, my cup would refill with wretchedness and rage. I would sense that level of blackest sludge rising in my soul and think, *Why did I do that again?*

The decision to pick back up my pain was never worth it. Forgiveness is always the better path.

Eventually, as I got better and better at making wise emotional choices, I noticed that the darkness remained receded and that I was being filled up with something good. It was peace. It was light. It was understanding, compassion, and love. And all of it was from the Lord; he was refilling me with clear, perfectly pure water.

As I began picking up other practices such as confessing my sinfulness and pride and meditating carefully upon God's Word, the clearer and purer that fresh water seemed. Who can gaze upon a crystal-blue sea without marveling at the beauty it holds? That is precisely how I felt as I took in my beautiful state. I had been freed from bitterness. I had been freed from fury. I had been washed clean and was seeing the fruit of transformation in my life. I was not merely saying I wanted to become more like Jesus; by his power, this transition was *actually becoming so.*

Part IV

A STORY REDEEMED

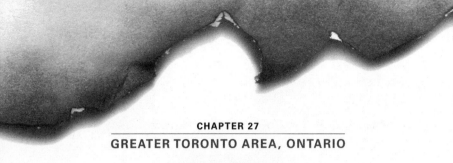

CHAPTER 27

GREATER TORONTO AREA, ONTARIO

REUNITED

SEPTEMBER 1997

I am a doting mother to two boys, a devoted wife, a grown adult of thirty-four years who is as stunned as anyone to be filling any of these roles, let alone all three. With baby Stephen squawking in the background to be fed, the phone rings. My documentary's line producer, Shelley Saywell, is on the line. "Kim," she says, "I received a message from Madame Ndèye Fall of Quebec. She wishes to speak with you."

I did not know who Madame Fall was, but after Shelley explained that Madame Fall worked with a very important global organization that strives to bring about world peace, I told Shelley that she could pass along my contact information to her. A day later, Madame Fall called me.

"Kim Phuc," Madame Fall said, "I have just seen your film here in Quebec, and I would like very much if you would consider serving with us here at UNESCO as a good-will ambassador.

Madame Fall's words meant little to me: *What is UNESCO, what are goodwill ambassadors, and why on earth is she asking me to be one?*

"Oh, Madame Fall," I replied, "thank you for reaching out to me today, but I do not have any desire to serve in a political role. I am not a good choice for an ambassador of any kind."

"No, no. You misunderstand," she explained. "This is not a political position in the least. It is an opportunity to serve as an ambassador who promotes a culture of peace."

It turned out that Madame Fall and her entire team at the Quebec office of UNESCO had seen the film and were touched by my story. "We all remember the famous photograph of you," she said, "but in your film, there was *another* photograph included from your life, one marked not by hatred and war, but by love and hope and peace. That is the picture we wish for you to present to the world, the picture of what life can look like when the choice is made for peace."

As humbled as I was to be asked, Stephen's screeching brought me back to reality. "But Madame Fall, I have just had a second baby, who is today barely one month old. I am a mother. I am not an ambassador! What am I to do?"

Madame Fall laughed, then said, "You do nothing for now. You just be yourself, be a mother to your baby. As opportunities arise for you, we will create a plan. For now, please know that we would be honored to work with you and to find ways for as many people as possible to hear your story and learn your ways."

I hung up the phone having no idea what I was about to sign up for. I did not know that my world had flipped over, that for me, all had just changed.

The second photograph Madame Fall had mentioned had been taken several years before, when Thomas was a baby. A photographer had offered to take photos of my family, and my favorite shot from the entire session was one of me holding Thomas, both of us with skin exposed. In the picture, which I had converted into an oversized business card, you see the back of my neck, my left shoulder, my back, the entirety of my scar—so angry and creased. And you see the back of Thomas's neck, his right shoulder, his back, his fresh, new skin so smooth and sweet. The contrast is striking.

I am holding Thomas close to my chest, my lips close to, but not touching, his right ear. My eyes are trained on Thomas, who is looking away from the camera, ahead. Between us a shadowed heart is formed by the lines and curves created by my shoulder, his neck, my chin.

When I first saw the proof of that photo, it took my breath away. "Toan, *look*. Do you see what I see there?"

My scars were undeniable—the evidence was staring at us both. But because of where Thomas was looking, those scars were in the past. Thomas was looking to the future, where war and pain were not in control. Looking back, it is as if my mouth was whispering into his ear the truth of things: "Yes, your mommy was horribly wounded, but she is still standing, and so must you. Stand for peace, Thomas. Stand for righteousness. And do you see this heart between us? Most of all, son, stand for *love*."

"We cannot change history," I say at every UNESCO speaking opportunity I go to, "but with love, we can heal the future." No matter the question posed, the answer, I believe, is love.

—m—

If there was any gap in my experiencing the love I was so passionately promoting back in 1997, it was the distance that existed between my parents and me. Communication with Ma and Dad had been a challenge ever since I left for Cuba in 1986. They did not own a phone, but there was one at the post office in Trang Bang, so just before I left Vietnam we agreed on an appointed time each week when I would phone them there. This plan worked for a time, but very quickly we all realized the folly of the arrangement. Sometimes, one or both of us was unavailable at the designated time; other times, the post office's line was busy when I finally called in, or I was unable to access a telephone on my end. Our best laid plans fizzled, and an unwanted period of silence ensued.

After I had successfully sought asylum in Canada, I wrote a letter to Ma and Dad telling them of Toan's and my defection (and also of Toan!), but because we were bouncing around from one residence to another, I could not always provide a reliable return address.

Now with an actual plan for a reunion taking shape, not to mention one that was *funded*, Toan decided to write a formal invitation to my parents, asking them to come to Toronto for a month-long stay. "Have a postal worker make ten copies of this invitation for you," Toan instructed my dad, "and keep them in separate places, in case one or more of the copies are confiscated by the authorities. You will need proof of our request for your visit. Be sure you always have a copy at hand."

My parents did as they were told, having copies made and keeping the copies in separate locations, always being mindful of communist officials who could prevent them from making the trip. On an appointed morning, my ma and dad took one copy of the invitation to the local Trang Bang officials to ask for permission in securing international traveling papers. They did not have passports or visas. They did not have *any* of the required documentation. All they had was a piece of paper from two defectors living in Canada and hearts overflowing with a driving, desperate hope.

"How dare you ask for permission to visit your daughter!" one of the officials boomed, clearly enraged by my escape from the communists' clutches. "She disobeyed us!" he said, ripping Toan's invitation into shreds. That official proceeded to pepper my father with questions about my whereabouts and my involvements, even as he kept yelling, "Shut up!" as my dad attempted to respond.

—⁓—

While this unfortunate situation unfolded back in Trang Bang, I waited in Toronto with eager anticipation, convinced I would hear from my parents any day. Days turned into weeks and weeks blurred into months, and still, I had not received a reply. *What could be taking so long?* I wondered. *Is everything all right?*

Just when I was prepared to give up hope, another Trang Bang official paid my parents a visit to report that he and his comrades had held a meeting and wanted my parents to file their paperwork again. It was actually a veiled bribe; the official was all but saying to my ma and dad, "You give me something, and I will give you something in return." My parents had nothing to give, and they did not want to ask me for money, so they told the official no.

The plan was log-jammed again, but things were about to break free. While my parents stewed over what to do next, Ms. Shelley Saywell phoned me to say that her father had a good friend who happened to work as a Canadian liaison to Saigon. "I would like to ask my father to write his friend a letter, requesting assistance for you and Toan."

I could not say yes quickly enough. Yes, I believed that God could sway the hearts of leaders who stand in the way of your dreams. And yes, I believed that God could open doors that no man could keep shut. But who was to say this was not God himself at work? I viewed Ms. Saywell as a conduit of God's favor.

Within a few weeks, my parents were handed Vietnamese passports and offered well wishes on their journey to the West. Three months later, on the twenty-fourth of September, 1997, with proper visas and other legal documents in hand, they landed at Toronto's Pearson International Airport, where Toan and I waited anxiously at the gate.

My parents must have been in the very last two seats on the plane, for Toan and I watched no fewer than two hundred people deplane before we spotted Ma and Dad. Toan and I were overjoyed that they had arrived safely. My ma wore her usual outfit—black, wide-legged pants with a crisp white tunic—and Dad had on a short-sleeved shirt and slacks, both outfits completely unfit for the chilly Toronto air. I nodded knowingly to Toan. Winter coats would have to be the first purchase on our errand list.

As Ma neared, all of the dissonance and distance we had endured for years was rendered powerless at once. "*Ma oi! Ma dang o day roi, Ma den duoc Canada roi!*" I cheered, once she stood before me, in the flesh. "Oh, Mommy! You are here! You made it to Canada!"

"*Cam on Chua Ba, Ma den Canada an toan,*" I went on, unaware that I had not stopped talking long enough to let Ma speak. "*Con that la sung suong gap lai Ba Ma!*" "Thank God you arrived safely. I am so happy to see you, Ma!"

I could see the pride in Ma's face as she looked at me—her little girl, all grown up, married now and a mother herself, making her way in a whole new world. She pulled me close, hugging me over and over again, as though trying to fill a love tank that for too many years had been dry. I introduced Ma to Toan, who was so overcome with the moment that he just laughed and laughed and laughed. Ma made her way to Thomas, who was toddling about our feet and then asked, "But, My, where is your baby? The little one—Stephen?"

I had been so distracted by Ma's arrival that I had completely forgotten about Stephen, whom I had left dozing in his car seat a good fifty feet away. "Oh, no!" I said, giggling over my foolishness. "My baby! How could I forget!"

I rushed to Stephen's side, hoisted the car seat onto my arm, and presented my baby to Ma and Dad: *Look what Toan and I made!*

Ma slipped her index finger into his chubby fist and

stared deeply into his eyes. "My beautiful boy," she said. "It is me, your grandma."

I do not remember walking from the terminal down to baggage claim, nor do I remember the car ride home. I only remember our happy throng bouncing along on air, feet barely touching the ground, hearts as light as a cloud. Ma and I were together again. Life was as it should be.

I had prayed for my parents for well over a decade—that our relationship would heal; that they would discover the person of Jesus Christ; and that God would redeem the years that the "locust hath eaten,"[30] as the prophet Joel put it, referring to whatever has been senselessly lost. So much had been senselessly lost between Ma and me. The prospect of her coming to stay under our roof, with me and my family, was equal parts wonderful and worrisome. If things went well, they could go really well. But if they went poorly? What were we as a family to do then? A month is a long period of time to cohabitate with an angry mob.

Through tears, I begged God for a beautiful outcome to my parents' visit, remembering my dear friend Thuy's assertion each time: *The more we cry, the more we pray.*

Well, within an hour of picking up my parents, all of the introductions had been made—Can you imagine your spouse first meeting your parents a full five years after the wedding has come and gone? Me either!—a tour of our modest home had been conducted, and I had put on lunch for my parents and me. "What can I make for you, Ma?" I had asked, to which she said, "Anything! We have not eaten in twenty-four hours."

Ma and Dad still followed the CaoDai tradition of fasting from meat ten days each month, and unbeknownst to me, the end of that month's fasting period fell during their day-long trip from Vietnam. "You did not eat a single bite on your flights—on your layover, even?" I asked, incredulous. No, Ma had explained, they did not, for fear that even the produce offered to them had been prepared using animal fat. I made a beeline for the kitchen, where I put together a simple vegetable-and-rice stew.

A little while later, with bellies full at last, I eyed Ma and said in our native Vietnamese, "You tell me everything, Mommy. How is everything back home?"

From that seemingly benign question, quite a tale of woe spilled out, involving my ma's loss of her business, her dignity, and her dreams. Evidently the government had come to my ma and informed her that a higher tax would be levied on her earnings immediately, to which my ma wrote a letter appealing the hike. The government responded by raising her taxes higher, prompting Ma to cry out in dismay: "But why?"

"Because you are so *famous*," came the answer. "Your daughter is *Kim Phuc*."

The taxes only continued to rise, until eventually Ma was out of money and the restaurant was no more. My parents filed for bankruptcy, eventually ending up at the temple of my youth in Trang Bang to request a place to stay. The answer was yes, but only after my parents were shamed by the temple keeper's prying questions, delivered with an icy stare. "You have no home of your own any longer?" "You have no business to speak of?" "You have no one else to take you in?"

At this part in my ma's story, tears sprang to my eyes. All those years when my parents were the ones funding the temple's food supply, the temple grounds' maintenance, the temple's care, only to one day be treated as less-than, as beggars, as dirt. The staff who had been there when my parents were among the best-resourced people in the village were no longer in the temple's employ. There was a whole new guard in charge now, made up of men and women who did not know my parents, my grandparents, or the standing in CaoDai any of them had held. They disrespected my parents so horrifically for those first few weeks when they were squatting inside the temple that eventually Ma and Dad relocated to a tiny hut out back. But that provided little relief; as soon as a single strong storm blew through the area, that hut was all but destroyed.

Little did I know that at the very time Toan's invitation reached my parents—hand delivered by someone somewhere who knew they were staying at the temple—they were suffering a level of poverty and despondence they previously had not known. "If we can only get to Kim," they had told each other, "then we will be okay."

My siblings, my aunts, my uncles, my parents' former neighbors back home—everyone had his or her fair share of problems to deal with already. How could any of them be expected to care for my ma and dad too? But Toan and I . . . we were the one bright ray of hope on my parents' darkest night.

That evening, after Ma caught me up on everything that had been happening to them, I did the same for her. As I looked at her sitting there, I thought, *Ma, you are so important to me, and I missed sharing so many important events in my life with you.* With patience and kindness I did not deserve, Ma listened carefully as I began with what had drawn me to Toan and why I had chosen him as my spouse. This was no small matter; from Ma's perspective, Northerners were still "the enemy," and yet now I had married one.

I could tell by Ma's first interactions with Toan—at the airport, in the car on the way to our home, in the kitchen during our shared meal, throughout Ma's and my conversation as Toan popped in and out of the room—that she harbored no ill will toward Toan specifically. In fact, the two of them, perhaps unified by their deep love for me, were the picture of consideration and care. But still, I wanted to honor Ma by explaining my reasons fully. She deserved as much, I believed.

Next, there was the matter of my children: Were they not deformed or somehow at risk because I had carried them in a compromised womb? I knew that Ma had held onto such fears all throughout my life. How many times she had told me, "Kim, you will never marry. Your body will never be able to bear kids." Again, I moved through the discussion slowly, patiently walking her into my life.

I told my ma how obedient Thomas was and what a snuggler Stephen was proving to be. I told her of the boys' various medical checkups and how our pediatrician had declared them free of any and all maladies. My boys were strong as oxen and as energetic as young ones could be.

"Ma, they are *perfect*," I said, even as Thomas mischievously spat a cucumber slice from across the room.

From there, I backtracked to fill her in on my defection, a topic that terrified her.

"You mean you just *left*?"

"It is not so much that I left, Ma," I said, "as much as that I simply did not go back."

We talked about my years in Cuba and about what had driven me to flee. We talked about my educational lapses and about how happy I was as a mom. And we talked about spiritual things, carefully, me going slowly out of deference to her.

"How is it you have fared so well?" Ma asked, truly wanting to know.

"Jesus! He is why everything for me has worked out," I enthusiastically declared.

It was during these first days with us that Ma began screaming out in the night, frightening the boys. "She is remembering the war," I would quietly tell them. I would go into the guest room and stand over Ma's bed, silently pleading for God to calm her mind. "Take these memories from her!" I begged my heavenly Father, even as my mother lay sweating and writhing in pain.

"Mommy," I said on countless occasions, "I have been where you are. I have suffered these nightmares too. I can tell you that God will help you. He will take away your bad dreams."

Ma would eye me skeptically, to which I would concede the point. "Okay, Mommy, listen. If you will not trust the Lord to do this for you, then at least for today, turn off the news." My ma adored watching the Vietnamese news feed on the TV that Toan and I had placed in my parents' room, but the steady stream of negativity was doing no favors for her mind.

During my parents' first few days with us, our homeland was mired in debate over the National Assembly's appointments for the positions of president and prime minister, and Vietnamese reporters were chomping at the daily political goings-on like sharks who had sniffed out blood. The question on Ma's mind was whether the communists would finally be pushed out of control, but of course that is not what occurred. She knew it would turn out this way, with the communist proponents cheering their inhumane causes and with their adversaries up in arms, and yet the coverage was captivating to her.

"Ma, today is a day for *Mr. Bean* or *I Love Lucy*," I would say to her on more than one occasion. "Or for calling one of your other beloved children. Today, we will saturate our minds not with darkness and heaviness and tragedy, but with laughter, lightheartedness, and joy."

Ma would nod in understanding, even as she rarely followed my advice. Over the ensuing month, Ma and I established an effective rhythm around the house—I would tend to Thomas while she helped with Stephen. My younger son weighed nine pounds at birth, and as he continued to grow, he taxed my physical strength. Ma was invaluable during those weeks, joyfully lugging Stephen here and there and everywhere, saving my arms, my hips, my back. Most days I would prepare a breakfast of eggs, fresh fruit, and tea; Ma generally took over the kitchen come dinnertime, when she would make a delicious soup, even if it wasn't her famous recipe. "You do the best you can with what Toronto has to offer, you agree?" I said to her with a laugh. Yes, we would have to make do.

When I needed to run out to tend to various errands, Ma gladly stayed behind with my boys. "I cannot speak the language," she said, "and I cannot drive a car and run your errands for you. But I can care for those grandsons of mine. That will be my service to you."

The month passed all too quickly. When it was time for Ma and Dad to head home, they could not bring themselves to leave. Yes, there was a bit of tension in the air from time to time due to the spiritual choices that Toan and I had made. But all in all, my parents were enjoying our company. And there was nothing waiting for them back home in Vietnam, save for family members who were now strewn hither and yon. Plus, there was the matter of my dad's health.

During the weeks leading up to my parents' visit, I had been very concerned about how my father would fare in our home. My dad drank and smoked, two habits that Toan had struggled to kick himself. We had banned both alcohol and cigarettes from our home so that Toan would not be tempted to fall back into his old ways. While I did not want those substances in my home, I was not comfortable forbidding my father from such habits. It had been so long since I had seen my parents, and I did not want to start things off badly.

Knowing no other course to take, I began to pray. "Father," I remember saying day after day, "please give me wisdom for this situation. Toan does not need alcohol and tobacco near him. None of my family should be breathing secondhand smoke. Would you please come up with a solution, while still preserving my relationship with my dad?"

In one sense, the situation felt hopeless to me; after all, people who are addicted to liquor and cigarettes rarely give up those things on the spot. And yet I had come across a verse that says with God *all* things are possible.[31] I was eager to see if this request would fall under "all things" or not.

On the advice of friends, Toan and I had purchased visitor's health insurance for Ma and Dad to cover them during their stay in Toronto. We never expected to use it, of course, but we had heard several horror stories of loved ones visiting from overseas who had become terribly ill, with no means for receiving medical treatment. We wanted to be prepared—just in case.

During the flight to Canada, my father was prohibited from smoking, which meant that for twenty-four hours (minus two two-hour layovers), his body began the process of withdrawing from his nicotine addiction. Soon after he and my ma landed, Dad became so sick that Toan and I feared he might not make it. He contracted a deep cough that was room-rattling in its severity, causing his body to shake violently, as though he were caught up in his own personal earthquake.

I rushed to Chinatown and purchased every herb for respiratory relief I could find and began giving them to my dad immediately, along with the few sips of soup he could stomach. Each time I left his bedside, I asked God, "Is this it for my dad? Lord, is he dying? Before my eyes?"

When it was evident that the herbs were not strong enough, Toan took my dad to the doctor, who said that Dad had picked up a vicious bug. When my dad did not recover in time to make my parents' scheduled flight back home, I helped Ma file for an extension to their visas, citing health reasons as the cause for their delay. Fortunately for us all, that extension was granted. Even had my father not fallen ill, I would have wanted him and Ma to stay.

For six full weeks, my father lay in pain, coughing and shaking, moaning and writhing. And then, one morning, Dad woke from his restless sleep, sat up in bed, and for the first time since arriving in Canada, he did not cough.

"Daddy, are you getting better?" I asked him.

He grinned and said, "My, light a lamp for me so that I can find my way to the washroom."

"Oh, Daddy, you only need to flip the switch!" I said, ecstatic that he wanted to be up on his own two feet. My father ate breakfast that day, and then lunch, and then supper, gaining strength with every meal. As that day slipped into the next, and those days unfolded into weeks and months, all covered by that extended visa, Dad realized that he no longer craved alcohol or cigarettes.

My ma thought I had put some sort of Christian hex on my dad. "Kim!" she would say to me, incredulous. "What did you do to your father?"

"I just prayed, Mommy, that is all," I would honestly reply, assuring her that Christians do not "hex" people.

I think Ma was a little miffed over the whole turn of events because she had suffered the effects of living with a smoker for years, having no idea that one day he could simply stop. "My whole life, I live with that smell!" she said, equal parts aggravated and amused. "And now, *poof*! No more smell!"

The moment I realized my father was going to survive whatever had befallen him—a respiratory infection, an especially harsh detoxification, or both—I cried tears of deep relief.

Sandwiched into the busyness of our October that year, my telephone rang again. "Kim Phuc," I heard Madame Fall say, "all of UNESCO's ambassadors are convening next month for a general assembly in Paris, and it would be an honor for you to join us as a keynote speaker."

My stomach began to churn. *Oh, how I wish I had been able to complete my ESL coursework and master the English language! How can I possibly address delegates from nearly two hundred countries, using coherent sentences?*

"Madame Fall," I replied, hoping to decline gracefully. "My baby, Stephen, is still nursing." I knew that I could leave breastmilk behind for Ma to give to Stephen from a bottle—that was not the problem. The real truth was that I did not want to be an ocean apart from my baby. "I do apologize, but I must not be away from him for a week."

Before I could say anything else, Madame Fall interrupted, "Oh, Kim Phuc, we have thought of this, yes. Please bring Stephen along."

I was momentarily speechless. She had whisked away my only excuse. With no logical recourse, I agreed, thanking Madame Fall for the opportunity. As soon as I hung up the phone, I began researching how to obtain a Canadian passport for my baby boy.

Four weeks later, Stephen and I boarded an Air Canada flight bound for France, leaving Toan, Thomas, and my parents at home. I did not realize it at the time, but with that singular seven-hour trip, my new life's mission was born. If I proved faithful in this role, I would now be known not as a victim of war, but as a grateful ambassador for peace.

Following that initial talk before UNESCO's general assembly—yes, I made it through, despite believing that I would either faint, throw up, or die there on the spot—I was asked to sit for media interviews in a hotel room that the organization had secured. They also had hired a babysitter for Stephen so that I could focus on the task at hand, and what a satisfying experience it turned out to be. I remained keenly aware of how good it felt to be asked questions directly and invited to respond in my own words. No handlers. No translators. No hidden agendas. No manipulation. No abuse. I took my time answering the reporters, measuring my words carefully, in hopes of articulating my thoughts well.

That speaking opportunity led to another and another, a whole string of them across that first year. And after each occasion, I saw greater evidence of God's protective ways. For more than half of those events, I was able to take questions at the end from the audience, and during those Q&A sessions I noticed a trend. People from all over the globe told me time and again that when they first saw my picture back in 1972, they began praying for "that little girl." They had been haunted by the image of a small child running naked up the road, being chased by an inferno.

By this point in time, I had laid perhaps thousands of questions at God's feet regarding the whys of my situation.

I understood the plain facts, to be sure: My own people had dropped bombs on Route 1 in an effort to cut off the trade routes for the Viet Cong rebels; I had not been targeted, of course. I had simply been in the wrong place at the wrong time. But as to the greater meaning behind my pain, for so long I had been in the dark. And yet here were so many people telling me that my picture had prompted them to pray. Had my suffering actually been the catalyst to bring me into God's family? Could such a thing be true?

In my heart, I knew the answer. *Those bombs led me to Christ.* Armed with that information, my passion soared for helping others make the connection between their pain and God's ultimate plan.

I returned from Paris to find that winter had descended on my hometown. By now, my parents had stayed on in Canada for two full months, and the routines the four of us adults had established seemed to be working well. Over tea one afternoon, I initiated a conversation with my ma. "Ma," I said slowly, studying her face for signs of receptivity, "would you and Dad like to stay with us here?"

I did not specify a timeframe, but Ma understood what was meant by the question: I was asking them to live with us permanently.

Ma's eyes widened at the proposition. "It is cold here," she said, more an observation than a protest. Then, a few seconds later, she added, "I think I will like the change."

Toan and I agreed that my parents needed to experience a Canadian winter before we asked them for a firm decision. Despite the cold-weather gear—coats and hats, gloves and sturdy boots—that Toan and I had purchased for them, we knew the plummeting temperatures and heavy snow would be hard for them to take. Toronto in the wintertime is tough on anyone, but when the only climate you have ever known is hot, hotter, and so hot you think you will melt, frigidity presents a special kind of pain. And yet I could not help but notice each time I passed through the living room and caught sight of Ma and Dad sitting by the window, watching the snow fall in delicate sheets, that delight was etched on their faces. It seemed they were adjusting just fine.

Perhaps it was having weathered Dad's incredible health ordeal, or else the unity we all felt upon making the collective decision to live under the same roof that fueled Ma's desire to approach Toan and me and hear us out on spiritual matters, to know more about "this Jesus" we had decided to follow. Whatever the reason, eventually, on an otherwise uneventful afternoon, Ma met my eyes over her cup of hot tea and said, "Your God is great, Kim. And your God? He is *real*."

Christmastime was soon approaching and, taking a cue from my old friend Anh's approach to spiritual development, I seized the chance to move things ahead. "Mommy," I said, "we need to get you to church." My parents both accepted Jesus as their Savior at the Christmas Eve service, leaving me ecstatic, grateful, and humbled again by God's care.

After my parents gave their lives to Jesus, the four of us— Ma, Dad, Toan, and me—with Thomas and Stephen scampering about at our feet, began to read Scripture and pray together each day before tending to obligations and chores. Especially touching to me was seeing my ma learn to read and write her native Vietnamese by studying Bible verses and then copying them down. It was a laborious process, but, as I told her, what could be better than memorizing God's Word and becoming literate at the same time? She continues the practice to this day.

It was not long before my parents craved salvation for *all* of their kids. "Yes!" I said, knowing just how they felt. "Once I met Jesus, I wanted you both to meet him! And once Toan met Jesus, he wanted all of his countrymen to meet him! We know the longing you feel, Mommy. It is a natural part of loving God."

"I will go back to Vietnam and I will *make* them follow Jesus," she said with force. "I am their mother, after all. They *have* to listen to me!"

I could not help but laugh. "No, no, Mommy. That is not how this works. The Holy Spirit must draw them to himself. Your job is simply to pray."

I explained to my ma that if she would begin praying without ceasing from Canada, God would begin working in the hearts of her children in Vietnam. "His hands are strong," I told my ma. "And his arm is never too short to reach those whose hearts are his."

To my ma's credit, she did just as she was told, praying fervently night and day for her other seven children to come to a saving knowledge of Jesus Christ and devote their lives to him. Five or six times each day, Ma would excuse herself from our company, find a quiet spot in the house, and lay out her request before God. She was just like the persistent widow described in Scripture, who kept knocking and knocking on the door of the town's judge, whom she hoped would rule in her favor in a dispute with an adversary of hers. Because of the widow's tenacity, the judge complied.[32]

I like to picture God as that judge in heaven, grinning over my ma's incessant pleas. "Yes," I envision him saying to her, "*yes*, I will meet your demands." And oh, did he ever meet them. By the year 2004, all seven of my brothers and sisters had come to faith in Jesus. One by one they came, with Ma cheering their every step.

Stephen was just a tiny baby when Ma and Dad arrived in Toronto and only months old when they surrendered their lives to Christ. He was toddling on his physical legs while Ma and Dad were toddling on spiritual legs; he was entering adolescence as my parents began deepening their faith-fueled walk and as they formalized their defection to Canada, marking that particular season with spiritual and physical freedom alike. I think about that parallel, how God simultaneously brought birth and rebirth to my home and family, marking that years-long era of disconnection, disunity, and distance with blessing and grace . . . and love. So much love we shared once again.

There is no power like the Lord's power. There is nothing as good as the goodness of God.

CHAPTER 28

HERE, THERE, EVERYWHERE

PROTECTED ALL ALONG

1998–2011

With each speaking opportunity I accepted, I asked God for wisdom in choosing my words. "Help me to help the people who are listening to find you," I would pray. "Let my story prompt them toward peace." And oh, how he did just that. In the span of a few years, I sat with world leaders and celebrities, with famous musicians and heads of state, and as often as possible, I told them about the love of Christ.

I remember dining with the grand duke and grand duchess of Luxembourg—Henri and Maria Teresa—during their International Peace Day celebrations and not even being able to eat because of the number of questions the duke asked me about my life. The wait staff would deliver the next course to the table and remove my full plate from in front of me. Finally, after five or six courses, I said to the duke, "Henri, you have asked much of me today; I wonder, might I ask a question of you?"

Henri laughed sheepishly, realizing he had been a little overzealous and said, "Oh, certainly. Please, Kim Phuc. Go right ahead."

I seized the opportunity to probe this very powerful man's spiritual life. "Henri," I said, "you are a king and have everything a person could want. Money, power, family, fame . . . but do you have assurance of salvation in your heart?" I paused for a moment.

"Henri," I continued, my tone quiet and sincere, "if you were to die today, do you know for sure that you would go to heaven? Or would you go to hell?"

Henri could not hide his shock. He laid down his fork, folded his hands under his chin, and said, "Oh, Kim Phuc, now *that* is a question. I am afraid I don't know my answer. I must think about that for a while."

After a moment of silence, Henri said, "Kim, would you tell me how one might receive this salvation?" And from there, we had a most marvelous conversation.

I thank God for every one of those opportunities. Most times, I do not know whether the person I am talking to goes on to trust Christ, but that is okay with me. "Salvation is mine," God continuously reminds me. "I, alone, bring it to pass. Faithfully sow the seed, Kim, and I will bring forth the fruit."

Yes, Lord, this is what I will do.

The fact is, we *all* are children of war, whether we have seen a single bomb fall from the sky. A battle is being waged inside of us, and the spoils are our souls. God was showing me that every person knows on some level what it is to suffer and strive, what it is to wear scars they cannot erase. "Tell them I will give them strength to bear their pain," the Lord has encouraged me daily. I had to say goodbye to my dream of becoming a medical doctor, but perhaps healing the soul is as important as healing the body. I consider it noble work.

My story seemed to be opening doors for me to tell of God's goodness and grace, of the miracle that had become my life. I wanted to extend this gratitude to those who had served me well along my journey, the men and women who refused to give up on me, despite the strong temptation I faced to give up on myself. First on my list was Bac Dong.

Toan and I planned a trip to North Vietnam. We wanted to introduce Toan's family to our two boys, now four and one. Also, I reached out to Bac Dong's staff to see if we could come by for a visit and perhaps enjoy a meal together. The former prime minister, now in his nineties, cheerfully agreed to the meeting, but when we arrived, my effusive and energetic friend was unusually quiet and reserved.

He greeted us all warmly and was clearly happy that I had found marriage and motherhood to be to my liking and that I was rebuilding a good life for myself. But across the years that I had been gone, his spark had faded. He was weary. He was near death.

I thought back on the last long conversation that Bac Dong and I had enjoyed, on the night before I departed for Cuba. "Bac Dong," I asserted that evening, "you should believe in the Lord Jesus Christ; if not, you will go to hell!"

I am not sure my approach was correct; perhaps every

young believer charges ahead through a locked door instead of quietly searching for the key. Fortunately, Bac Dong had chuckled, forgiving my brashness without a second thought. "Ah, is Jesus the one from America?" to which I rolled my eyes with mock impatience and said, "No, Bac Dong! Israel! Jesus Christ is from Israel."

We shared a good laugh over that memory now, with me exhibiting a little more gentleness this time around as I shared the gospel with him.

"My daughter," Bac Dong said quietly to Toan, pointing his index finger toward me. "This one will always be my kin."

I beamed with pride. Whether Bac Dong knew Jesus or not, he had been divinely sent my way.

Two years later, Bac Dong passed away. Bac Dong had served as Vietnam's prime minister from 1955 until 1987, when he retired. Condolences came from throughout the world; he was considered one of the greatest, most influential allies of Ho Chi Minh, the founder of communism in Vietnam. Ironically, Bac Dong had also been one of my greatest allies. Oh, the mysterious ways of God.

Toan and I also returned to Cuba so that we could show our boys the sights from that stage of our lives, and so that I could visit Mami and Papi, who were still stuck in the throes of communism. "*Tienen miedo.*" "They still have fear," I whispered to myself as the door to the airport's terminal shut behind me, leaving them in hellish conditions on the other side. I would also reunite with Perry Kretz in Germany, who was suffering from Alzheimer's. And while those get-togethers were profoundly touching to me, nothing could eclipse seeing Bac Dong. Not my weekly interactions with Nick Ut. Not my daily interactions with my loving ma and dad. No, it was Bac Dong who had called in a real rescue operation for me back when all was terribly bleak. Being able to sit with him, his fragile hand in mine, before he passed from this reality to the next, was a privilege I shall never forget. I like to think I helped walk him home.

—∾—

To be sure, alongside all of the joyous occasions were some devastating sorrows. The Lord was teaching me to rely on him more fully, to look to him alone to meet my needs. Yes, those lessons would help me grow in wisdom and grace, but they were not fun when they were happening.

Even as I was learning to trust God to redeem all of the difficult circumstances I had faced throughout my life, my story is still my story, and that story is saddled with pain. Once we see something, we cannot unsee it. Once we hear something, we cannot unhear it. Once we live something, we cannot unlive it. This is certainly true for me. And so, while I have grown in my faith in Jesus to the point of knowing that all of the bad things really are being worked together for good in my life, the residue of those bad things still exists.

On September 11, 2001, I watched the tragic events unfold on television, along with the rest of the world. As people fled the World Trade Center towers in New York City, I was taken back in time, running in front of the CaoDai temple, trying desperately to escape the fire. I looked up at my bedroom ceiling and saw bombs falling, hearing the distinctive *whump-whump* of the napalm canisters instead of the news reporters covering the horror unfolding in New York; my bedroom walls disappeared, and I saw a soldier carrying my three-year-old cousin, his flesh falling like ash. I glanced down at my arm and saw licks of fire engulfing my skin. There in my climate-controlled Toronto residence, I felt the sweltering Vietnam heat. I was so traumatized by the images, I could not leave my bedroom for a week, holing myself away from even my family to think, to cry, to pray.

I do not begrudge the truth of my story, for it is that story that has brought me to God. But oh, the sobering reality it always is, to remember that, yes, this is really my life.

A second sorrow was being financially stretched thin. My role with UNESCO has given me access to famous and powerful people, but it is not a paid position. The speaking engagements for which I am paid usually cover little more than my travel expenses. It has been this way since the beginning, simply a reality that Toan and I accept, which is probably why I was so elated when an artist [33] said he wanted to help us.

I shall call the man Robert. Robert reached out to me after seeing my documentary on television. He had an idea for how to help Toan and me secure our children's future financially, which was a top priority for us. So we arranged a time to discuss it.

Robert arrived, and Toan and I received him warmly, finding him to be very smart, compassionate, and talented.

"Kim, here is my idea: I will paint you and give you a percentage of every print I sell," Robert explained. "We could set it up as a trust fund for your sons, so that you are assured that the monies will not be used for anything other than their education."

I was not the first person that Robert had approached with a similar idea, and based on his previous successes along these lines, he offered Toan and me $20,000 in exchange for the rights to the original work. Ten thousand dollars would go to Thomas, and the other ten would go to Stephen. For the next ten-plus years, those monies would earn interest, turning into a real lifesaver for my entire family. Toan and I gratefully agreed.

Everything unfolded as planned, sales were made, and the trust fund grew. Each year, Toan and I would receive a statement from the bank where the monies were held, and each year we would thank God for the incredible gift on our children's behalf. Thomas's and Stephen's education was taken care of.

When Robert and I struck our deal, he was careful to look me right in the eye and say, "Now, Kim, I know that the time may come when you and Toan are tight on money and you are tempted to pull some of this money out just to get through the month. Please, do not do that. This money is for your boys' education, Kim. You must never touch this fund."

I nodded. Yes, Toan and I would honor that request.

Ten full years passed, and Thomas had decided to attend Faithway Bible College, following in Toan's footsteps. Thomas was happy to live at home, which would save us a lot of money. Thankfully, Toan and I knew that we would not have to repay the student loans Thomas received until he had earned his degree. During our discussion, it dawned on Toan and me that we had not received the most recent statement from the bank. Thinking there had simply been a mix-up, we phoned the bank and asked for them to send us the statement.

"I am so sorry," the woman at the bank said, "but the money from this account was cashed out months ago." By my best estimate, that amount totaled more than $40,000. There was only one other name on the account; only one other person could withdraw the money without Toan's and my knowledge. I picked up the phone and dialed Robert's number, feeling sure there had been a mistake.

Robert did not pick up the phone that day . . . or the following day . . . or the day after that. In fact, Robert avoided my phone calls for six years.

Finally, one afternoon, he answered my call. "Robert, we need to meet," I said. And he said, "Yes. Yes, I agree."

Toan, the boys, and I got into the car to drive to Robert's house. I felt jittery and unsure the entire trip with two big questions swirling in my mind. *Why did Robert avoid my calls for so long? And what on earth had happened to our boys' money?*

I used my concerns as fuel for prayer, asking God to oversee all that would soon unfold.

Soon enough, we arrived at Robert's house and were welcomed by him and his wife. Robert was an excellent cook and had prepared us a truly magnificent feast, acting the entire evening as though nothing at all was amiss. Following dinner, however, the mood changed. "Kim," he whispered to me privately, "I need to talk with you."

Robert and I retreated to a side room, out of earshot of

everyone else, and within seconds of being alone, he looked squarely into my face and said, "I am so sorry, Kim, but the money is gone."

I was so shocked I thought I was going to faint. "I had put so much hope in that money for my children, Robert!" I said, incredulous.

"I know," he said. "And I am truly sorry. Kim, I drank every last dime that was there."

Neither Toan nor I knew Robert was an alcoholic, and although his home was worth millions and his combined assets still more than that, he had liquidated all he could liquidate and had had nowhere else to turn. "My life makes me look wealthy," he said to me, "but in fact, I am very poor. I have spent everything on my addiction, and I have nothing to show for it now."

I looked at Robert intently, who was looking intently back at me. As my eyes met his, I saw terrible pain. I had every reason to be angry for what he had done to my family, but instead, I simply felt sad. "Poor you," I whispered to Robert.

I gave him a warm embrace and said, "Robert, I forgive you. I do. But I must ask one favor of you: Please, you be the one to tell my boys."

Robert agreed. He pulled Thomas aside first and then Stephen, explaining to each of my sons exactly what had happened. Thankfully, my boys responded to the news with compassion and tenderness, forgiving Robert too. But oh, how the truth stung us all. So much money! And then *poof* . . . gone.

Ironically, Robert had never given me a print, which may have been divine intervention. Now I would not be constantly reminded of this injustice.

"I will make a way for you, Kim," God assured me on the way home. Honestly, I was not so sure about that. Thomas was nearing graduation from Bible college and also preparing to marry his love, Kezia, even as school-loan bills were coming due. And Stephen was hoping to begin college in seven short months—how could we pull together funding so fast? And yet I knew what I had been told by God, and I chose to believe it word for word. "This is a good reminder," I said to my sons. "It is the Lord, not man, who provides."

As difficult as it was to learn that the money we had been counting on was gone, I felt an odd sense of joy intermingling with my sorrow. All those years mothering my boys had left me wondering if I was getting it right. Was I striking the balance between holding them accountable to biblical values while still being merciful, gentle, and kind? Was I teaching them critical life lessons? Was I modeling humility, wisdom, and love?

In one fell swoop, every last maternal apprehension I had held was laid to rest. My boys had been wronged in a way that mattered deeply to them, and yet they had replied with understanding and grace. I looked at Thomas and Stephen and smiled. *My sons are honorable young men.*

I thought back to a decision I had made when Thomas and Stephen were preschoolers, back when mommying days could be awfully long. One boy or the other—or, during especially challenging moments, *both* of my sons—would refuse to listen to me, and I would grow so angry inside that it was all I could do not to scream. *Why are they not doing what I ask them to do?* I would fume internally. *They have defied my authority again!*

I could feel my face wrenched in fury, eyebrows stitched together, eyes squinting, lips pursed, ready to release my rage. One day when this happened, I suddenly thought, *I wonder what I look like right now.*

I pushed pause on my irritation and headed for the bathroom mirror. Oh, my face looked ugly! So angry. So out of control.

I relaxed and let my features soften. I took a deep breath and practiced gently grinning instead. I thought about how much I loved my boys, and my eyes began to reflect that love. I pushed my cheeks up with the tips of my fingers and then massaged out those deep forehead lines. "There," I said to myself, at last satisfied with my face. "*That* is a mother's expression—accepting, warm, at ease."

I returned to my boys and told them I was done with my "angry face." They were busy playing, so I am not even sure that they heard me, or if they did that they could understand why this was such a weighty decision for me. Certainly, they would still occasionally defy me. And certainly, I would grow frustrated with them. But in terms of allowing myself to feel rage to the point that it registered disgust on my face, I determined those days were done. Even when I was irritated, I would reflect the light of Christ.

As I sat in the car with my almost-adult sons riding in back, I experienced the fruit of that single decision: Those who are well loved can love others well. This day at Robert's house, they had loved very well.

"You will be blessed for how you responded today," I remarked with confidence to both of my sons. Thomas and Stephen both nodded and smiled.

The entire ordeal regarding Robert reminded me that the Lord's ways really are different from our ways[34] and that often we are not able to see precisely what God is up to in our lives or why. "His way" for me always seemed to include chronic, inconsolable pain. "If I had my way," I frequently would say to the Lord, "this pain would be resolved."

I began to pray peace over my pain with greater frequency, saying, "There, there. No need to scream." The more I prayed, the more I could truthfully admit to my audiences, "Pain is my partner, just as in a marriage"—a partner not to be scorned but rather embraced.

In 2000, I was still regularly taking painkillers in an effort to relieve my chronic pain, when the question came to my mind, *Why am I taking medicine if I do not consider myself sick?* A burned person is supposed to feel pain; pain is simply part of the deal. And yet here I was swallowing one pill after another and yet *still suffering* with that thing called pain. "This is crazy!" I said to myself in that moment. "I will no longer take these pills."

Certainly, I am not opposed to medicines; they are so helpful for many people in many cases! But for me, they only dulled my senses. They did nothing to remove my pain.

"Lord," I prayed as I tossed my medicines into the trash, "please give me replacement methods to help me ease this pain."

Again, the words from the prophet Jeremiah ran through my mind.[35] "Yes, Lord, show me great things."

God showed me his promises in his Word to help retrain

my mind. He placed friends and family around me who were willing to help me in times of need. He prompted me to *sing*, of all things, when the pain came to me; even something as simple as, "Jesus loves me, this I know," can work wonders on a wrenched arm and back.

I took great comfort in the promises of God when my body was failing me. On one occasion, I sat at the dining room table, my Bible opened flat before me, my pain strong. I was reading Psalms, I think, when a memory suddenly took me back to another time in my life, when it was just a book and me.

I was a little girl living joyously, long before the war had settled over Trang Bang, curled up with a book. That day I had been transported into the world described in its pages. I was so absorbed in the story that when my father called me from another part of the house—"Phuc, please do come here!"—I stayed put. I heard Daddy on the edge of my subconscious, but I did not respond.

I should have known he would come looking for me. "Phuc!" he said, seeing me in my room. "Did you not hear me calling for you?"

"Mm-hmm," I said, my eyes still on the book in my lap.

I rarely saw Daddy frustrated, but that day? Oh, he was very angry with me! He grabbed my book, walked out of the room without saying a word, and threw it away.

"Daddy!" I remember crying out to him. "How could you put my book in the trash!" He did not respond, treating me with the very disregard that I had shown to him.

As I recalled the memory, I giggled to myself. What a mischievous girl I was! And what a loving father I had been blessed with—well, except for that day when he threw out my book. The memories cascaded in a beautiful flow, filling twenty or thirty minutes' time. When I rose from the table, I was able to carry on with my day with much less pain.

This is how it has been for me: daily pain with daily remedies from God.

On one day I would hear him say, "My child, try smiling. Let your face tell your body how to feel."

On another day, "Kim, go walking. Motion always changes emotion, and movement will move out your pain."

On another day, "Beloved, simply call a friend. Talk about something else for a half-hour."

On still another day, "Kim, just come sit with me. Let me bear your pain for a time." There, in the presence of my Father, he would remind me of his faithfulness in my life, just like the stones of remembrance in the story of Joshua.[36] God would help me recall those times when he showed up for me, the rescue missions that saved me many times.

"God, remind me that I was not killed by that napalm bomb but instead lived to tell of those events," I would ask him. I would stand up a stone.

"God, remind me that although my clothes and my skin were singed right off of me, my internal organs were unharmed." One more stone placed.

"God, remind me of the doctors' compassion toward me at the Barsky Unit all of those months." Another stone lifted up for God and me both to see.

"God, remind me of how you brought me through those torturous burn baths, which aided my healing."

"God, remind me to be grateful that enough of my body

was untouched by napalm that I had skin available for grafting, to piece me back together again."

"God, remind me of this beautiful smile you have given me. With it, I can minister to everyone I meet."

"God, remind me that this entire journey directed me to your invitation of salvation by grace through faith—my entire family and I have been forever changed because of the path I have been on."

If I recounted all the blessings, my pile of sacred stones would kiss the sky. *Oh, Father, may I hold fast to your faithfulness. May I never forget.*

In those private moments with God, I began to sharpen my ability to spot evidences of God's faithfulness in my daily life. When people would tell me that they had prayed for me when I was a child, I would hold fast to that admission, weighing each word. I would learn of yet one more doctor, one more nurse, who had tended to my scars, and deep gratitude would rise up from my bones. I would hear of one more plot twist to my story line, and another critical piece of my life's puzzle would blessedly fall into place.

I was handed one such puzzle piece three full decades after the napalm attack on Trang Bang, the answer to a maddening question I had carried all those years. Yes, I had wanted to know why God allowed wars and why so many people had to die. I also had wanted to know why those bombs had been dropped over my South Vietnam village by one of our own countrymen. And why, out of all the people who could have been burned that afternoon, the napalm found *me*. But there was one question that tormented me above them all:

Why did the people at the hospital put me in the morgue, leaving me to die?

Over and over, I begged the Lord for insight. "Why was I left for dead, Father? I was still breathing! I was still alive! I thought doctors took an oath saying they would take all measures to help their patients! This was true, was it not?"[37] I was speaking for UNESCO at a conference in Spain, and I was seated at a table with the other featured speakers. Next to me was a renowned scientist who had spent the majority of his career studying the weaponization of certain chemicals and chemical combinations, one of which was napalm.

As you might imagine, we had much to talk about. He was already familiar with my story, and after we exchanged initial pleasantries and delved into a bit of more meaningful conversation, he leaned over to me and said, "Kim, there is something you need to know about the treatment you received immediately following the napalm attack."

He had my full attention now.

"The fact that you were left unattended for three days' time, your wounds wrapped tightly in bandages, your body laid to rest, is precisely what saved your life."

The scientist explained that if the nurses in Saigon had removed my bandages as soon as I arrived at the hospital, the oxygen in the air would have set me on fire, and I would have died on the spot. Of course: *Napalm can reignite.* How had I never made that connection?

In fact, several years after that conversation, I attended a conference in Chicago and met many Vietnam veterans. One of the men I met—an American—had lost his brother in a napalm attack. The soldier had been flown from Vietnam directly to Hawaii, and when he was admitted to the hospital, well-meaning triage nurses removed his bandages to inspect the burns. Within minutes of the air hitting his napalmed skin, he took what would be his last breath.

Years later, when my younger son, Stephen, was in college, I reminded him of this part of my story. He was home for Christmas break and told me about someone who had made some personal remarks that had hurt him deeply.

"For decades I harbored bitterness toward the doctors and nurses who had left me in the hospital morgue," I said. "It was only when the scientist gave me greater perspective that I understood why they did so. I wish I had trusted God earlier with that hard part of my story, so that I could have been spared from carrying that awful burden of bitterness."

I looked into my son's eyes, holding his tender, attentive gaze. "Stephen, you can choose more wisely than your ma did. You can choose right now to trust God and extend love and forgiveness and grace to the person who has hurt you, even though that hurt is real. You can do this as an act of faith, believing that God is in this situation, and that he is working it together for good."

To Stephen's credit, he did just that, effectively avoiding years of pain.

I try to "take my own medicine" here, I must say. For some reason that only God fully understands, I am not finished with life on earth just yet. I am meant to be here, right where I am. And so, despite the pain I suffer on days such as today, when every instinct is telling me to curl up in the fetal position and groan, I look up to heaven, let the corners of my mouth form a smile, sing praises from a thankful heart, and

I remember that somehow, in some way, all things are being worked together for good. It is the Lord, alone, who heals.

And that healing he provides? Sometimes it comes through human hands. That has been the case for me for these past two years. A new procedure by a skilled dermatologist is promising me the unthinkable: *life with far less pain.*

MORE PAIN TO GET TO LESS

APRIL 2015

I think of the treatment as a kind of intensive "anger-management" program to soften my singed, scarred skin. The medical term for the process is *fractional ablative laser therapy*. As of today, I have completed the fifth of seven pre-scribed laser treatments with my dermatologist, Doctor Jill Waibel. During recovery, the pain was overwhelming, more so than previous times. *Why is this happening?* I have let my scars breathe overnight and kept clothing and blankets from touching them, as I always do, but this time, the pain is out of control.

I phone Doctor Jill, who listens to me describe where the pain is coming from. With that information, she tells me she is almost positive that the culprit is the beginning of a thin, singular strand of hair wanting to pop out from a follicle on my left arm, a follicle that has been reawakened after a deep, dark, four-decades-long sleep. "A stimulated hair follicle means new growth is happening," Doctor Jill Waibel assures me. "This means *progress*, Kim!"

It also means pain, I think to myself. And yet it is pain I will gladly take. Pains are not all created equal. This particular one is pain with great promise attached.

I had met Doctor Jill through a friend of her father-in-law's, who had heard me speak at a church in Ohio at the beginning of the year. It was a circuitous connection at best, but when I finished my presentation, the man approached me. "I think my friend's daughter-in-law can help you," he said to me, tenderness in his voice. "She has a dermatology clinic down in Miami and is seeing positive results with the treatments she does."

Within a matter of days, I was in touch with Doctor Jill.

"Fractional ablative laser therapy," Doctor Jill explained to me during that first meeting, "uses concentrated light and radiation to heat up the affected area and steam off tiny portions of the scarred tissue—the bad skin—so that new skin can grow."

Wait. What did she say? She is going to "heat" me up? I was certain that I did not want to be burned all over again, even in this controlled and therapeutic environment, but for reasons I could not fully explain, I did not move. "Because of the extensiveness of your wounds," Doctor Jill continued, "I recommend seven treatments spaced out over about a year's time, and then we will evaluate the results to that point."

My wounds were extensive, covering more than a third

of my body, which had necessitated another third then being sliced and diced and repositioned during the seventeen skin-graft operations I had undergone as a child and teenager. As a result, in addition to the more visible scarring on my left forearm, the backs of my legs looked like the impossibly rough terrain of the unpaved roads so common in my South Vietnam homeland. While Doctor Jill walked me through the details, I became more open to the idea, thinking of it as a grand "resurfacing." I simply had to give the laser treatments a try.

My excitement was deflated when I heard the cost of the procedure—two to three thousand dollars per visit. That meant that Toan and I might have to come up with $20,000 for the first year of treatments. *What if I need more than the initial seven visits?* Now my mind whirred and fretted. *How can we possibly afford it?*

I was defending my desire to pursue the treatments to my ma, who could not for the life of her understand why I would want to invite further stress and pain into my life, when my phone rang. On the other end of the line was Doctor Jill's New York–based publicist, Ms. Rok. She had a proposition for me: If I would permit the media to follow my progress during and after my laser treatments, then the treatments would be provided free of charge by Lumenis, the company that makes the laser machine. Once again, my story had thrown open an unexpected door for me.

I have talked with God about this curious dynamic often, how my terribly old picture continues to affect my current life. More times than not, I sense God saying that in the opportunities he is providing me, and in the people he is allowing me to meet, he is restoring bits and pieces of what the bombs took from me—my childhood, my confidence, my peace. It would take me many years to see the media as restorative agents in the hands of God, exempting Uncle Ut all the while, since he was *rescuer*, not "media" in my eyes. But in time I would get there, grateful for the people and their craft.

With gratitude, humility, and relief, I told Ms. Rok yes. One of my first pretreatment interviews was in early June with Ms. Jane Pauley for CBS *Sunday Morning*, a segment that would air on October 25, 2015, a month after my first trip to Miami.

Toan and I flew from Toronto to Miami the day before my procedure. We landed at Miami International Airport, where Uncle Ut, on behalf of the AP, awaited our arrival. Even though I knew Uncle would be there, I was overjoyed when I saw his face. Ms. Rok was there, too, to facilitate a press conference before Toan and I were driven to the Miami Hilton.

Our driver dropped us off at the clinic at 8:00 a.m. sharp the next morning. Once again, Ms. Rok helped me navigate media interviews before I was led into an examination room and prepped for my process with Doctor Jill.

The preparation for a laser treatment seemed more complicated and time-consuming than the treatment itself. First, a member of the staff took photographs of the areas on my body that would be treated. A nurse gently applied numbing cream to my skin and then wrapped my scars in plastic wrap, making me feel like a mummy. The plastic kept my body heat trapped inside, which helped the cream seep deep into my skin. Next, the anesthesiologist explained that I would be receiving something to dull my senses.

But before that happened, Doctor Jill and I prayed together. We share a love for Jesus Christ, and I was soothed by her earnest entreaties on my behalf. She asked God to be near me in a way I could detect, to give me peace that passes understanding and for her skills to be used for good—to heal my body and remove my pain.

When Doctor Jill said amen, I closed my eyes, begging the anesthetic to kick in quickly and do its numbing magic. As I tried to focus my hazy attention on releasing the tension that had gathered in my shoulders and slowing my breath, I could hear the clicks of photographers' cameras, the lenses trained on my every move.

Each treatment ran from morning until later afternoon—four o'clock, or so—and while I was undergoing the procedure, Toan and members of the media enjoyed a marvelous buffet provided by Doctor Jill's office featuring sandwiches, salads, side dishes, and plenty of chocolate desserts. Everyone ate very well while I was in another room having my burns voluntarily reburned. The way I saw it, all of us were being nourished—some with food, and one with light.

Still, it was not an ideal situation for me, given the media's demands. For starters, there was rarely enough time for the anesthesia to work itself all the way into my system. I could not be administered the drug until the last reporter had asked his or her final question, and yet Doctor Jill could not hold up the procedure that takes multiple hours to complete. "It will never be enough time," Doctor Jill told me during that first visit. "But we will accept things as perfect enough."

The moment each procedure was finished, someone's microphone was there to greet me. "How are you feeling,

Kim?" a well-meaning reporter would say softly, to which I would groggily grunt and groan. I did my best to answer the questions, even as progress seemed subtle and slow. "Give me a full year," I would always tell them. "In one year's time, we shall see how things look."

Secretly I had high hopes for healing, although I never said those things aloud.

The possible side effects of fractional ablative laser therapy include redness, swelling, itching, peeling, susceptibility to infection, and extreme sensitivity to sunlight. After every treatment, Doctor Jill would graciously drive Toan and me back to our hotel room, passing on strict instructions to me each time: I must remain indoors with my skin uncovered as much as possible so that it stays in contact with the air (and not with the sun); I must apply a specific type of cream to my scars as often as possible and as thick as I can withstand; and I must take two twenty-minute showers a day, using a liquid soap Doctor Jill has approved.

It is those showers that would do me in.

For so many years, long after scar tissue had formed and covered my nerve endings and organs, showering was a solace for me, the only place where I found relief from all my pain. The warm water temporarily softened my vast scar tissue, tissue that was four to five times thicker than healthy skin. But here? Now? Punctured by so many laser holes? The steady stream of water may as well have been the Great Flood that Noah and his family survived, a savage rush destroying all in its path.

If you have ever been badly sunburned and quickly got

in the shower to cleanse your angry red skin, then you know the pain I was suffering. You dance in and out of the stream of water from the showerhead, desperate to avoid the sting. "Too hot! Too hot!" I had cried in 1972 when napalm had its way with me. I would repeat those words in the shower after my treatments, even when the water temperature was tepid or even cool.

The place that once was my best friend—the shower—seemed to have turned on me and become my worst enemy. "Love your enemies," I would tell myself in those moments, a distraction that sometimes made me laugh.

Other times, I meditated on the Bible story of the Syrian commander, Naaman, who found miraculous healing from leprosy when he followed the prophet Elisha's instructions to wash in the Jordan River seven times.

Naaman was angry that Elisha wanted *him* to do something, rather than the prophet waving his hand and healing Naaman himself, but Naaman eventually came to his senses. Amazingly, by the seventh "treatment" in the Jordan River, Naaman's skin was clean, with no sign of leprosy.[38]

There in the shower, I scrubbed and scrubbed. "Be faithful to wash and wash and wash," I would tell my still-burned, still-scarred self. "Do this with diligence, Kim, and your skin will be restored."

I chose to believe it was true.

After each shower, Toan would diligently rub the medicated cream into my skin to keep it hydrated and supple. After the first treatment, we realized that my long hair was getting in the way, covering the scars on my neck that needed the cream, too, so I had it cut into a short bob. "Much easier," Toan said to me afterward, rubbing the cream as gently as possible in long, slow circles.

Once we returned home, Ma assisted me during the week when Toan was at work. "Kim," she would say with a grimace, while I groaned and squirmed, "why would you put yourself through this new pain after all of the pain you have known?"

"Mommy," I said, "this pain is little, given the big result it will yield." It is true that neither Doctor Jill nor I knew for sure how my body would respond to these treatments, but already I saw glimpses of the improved appearance, improved texture, and improved circulation. Now, if we could just claim that "reduction of pain."

Two months after the bombs dropped on Trang Bang, the Associated Press reported that I was "nearly recovered"[39] from my burns, but in fact, I am still actively recovering—it is present tense, not part of my past. The scarred nerve endings throughout my body can misfire without any obvious cause, sending a penetrating jolt of pain through my neck, my back, and my arm. This is the reality I have been trying intently to redeem, by God's grace and the gifting of Doctor Jill. And this is why I flew to Miami not seven but eight times in all.

It is with joy that I report this truth: Some days—not all of them, mind you, but on *some*—I know relief. Some days, I wake at seven in the morning, feeling rested, refreshed, and energized to take on the day. I have slept well for a change.

Some days, I climb out of bed—pain-free . . . *yes!*—and after tending to personal needs, I head downstairs. I read and read and read Scripture at the dining room table, and when my mother and my husband rise and join me, I read some more aloud. We have breakfast together, and then I go into my home office, where I return emails. Two, sometimes three times a day, I drive my mom to visit my dad, whose health has declined to the point that he requires more assistance than Toan and I can provide and now lives in a nursing home nearby. I keep my Bible app open on my oh-so-smart phone, so that throughout the day I can connect and absorb God's Word.

I pray whenever problems surface, because don't they *always* find a way into our lives?

I nap . . . most afternoons, I nap.

And every two weeks, our family hosts a Bible study in our home for Vietnamese families. I make the arrangements for the food, beverages, and childcare. My ma prepares her famous soup for those meetings, Toan delivers a message from the Scriptures in our native tongue to the adults, Thomas speaks in English to the young people, and Stephen assists with the youngest children, playing with them and making them feel at home.

You can imagine how this mama's heart always swells, as I watch my two sons serve. Toan and I never knew what life path the Lord would ultimately call them to, since both Thomas and Stephen have expressed a number of possible dreams. At various times, adventure-seeker Thomas was determined to be a lawyer, a pilot, or a professional basketball player, just a few options from a long list. Stephen, who has always been content to be home, close to his ma, was dead set on a professional football or mixed martial arts career, provided the path would occasionally bend Toronto's way.

But eventually, both of them came to Toan and me to

share their mutual decision. "Ma. Dad. We want to go into full-time ministry." What that will look like is still a work in progress, but our family's love for serving the Vietnamese in our community has ignited something special in their hearts.

Oh, those are some of the days I have known, and I treasure each and every one! My prayer, then, is to string a few pain-free days together . . . to know *some* weeks, *some* months, *some* years when I feel great.

Until then, I sing, and I smile, and I praise God. I have learned to manage life's bigger challenges—terror and tragedy, abandonment and abuse, poverty and wrenching pain—and let the little inconveniences amuse me instead of annoy me.

An occasion comes to mind just now. I had been invited to speak about peace in a world at war at the University at Buffalo in New York. One of the professors who helped lead the campus organization that was hosting me offered to make the two-hour drive to my home to pick me up for the event. He and two student leaders arrived on the appointed day, and off we went.

From the moment I got in the car, I was engaged in an incessant and enthusiastic conversation with my car mates. When we got to the 403 interchange heading east, the professor missed it completely and we continued heading west . . . toward Detroit, not Buffalo. Two hours later, there was a lull in the conversation, and the professor said in alarm, "Kim! Did that sign say that we are headed westbound?"

Well, I rarely have any idea where I am when I am not driving. "I do not know!" I said. "Do you think that we made a wrong turn?"

Once we got our bearings, we realized that we would officially be late. As in, *sixty minutes late*, the same time allotted for my talk.

The professor turned the car around and began heading eastbound, muttering that he wished we "had a helicopter" and how "burned up" he was over his mistake. I waited until his initial rage simmered down before offering up my thoughts.

"Professor, I know that we will be late to the event. But even if one person is left in the auditorium, I will count the evening a success. I will speak from my heart to that one person, and who knows? Perhaps my words will matter to him or her."

The professor was still fuming. "Whatever mistake you make, my friend," I added, "simply start back up and try again. Do the next right thing . . . that is all we are able to do."

At eight-thirty that evening, exactly one hour after my speech was scheduled to begin, we arrived at our destination. The four of us rushed into the auditorium, where five hundred people sat patiently. All in all, it was a truly wonderful experience.

Afterward, the professor said to me, "Kim, I was on fire on the way here, as you know. But your words and your attitude—they really cooled me off." He gave me a hug and thanked me.

It occurred to me in that moment that perhaps that is my sole mission in this life—to help put out whatever fires I find. We all are walking one fire road or another, be it paved by relational upheaval or financial upheaval, physical or emotional or the general inconveniences of life. But when you and I come along with a posture of peace, or with gentle and kind words, or with an offer of prayer or a hug, or with anything that looks and acts like Jesus, it is as though we have used a fire extinguisher—the flames that burned hot settle down.

The education, the money, the food, the family, the healing, the freedom, the reunion with my ma—all of the things I craved along the way were never going to satisfy my soul. It was only the peace that Jesus offers that could settle the flames inside of me. "Believe me," I told those university students, "I really want relief from my pain. But do you know what I want even more than that? I want to remain close to Christ."

As hard as this may be to believe, I meant every word that I said.

CHAPTER 30

NECKER ISLAND, THE CARIBBEAN

BARING MY SCARS

AUGUST 2015

"We will pay all expenses for you and Toan," the event coordinator said to me, as I absentmindedly ran my index finger along my left-arm scar. *I am almost sure my skin is softer there. Maybe the laser treatments are working, thinning out my scar tissue.*

"Kim," the coordinator said, bringing me back to the reason for her call. "It would be such an honor if you would come share your story with us." The "us" happened to be fifty of the world's most influential leaders who were attending billionaire Richard Branson's multi-day seminar, "The Power of Forgiveness and Gratitude," on his private Caribbean island.

"I am the one who would be honored," I said. "Toan and I accept your kind offer."

For the past twenty years, regardless of where I am

speaking, when I am speaking, or to whom I am speaking, I have almost always worn a traditional Vietnamese *ao dai*, complemented by a pair of black shoes. It is such a contrast to the secondhand blouse, polka-dot skirt, mismatched scarf, and mid-length beige trench coat that I wore for the Veterans Day speech in 1997. I did not feel put together at all, but what was I to do at the time? I had no money to purchase clothing; Toan and I were trying to survive!

I remember crying out to the Lord one night. *I want to look professional. I want to look beautiful. But most of all, God, I want to hide my skin.* Of course, the entire reason that people were inviting me to come speak in the first place was because of my scars. *They must simply use their imagination, God. That is the best that I can offer them.*

One week after I began asking God for help in this regard, I met a Vietnamese couple at a church service. I did not know either of them, but I felt an instant camaraderie with the wife . . . as well as an instant affinity for her beautiful outfit. "I must tell you how lovely your *ao dai* is," I said to her. "Did you get it overseas?"

She smiled conspiratorially and said, "I will give you a lady's number, and in two days' time, you shall have one for yourself."

As you might guess, I could not phone the lady fast enough. In less than a week, she had met with me, taken my measurements, and whipped up seemingly from thin air the most gorgeous *ao dai* I had ever owned. I believe I paid fifty dollars for the outfit, which I still wear to this day. I am comfortable when I wear it. I look professional. I look beautiful—at least, that is what many people have told me. And most important, not one inch of my scars can be seen. This has been the perfect outfit for me.

When Toan and I arrived on Necker Island, we were greeted by scorching heat. But the weather had nothing to do with something I had already decided to do. For the first time, I was going to wear short sleeves in public. With armfuls of courage, I had packed a lightweight sundress for this esteemed event.

I had hated my buffalo-hide skin for most of my life, and yet I had indeed made peace with my pain. I had come to accept the napalm's effects. I had learned, yes, even to love my scars. "You humble me," I would say to them. "You help me to *live*."

But here on Necker Island, I felt some trepidation: *What will people think of me? What will they say?*

I thought back to another prestigious invitation I received in 2000—to meet Queen Elizabeth—an event I nearly turned down. When one of the queen's representatives phoned and asked me to come to London in two weeks' time I said, "Oh, I am so very sorry, but I cannot be there that day."

There was a long pause, and then she said, "You cannot come for the queen?"

"I am honored by this invitation," I replied sincerely, "but I have another commitment in the United States that day."

I was scheduled to speak at a university in California. How I loved speaking to university students! Not only did their youthful optimism inspire me, but being in an educational environment was personally gratifying. I had spent so much time wishing for, but never seeming to obtain, a solid education, that being in a large lecture hall full of eager students felt almost like it closed that gap for me. As only God could orchestrate it, on six occasions, the university higher-ups actually presented me with an honorary doctorate. Really! Me, Kim Phuc, the one who never earned even a bachelor's degree because of governmental shenanigans? Each time I returned home with another one, I insisted with a twinkle in my eye that Toan, Thomas, and Stephen address me by my title. With the titles adding up, the boys finally referred to me as "Doctor Doctor Doctor Doctor Doctor Doctor Mommy." Oh, we had some good laughs over that one.

On the other end of the phone line, I heard the queen's representative say with a bit of an edge, "I see," before assuring me that she would pass along my regrets.

Which is precisely what I told Uncle Ut when he phoned me moments later. "Kim, you must go to England. This is the queen, Kim! The *queen*." I could imagine the look on Uncle Ut's face from the tone of his voice.

Uncle Ut said that he, too, had been invited and explained why both of us needed to be there: A permanent exhibit featuring my picture was being installed in a British museum.

"But Uncle Ut," I said, "if they knew they would be inviting us, why are we only learning of this today?"

"Kim," he said, "this is how things must be—possibly for security reasons, we could not know."

I felt terrible that I could not make it, but Uncle Ut would have none of my rationale. "Kim, you must change your plans," he told me.

Knowing Uncle Ut would never lead me astray, I said, "Oh, Uncle Ut, I do love you. I will do what you ask. I will change my plans and go." Toan was to travel with me, and so we set about making our plans.

Toan and I finally made it to the welcome wing of London's Science Museum, where elegant preparations had been made. Everyone in attendance was on pins and needles, waiting for the queen and her husband, Prince Philip, to arrive. Behind the receiving line, onlookers watched eagerly to catch even a glimpse of the British royalty. I had landed in quite a whirlwind of activity and now understood just how rare it was to have this wonderful opportunity to meet such a famous leader.

I had chosen a beautiful black *ao dai* for the occasion, its bodice accented with thick crystal clusters, its fabric covering every inch of my scars. I had been prepped on the protocol for how the queen would move through the receiving line— "She will move rather quickly, in order to have time to greet each guest; do not offer your hand until she first offers hers; keep conversations brief, supplying only the information that the queen asks of you."

But when she arrived at the museum and began greeting guests, I was not prepared for what happened when she reached me.

Queen Elizabeth extended her gloved hand for me to shake, looked intently at my face, and said, "Kim? Is it really you?"

I laughed while still holding the queen's delicate hand. "Yes! It is me, Kim Phuc, your Majesty. Truly! Here I am!"

"Kim, I can hardly believe it," she replied. Then it dawned on me. *She cannot see the evidence of my burns.* I wanted to roll up my sleeve to show her that I really was that little girl, but I knew it would be violating proper etiquette.

Still, the moment stuck with me, long after the event. *Why am I so ashamed of my scars?* I wondered. *What am I afraid will happen if I reveal them?*

Here, at Mister Branson's event, I was ready to come out of hiding. I was ready to walk by faith, not fear regarding my appearance. I was ready to bare my scars.

I will never forget the warmth on Necker Island—not just the tropical temperatures outside, but also the spirit of acceptance and love in the room when I was giving my talk. "Choose to free your heart from hatred," I said to those gathered, the first in my list of five important decisions I wanted the audience to consider making too. "Yes, we will be wounded in this life," I acknowledged. "Yes, we will feel we have every right to make our perpetrators pay for the wounds we received. But this is the truth: Only God can right the wrongs we have known. And to carry around hatred and bitterness is to forfeit our one beautiful life. Come to God. Choose to love God. Lean into God's supernatural strength, knowing it is the only means for doing supernatural things. Let go of the hatred. Let go of the bitterness. Allow God to do what is his, alone, to do."

I had worked through four of my five points—free your heart from hatred; live a simple, not complicated, life; give more to those in need that you meet; expect less, and you'll know less dissatisfaction—and when I arrived at the fifth one, the topic I knew so intimately, I smiled. "Walk by faith, and not by fear," I said to the crowd.

"I spent too many years tied in knots because of plain fear. I feared my pain. I feared my appearance. I feared my destiny. I feared myself. And where had all that fear taken me? Right to suicide's front door. You cannot imagine how gripped by fear I was," I said. "I could not breathe, for the fear I knew." I paused, then continued.

"But then," I said, "I found faith. Not a nondescript sort of faith, but the faith of a person who has met and surrendered to God. And do you know what I discovered, upon being swept up by the God of love? Fear cannot be present wherever faith is exercised."

I told the men and women that I wanted to demonstrate what walking by faith instead of fear means to me. "Today," I said, as I held my left arm aloft, "I am showing my scars in public for the first time. Before this, I have always worn long sleeves. But I am no longer afraid. These scars, they are part of my journey. They are part of my story. They are part of *me*. And I have decided that in order to walk by faith, I must let go of my fears—the fear of what you might think about me as you see my unusual skin; the fear of what you might say about me, long after we part ways from this event; the fear of what you might feel toward me, now that you see how disfigured I am . . ."

Before I could say anything more, a smattering of applause began across the quiet room. That smattering gave way to louder applause, which turned into a standing ovation. These wildly successful men and women had tears in their eyes. "I love you, Kim!" several of the participants shouted above the raucous applause. I smiled broadly and whispered, "Oh, how I love you, too."

PEACE AT LAST

JUNE 2016

China's International School of Dongguan, a preparatory school for Asian students planning to attend university abroad, had invited me to come and speak on the subject of peace. I enthusiastically accepted their offer and immediately began scheming a way to tack on a trip to Trang Bang. "It is so close to Vietnam," I said to Toan, who agreed wholeheartedly to my plan.

"We will spend three days with my family in Hanoi," he said, "and three days with your family in Saigon." And with that, a plan was hatched.

It had been twelve years since I had visited the village of my youth, my last trip booked in order to pay my respects to the family of dear Number 5, who had unexpectedly passed away. I was prohibited by the Vietnamese government from traveling there in time for his October funeral, but I did make it for the Christmas holiday. Perhaps that was better, in the end. Now that my entire family had chosen to center their lives on the Christian faith, celebrating the Christ child's birth together at my sister-in-law's made for a memorable and gratifying experience indeed.

This time around, Toan's and my trip abroad was blissfully uneventful, as were the days we spent in the North. My sole recollection from those three days is just how hot the weather was. The word *sweltering* comes to mind, which is, of course, characteristic for that part of the world in June. Only one area in Toan's family's home had fans, and so for seventy-two hours straight, I planted myself in front of those whirring fans. "I am so sorry to do this to you," I would whisper to my scars. How they despised such soaring temperatures.

When we boarded our two-hour flight from Hanoi to Saigon, it brought back memories of my week-long journey from Saigon to Hanoi to enlist Bac Dong's aid when I was nineteen years old. "Oh, Toan," I said, making myself comfortable in my airline seat, "this way is much better. I would not want to go by road."

In Saigon, a prearranged van picked us up from the airport, a nice gesture provided by my brother Number 8, one of the two who had run with me along that fire road. Toan and I had FaceTimed with him prior to our departure from Toronto, and he had requested various Western treasures for us to bring. At the top of the list? Omega 3 capsules. "Out of all the goods available in Canada, brother, *that* is what you desire?"

We had shared a good laugh then, as I dutifully jotted down the supplement on my grocery list.

After visiting with Number 8 for a few hours, we climbed back into the van and headed east, toward Trang Bang, where we would meet up with my sister-in-law, the one who still grieved the loss of Number 5. Her house was located on a corner of the expansive property owned by the CaoDai temple.

That evening, all the local relatives—my aunts and uncles, my in-town siblings, my nieces, my nephews, all of their spouses and kids—were convening for a delicious family feast. So much food, so much drink, so much levity, so much joy . . . how far we all had come across the decades. Our lives had not always been so abundant. "We are so blessed," I said to my family that evening. "Do you see it? *Richly* blessed."

As I looked at those precious faces surrounding me, now believers in the true God, I teared up. Those of us who had grown up together had known great heartache over the years and such pain. We had been impoverished. We had been despondent. We had been mistreated. We had been displaced. But now, here we were—safe, secure, and with bellies full. For such a long time, I could not see that God was working things together for good, but here the evidence was all but shouting: "The challenges you faced did not overtake you. You made it! You are still standing! And most important, you are at peace."

The following morning, Number 5's two daughters accompanied me on a walk flanking Route 1, heading toward the CaoDai temple. To walk on the road itself would be a death wish, since what once had been a primitive dirt road is now a divided, four-lane highway jammed with cars and trucks.

As the three of us walked together, I reached out to brush my hand across the leaves on the lush trees that formed a natural wall along the edge of the road. I had loved climbing those trees as a child. The years of war had demolished every last inch of the lovely landscape I had known the first eight years of my life; after the bombing, I felt like I was living in the apocalypse. But to look at Trang Bang now, you would never know it had suffered so greatly. There were scores of people zooming along to wherever they were going, windows rolled down in their cars, radios blaring, cell phones in hand, hardly a care in the world.

When we reached the temple, my nieces shouted above the roar of the traffic, "You like to go inside, Auntie?" I hesitated at first, but then agreed. How many times had this place been bombed to within a remnant of itself, only to be rebuilt once again? As soon as I set foot on the temple grounds, I paused, remembering in a flash where the color mark for the bomb had been dropped. I nodded to myself—*Yes, that was the day, the day that changed everything for me.*

We entered the temple building, and I felt nearly assaulted by the many idols that I had adored when I was young. Oh, I had been devoted to CaoDai, the most devoted child anyone had seen. With our footsteps echoing through the vast room where worship took place, I made my way to a side window and peeked through the small frame. Suddenly, it all came back to me, a rush of memory, an ache. *There was the place*, I murmured to myself. *On that emotionless patch of road.*

The bombs.

The fire.

The shrieks.

The fear.

The picture that made the world gasp.

Oh, that picture. *My* picture. The picture I had longed to be separated from. The picture that, in the end, had given me a mission, a ministry, a cause.

As I stood inside the temple, staring out the window, I remembered the horrors of 1972 and the trials and torment that followed, the scars which I still painfully bore. But then I thought about how far I had come, discovering freedom, aliveness, peace. I thought about the contentment and patience and joy I had gathered along the way. "Thank you, God," I whispered. "Yes, even for that road."

Three weeks after my trip to Trang Bang, Toan and I were seated at the head table of a lavish event in Los Angeles, where my friend Nick Ut was being presented a lifetime achievement award by the LA Press Club for his marvelous work in the field of journalism. When the presenters introduced Nick to the packed auditorium, they projected his Pulitzer Prize–winning photograph of me onto a giant screen.

I knew every nuance of the picture—the puddled roadway, the expressionless soldiers, the contour of the napalm clouds—as well as I know the back of my own hand. It was the photograph that had defined my life. And, yet, as many times as I had seen it, on that evening, mere moments before I was introduced to join my dear friend on stage as he accepted his award, tears began streaming down my cheeks.

I looked at my feet in the picture, running as fast as they could possibly run, and I thought about the race I had run for so long—a desperate attempt to flee the bombs and the war, my picture and also my pain. I had run from my religion. I had run from communist control. I had run from Vietnam. I had run from Cuba too. Motivated by sorrow, and then by rage, and then by fear, and then by resolve, I had spent so much of my life running, convinced that for me, there was no other choice. And yet the path I had been racing along all that time had taken me straight into the arms of God.

I squeezed Toan's hand before I got up. "My tears, they are not from sorrow this time. They are tears of gratitude, Toan. Gratitude to God that I lived."

HOLDING FAST TO HOPE

I deliver more than forty talks every year, and each time I travel, a flash of regret grips my heart. *I would rather simply stay home*, I think. Our home in the suburbs of Toronto is a safe haven for my family and me. I finger the delicate gold chain 'round my neck, the one a friend had made for me. Two tiny charms—a simple cross and a maple leaf—dangle from it. *Oh, Jesus, just you and me and Canada. Life is so straightforward here!*

But then I see the faces of innocent sufferers, those whose lives have been traumatized by ignorance and outrage. *If I do not go, who will?*

And so once more I say yes to the speaking engagement. Once more I pack my bag. Once more I head for the airport. Once more I travel to "there," wherever there happens to be that time.

The toll on my family has been significant, and the price quite often has been high. When my young Thomas was asked at school to draw a picture of his ma, he crayoned an airplane soaring through the sky. I cringed inside when I saw it, but I was not altogether surprised. My mind flashed back to a poignant moment with Thomas when I was leaving for another speaking engagement, this time in Hong Kong.

"Mommy, this is the last hug and kiss I will ever give you," he said, his eyes brimming with tears.

I was stunned. "What! What on earth do you mean, Thomas?"

The concern on his face was unmistakable. "There is Asian bird flu in Hong Kong right now. You will catch that disease and die."

As I wrapped my son in a tight hug, I asked, "Thomas, do you trust the Lord?"

Thomas sniffled and replied in a tear-choked voice, "Yes, Mommy."

"I do too, Thomas. And because we both trust God, we can believe his promises, right?"

There was more sniffling and then another quiet yes.

I squeezed Thomas tighter. "One of God's promises says that he will protect us, carrying us under his wings of safety, all the days of our lives. Whenever we feel fearful, we must turn that fear into fuel for prayer. So I would like you to pray for Mommy while I am gone. Will you do that?"

He nodded in agreement.

I like to think that the commitments that took me away from my family made all of us—Toan, me, and our boys—rely on God more deeply.

Ma also would worry frantically whenever I traveled to places with supposed terrorist threats. "Ma," I would tell her, hopeful she would take my advice, "turn your worry into prayer. If you worry, you harm yourself and you neglect to care for me.

But if you pray, you bless us both. You get to come nearer to God in conversation, and you get to minister to me from afar."

As Ma took in my words, I couldn't help adding, "Besides, if anything bad goes down on earth, to heaven I go up!"

My ma was not amused, but from that moment on, she prayed.

I feel called to this ministry God has given me, and to refuse to go to the people who wish to hear my message would be the worst kind of defiance of all. And yet, I am not always welcomed with open arms. Recently, when Toan and I offered to return to Vietnam to build two orphanages and a library in conjunction with The KIM Foundation International, we were denied. We had carefully completed the necessary paperwork, humbly asked permission for the appropriate licenses, dotted all of our i's and crossed all of our t's, only to be told by the Tay Ninh officials, "There is no need here." Whew, that was difficult to hear. We knew there was need, great need. And yet what else could we do, except find someone somewhere to serve? There are *many* in need, it turns out.

In December 2016, Toan and I arrived in a truly tumultuous part of the world. Turkey sits below the Black Sea, beside the Mediterranean Sea, and just above Aleppo, Syria, from where thousands of refugees were fleeing for their lives. I was not in Turkey to speak about or assist with the refugee crisis explicitly, but to promote peace.

Still, at that time, some news outlets had reported that more than 2.5 million Syrian refugees had taken shelter in Turkey, which perhaps explains why every single Turkish media interview I had wound up landing on the subject of the Syrian War. A cease-fire had just been reached between the warring forces—Syria's official government backed by Russia and Iran, and the Syrian rebel groups, backed by Turkey, Saudi Arabia, Qatar, and the United States. But this had hardly stopped the insanity unfolding all around.

On the very day that Toan and I and our hosts arrived, there was a suicide bombing in a Syrian stadium that killed scores of people and terrorized the rest. How well I could empathize with those war-torn people. The senseless violence to protect one's power, the irrational activism, the wake of destruction and death—the scene was all too familiar to me, reducing me to tears, and also to prayer. "Oh, Father, protect these dear people," I cried. "Father, please protect Toan and me."

After multiple days of one unscheduled interview after another, I was exhausted. My scars were upset. I needed rest, and silence, and peace. We had only one more appointment— a visit from the mayor of Sariyer—before we would be heading home the following day.

I assumed the mayor's visit was a courtesy call, to bid me farewell. But when I answered the knock at our hotel room door at 10:00 p.m. and opened it, I was surprised to find the mayor with his assistant, several staff members, and a full media entourage. Ah, sleep would have to wait.

That final interview was conducted by a reporter who spoke broken English at best, but I understood clearly what she was after—she wanted me to take a political stance on the situation. "Kim Phuc," she finally said, exasperated, "as an ambassador of goodwill, you are obligated to say what your position is on these tragic matters of war."

I swallowed hard at her intimation. Whatever I said would be broadcast to tens of millions of people across the region and would live forever in media history. I wanted my words to matter. I did not want to shrink back from the truth.

In the space of a precious few seconds, my thoughts chased back to when Thomas and Stephen were young boys. Every night, when Toan and I put them to bed, we prayed the Aaronic blessing over our sleepy sons. "Lord, please bless them and keep them. Please make your face to shine upon them and be gracious to them. Please, Father, lift up the light of your countenance upon their lives, and always, Lord, give them peace."

Praying that blessing would become as natural as breathing to me—and not only for my sons. Almost daily, someone would come to my mind, and I would be prompted to ask the Lord to bless that person and to keep him or her in his forever grip of peace. "Help them to feel no rejection this day," I would ask the Father. "Keep them from isolating or withdrawing. Remind them that you adore them, that you seek them out, even when they feel unloved."

God sees us! He loves us! He has good things in store for us!

Sitting in the hotel room in Turkey, I found myself praying blessing over my own life: "Father, bless me and keep me as I answer with truth. Keep me here in your grip of peace. Make your face to shine upon me. Help me to shine with Christlike love."

Steadying myself with a deep breath, I looked directly into the interviewer's eyes and said with quiet confidence, "My 'position' on this, and all matters, is *forgiveness*. My 'position,' if you will, is *love*. My faith in Jesus Christ is what enabled me to forgive those who had wronged me—and as you know, the wrongs were severe. My faith in Jesus Christ is what enabled me to pray for my enemies rather than curse them. And my faith in Jesus Christ is what enabled me to love them. I do not just tolerate them, nor am I merely civil toward them. No, I *love* them. It is this love, alone, that ends wars."

The woman, who had been very professional, very serious, very stoic at the beginning of our discussion, now had tears in her eyes. Several silent seconds passed before she cleared her throat and spoke. "You are an amazing person," she whispered to me.

"It is only the Lord," I replied.

Twenty-four hours after Toan and I returned home, we would learn from a CNN news alert that Andrei Karlov, the Russian ambassador to Turkey, had been assassinated during a speech he was giving at a modern-arts center in Ankara, just minutes from the city center where we had stayed. Twenty or so people had been allowed into the room for the opening of an exhibit and were listening intently to the live broadcast of Mister Karlov's comments when one of the bystanders, a Turkish police officer assigned to the event, opened fire. With media cameras capturing every frame of the action, the ambassador fell to the floor while onlookers cowered in fear.

Like countless others around the globe, I scrolled through the photos that surfaced immediately on the Internet. Oh, the futility of such a treacherous act. "Allah is greater!" the gunman had shouted, just before discharging his weapon. "Remember Aleppo!" he screamed. "Remember Turkey! Allah is greater!"

I imagined my great God was greatly grieved. Honestly,

so was I. Had my message made any difference at all? Would peace on earth ever prevail?

I couldn't take my eyes off one photograph, showing the people who had run for cover huddling underneath a table in the gallery. As I studied their faces, I nodded in recognition. "I know that look," I said to myself. "I know the terror. I know the despondence. I know the fear. I know how wearying wartime experiences are. I know how hopeless life can feel."

"Do not give up!" I whispered to those faces on my computer screen. "I know this peace I have found can be yours. I was a little girl who suffered much, but today, I live at ease. Yes, my circumstances can still be challenging, but my heart? My beating heart is 100 percent healed.

"Hold fast to hope," I urged them. "It is *hope* that will see you through."

Acknowledgments

I humbly wish to thank Nick Ut, Pulitzer Prize–winning photographer, who took my picture and then took me to the hospital. For so many years, Uncle Ut, I could only thank you for one of those choices, but given how God has used your photograph—my photograph—I now hold gratitude in my heart for both. You went beyond the call of duty on that June day in 1972. I praise God for the compassion you showed.

The Associated Press first chose to run my picture, and soon thereafter, the entire world had seen it, it seemed. Thank you for deliberating over the appropriateness of publishing such a shot and for ultimately choosing to do so. I like to think that this unusual partnership between us has done some good in the world.

CBS, you, too, have been part of my life for many years now, and I remain grateful for the opportunities you have afforded me to tell my story and in doing so to reach others who are suffering and in pain. You should be proud of your approach to broadcasting. I surely am.

Christopher Wain, we all need a witness to our suffering in this life, and you, my friend, were mine. Thank you for coming to visit me in the hospital when so few would. You are a gift to me.

Pastor Ho Hieu Ha, you led me to the most important decision a person ever could make, that of surrendering herself to the lordship of Jesus Christ. I will always remember your kindness during that Christmas Eve service, when I was a nineteen-year-old in search of peace. Because of your faithfulness to communicating truth, I found it. May many others find it as a result of this book.

Pastor Nguyen Viet Anh, thank you for so patiently and graciously answering all 8,734 questions I had regarding what it means to follow Jesus Christ. You are a good and godly man.

Papa Perry Kretz, journalist extraordinaire, you truly drew out a broken stone from the bottom of the sea as you searched out an answer to your question, "Is that little girl still alive?" You brought public awareness to my suffering, and thus to the suffering of all who have been wounded by the horrors of war. I will forever be grateful to God for your persistence in finding me and for your selflessness in securing treatment for my pain.

Norm Keith, my lawyer and friend, thank you for undergirding all of my business efforts with both strong systems and devoted prayer. Thank you for finding me the perfect literary agent in Lisa Jackson. I consider it a great blessing to count such professional and wise people as my friends.

Lisa, you and Michelle Alvis and the entire Alive Literary Agency team supplied me with constant kindness, generous grace, deep understanding, and all the handholding a woman could need. Thank you.

Ashley Wiersma, without you, there would be no book. The Lord brought us together, and you have proven to be the ideal writing companion for me. You fueled me when I was weary and put words to my vision for each page. I love you, my dear friend. Tell Perry and Prisca hello.

Jan, Sharon, Nancy, Todd, and all of Team Tyndale, thank you for believing in my story and in the power of this book to change lives.

Bonne and Sarah, thank you for providing editing expertise to this project. You women mean business! This book is far better because of that.

Andy, you and your family inspired me to rally a prayer team as I worked on this book, an idea that bore so much needed fruit. Dan and Joy Loney, thank you for heading up those prayer efforts. What faithful friends you are.

Anne Bayin, my sister and friend, thank you for dedicating your life to helping me thrive. Everyone needs an Anne in her life.

Liesa and Enzo Cianchio and family, my dear friends in Canada, thank you for believing in me and for loving me well.

Reg Reimer, my "big brother" in Canada, thank you for living your life with courage and devotion to Christ. And for loving my homeland, Vietnam, as much as I do.

My friend Tran Thi Trieu, thank you for the decades-long companionship you have afforded me. I adore you and pray for you daily.

I still do not know the name of the pilot who was responsible for those napalm bombs falling on my village in 1972, but I do not need that detail in order to convey these thoughts: I would love to meet you someday. I would love to offer you a warm smile and a long hug. I would love to look you in the eye and say to you, "I forgive you. It is in the past. Let us move forward in peace." War is hard on all involved, and so my country's war surely wounded you too. I pray that you have found healing across the years that have passed. And that you will carry my forgiveness with you always.

Oh, Canada! How I do love you. Thank you for accepting my husband, Toan, and me in 1992, when it seemed we had nowhere else to turn. Thank you for freedom! Thank you for the ability Toan and I have had to build a new life for ourselves within your borders. Here, we are truly at home.

To my friends and co-laborers at The Kim Foundation International, thank you for furthering my work around the globe and for believing, as I do, that all children deserve to know health, wholeness, freedom, and peace all the days of their lives.

To my friends at UNESCO, thank you for affording me countless speaking engagements across the last twenty years. Let us always be ambassadors for peace.

To the believers around the world who saw my picture in the newspaper decades ago, laid hands on that little girl's fragile frame, and prayed to God that I would survive—even thrive—thank you. Thank you for holding out hope for me when I was too wounded to hope for myself.

To the doctors, nurses, medical assistants, physical therapists, dermatologists, and laser specialists who have walked with me all these years. Your treatment has improved my quality of life, and your kindness has expanded my heart. I must especially thank Doctor Le My, who admitted me to the Barsky Unit all those years ago. God placed you in a position of power when I was most impotent, and I will forever thank him for your mercy, tenderness, and care.

To my friend Steven Stafford for your love and friendship.

To my wonderful niece Danielle (Hong Duc) whose father, my brother Phuoc, ran with me along that awful, fiery road. I praise God for you, and pray his rich blessing on all of your days. Toan and I were overjoyed to sponsor you here in Canada for those seven years and now regard you not as our niece, but as our daughter.

To my husband, Toan; my sons, Thomas and Stephen; my daughter-in-law, Kezia; and my precious little grandson, Kalel Bui, thank you for consistently demonstrating unconditional love, unwavering prayer support, and sacrificial selflessness as I have shared my story with the world.

Finally, to my Lord and Savior Jesus Christ, thank you for rescuing me from the physical, emotional, and spiritual darkness I found myself in at age nineteen—and for purposing me for a life that counts. I treasure you. I live for you. I have found peace, at last, in you.

Notes

1. Philippians 4:7. All Scripture quotations are from the Holy Bible, King James Version.
2. 1 Peter 4:12-13
3. See caodai.org.
4. See http://adst.org/2014/07/the-vietnamese-boat-people/.
5. See John 14:6.
6. Anh pointed to two Bible verses as proof: "For there is one God, and one mediator between God and men, the man Christ Jesus" (1 Timothy 2:5); "And this is the record, that God hath given to us eternal life, and this life is in his Son" (1 John 5:11).
7. See Romans 10:17.
8. "For with the heart man believeth unto righteousness; and with the mouth confession is made unto salvation" (Romans 10:10).
9. "For by grace are ye saved through faith; and that not of yourselves: it is the gift of God: Not of works, lest any man should boast. For we are his workmanship, created in Christ Jesus unto good works, which God hath before ordained that we should walk in them" (Ephesians 2:8-10).
10. See Ephesians 5:25.
11. Based on Psalm 26:11-12: "But as for me, I will walk in mine integrity: redeem me, and be merciful unto me. My foot standeth in an even place: in the congregations will I bless the Lord."
12. A reference to the fact that Jesus' birth came to mark time: BC meaning "before Christ," and AD, Latin for *Anno Domino*, or, literally, "in the year of our Lord."
13. See 1 Corinthians 10:27-28.
14. "If any man come to me, and hate not his father, and mother, and wife, and children, and brethren, and sisters, yea, and his own life also, he cannot be my disciple" (Luke 14:26).
15. Matthew 6:34
16. Psalm 46:1; Psalm 9:9; and Isaiah 41:10, respectively.
17. See 2 Corinthians 11:23-27.
18. See Romans 8:28.
19. See Hebrews 10:16.
20. "I know both how to be abased, and I know how to abound: every where and in all things I am instructed both to be full and to be hungry, both to abound and to suffer need. I can do all things through Christ which strengtheneth me" (Philippians 4:12-13).

21. Matthew 5:6

22. Uncle Ut was correct in his assessment! Across his five-decade-long career with the Associated Press, he took many, many "good pictures," including photos of actor Robert Blake, actress Joan Collins, singer Michael Jackson, and media personality Paris Hilton. When Uncle announced his retirement on March 13, 2017, he summed up his accomplishments in four words posted to his social-media accounts: "From hell to Hollywood." I regret that my picture falls under the first place mentioned, even as I acknowledge that of the many scenes dear Uncle captured for posterity, mine was the most famous of them all.

23. 1 Thessalonians 5:17

24. See Romans 8:15.

25. Luke 6:27-28

26. See Matthew 6:14-15; Matthew 18:34-35; Romans 12:19; Ephesians 4:32; 1 Peter 3:9.

27. Matthew 18:21-22

28. When several questions were subsequently raised about Captain Plummer's statements about his involvement on some level with the bombing of Trang Bang, he still maintained his culpability, and I believe him. At the end of his military service, he received a Bronze Star for Service with the accompanying citation that stated he "assisted in the coordination of a tremendous number of air strikes and support activities" during the Vietnam War. What is most important to me is that Captain Plummer was the first person I had the opportunity to forgive face-to-face, which began the healing in my heart.

29. Jeremiah 33:3

30. See Joel 2:25.

31. See Matthew 19:26.

32. See Luke 18:1-5.

33. Over the years, there have been several artists who have created different pieces depicting me in some way, but only one—"Robert" (whose identity remains undisclosed)—was involved in this part of my story.

34. Isaiah 55:9 reads, "As the heavens are higher than the earth, so are my ways higher than your ways, and my thoughts than your thoughts."

35. See Jeremiah 33:3.

36. See Joshua 4:1-7.

37. See the history of the Hippocratic Oath at http://www.pbs.org/wgbh/nova /body/hippocratic-oath-today.html.

38. See 2 Kings 5:1-14.

39. https://news.google.com/newspapers?nid=1842&dat=19720807&id=2Aws AAAAIBAJ&sjid=SsgEAAAAIBAJ&pg=5773,1418544&hl=en.

About the Author

KIM PHUC travels to hundreds of events every year around the world. She has received numerous awards and recognitions for her commitment to global peace and reconciliation. This includes six honorary doctorates for her work in supporting child victims of war around the world through the nonprofit organization KIM Foundation International. She helped launch the Restoring Heroes Foundation, an organization that serves military and first-responders who have suffered traumatic scars, burns, or amputations by providing them access to state-of-the-art medical treatment. Kim and her husband, Toan, have two grown sons, Thomas and Stephen, and live in the Toronto area.

"I want to help other children of war discover the peace that I have found."

The **Kim Foundation International** (KFI) is a nonprofit organization that works with existing organizations to serve the youngest among us who are disabled, disenfranchised, or displaced. Our mission for the past twenty years has been to extend hope and healing—both medically and psychologically—to these innocent children.

Ongoing projects include:

- Emmanuel Orphanage (India)
- Ongutoi Project, a series of medical clinics for expectant mothers (Uganda)
- Bethany Kids Project (Kenya)
- Tajikistan Refugee Camps (the Middle East)

You can bring hope to a child today!

For more information on KFI, or to donate to KFI's work around the globe, visit www.kimfoundation.com.

The Kim Foundation International
P O Box 31025
15 Westney Road North
Ajax ON L1T 3V2, Canada

CP1281

Online Discussion *guide*

TAKE *your* TYNDALE READING EXPERIENCE *to the* NEXT LEVEL

A FREE discussion guide for this book is available at bookclubhub.net, perfect for sparking conversations in your book group or for digging deeper into the text on your own.

www.bookclubhub.net

You'll also find free discussion guides for other Tyndale books, e-newsletters, e-mail devotionals, virtual book tours, and more!